The
Betrayal

More historical fiction by Douglas Bond

The Crown & Covenant series:
Duncan's War
King's Arrow
Rebel's Keep

The Faith & Freedom series:
Guns of Thunder
Guns of the Lion

The *Betrayal*

A Novel on John Calvin

DOUGLAS BOND

P U B L I S H I N G

P.O. BOX 817 • PHILLIPSBURG • NEW JERSEY 08865-0817

For my wife

"Let us banish from France this hateful doctrine of grace."
—NOEL BEDA, *Doctor of the University of Paris*
Chief opponent of reformation

"A system of terror was set on foot throughout France. . . . The spies of the Sorbonne and of the monks [crept] into churches, colleges, and even private families to catch up any word of evangelical doctrine. . . . In vain did the king's soldiers arrest on the highways . . . hunting down and treading underfoot . . . everything that seemed to bear the stamp of the Reformation."
—M. MERLE D'AUBIGNE

"My heart I offer thee, O Lord, promptly and sincerely."

—John Calvin

"Take heed: he who strays away from the Word of God may run as fast as he likes, yet he will not reach the goal because he will wind up in the wrong path. It is better to limp on the right way than to run on the wrong. . . ."

—John Calvin

Contents

Note to the Reader   11

1. April 1918: The Bombardment   13
2. The Confession   19
3. The Accusative Case   21
4. Shorn Head   29
5. The Voice of God   37
6. The Scourge of God   41
7. The Plague Closes In   47
8. Frank Next Door   59
9. Carriage Ride   65
10. My New Gown   75
11. The Price of Learning   85
12. Fleshed on the Prey   93
13. Paris Burning   99
14. My Chapeau   109
15. My License   117
16. Changes Afoot   125
17. Orleans   139

18. Light in Bourges   153
19. Seeking Calvin   171
20. Cost of Quietude   183
21. Providence   191
22. Martyr Burning   209
23. Cop Speaks Out   217
24. Flight!   227
25. To Angouleme   235
26. Caves and Wine   245
27. Royal Feasting   257
28. The Institutes   265
29. A Violent World   277
30. Fiery Farel   287
31. Geneva   295
32. Lausanne Debate   305
33. Banished!   315
34. Strasbourg   331
35. One Hundred Deaths   345
36. Triumph at Last   359
37. The End   373

Timeline of the Reformation and John Calvin's Life   377
Guide to Further Reading   381

Note to the Reader

THIS IS A WORK of historical fiction, set in the times and places when and where John Calvin lived and worked. Though it is fiction, the reader may accept Calvin's words in dialogues, sermons, discussions, and debates with confidence. In nearly all places where Calvin speaks I have drawn and shaped his words from his letters, commentaries, *Institutes*, and other writings. For cohesion and grammatical accuracy, I have altered tenses and pronouns, and for brevity I have excerpted Calvin's far lengthier theological investigations. Though shaped for fiction, Calvin's voice in this novel is a faithful attempt to reflect accurately his own verbiage, piety, and theology. Frequently, I use Calvin's written summations of his critics' views as grist for their voice when debating or deliberating with him. Wherever possible, I have attempted to faithfully represent other historical characters, often shaping their voices from their letters, journals, and other writings. To read Calvin in his context, readers may want to consult the Guide to Further Reading at the end of this book.

Douglas Bond
July 10, 2008

1

April 1918: The Bombardment

IN THE WAR-TORN VILLAGE of Noyon-le-Sainte in northern France an old man, clutching the hand of a little boy, mused on the war to end all wars. After three and a half years of bloody stalemate, it seemed less like a war to end war and far more like a war that would just never end. In spite of the endless cycle of artillery barrage, infantry advance, and entrenchment, inexplicably the cathedral, the town hall, the Renaissance library, and various medieval buildings remained standing, awaiting the next cycle of war. Still more importantly to the old man, his house, Grain Place, as it had been known for centuries, remained standing. And he had his music and his books.

That night, windows shrouded in black, he opened the volume he had been reading. A biography originally penned in 1577 by Jérôme-Hermès Bolsec, the old man's copy had been printed in 1875. Far more a vengeful diatribe than a proper biography, the old man had read enough not to think of it as real history; nevertheless, the scandalous rant against a man Bolsec must have intensely hated was entertaining. Perching his reading glasses on his nose, and leaning toward the lantern, he had only just recommenced reading when suddenly the house shuddered to its foundation stones.

"Grand-père!" cried the little boy at his feet. "Qu'est-ce que c'est?"

The old man knew what it was. Snatching the boy's hand, he ran through the house into the back garden, hoping to get the little one to the bomb shelter in time. There was nothing an old man or a mere boy could do; the defense of the town and of the Oise valley was entirely up to the British Fifth Army.

Shifting troop strength to the Western Front in April of 1918, Kaiser Wilhelm II ordered his German army to redirect the gaping mouths of its massive artillery, capable of firing one-ton ordnance over nine miles, and to commence thundering destruction on the Allied defenders and on what remained of the town of Noyon-le-Sainte. The apocalyptic Hindenburg-Ludendorff Offensive had begun.

Holding the trembling boy in his arms, the old man listened to the earth-shaking staccato of German artillery raining death and devastation on the village above them. And then would come the infantry advance. With deadly accuracy, the British defenders who had survived the barrage valiantly went to work with their Enfield rifles, *pee-oohing* death into the waves of German infantry advancing on the town. The Germans responded with the heavy gut-lurching chattering of machine gun fire, cutting down all life in its path, valiant or otherwise. But the old man had seen enough of modern war. He knew that at the last it would be the coordinated artillery fire, the molten shrapnel, and the erupting debris that would carve out a path of death and devastation for the German advance through his village, his home, and his life.

When at last the echoing of heavy guns had lapsed into an eerie silence, the old man and the boy slowly emerged from the bomb shelter. What met their senses seemed like a microcosm of the death of civilization. Everywhere the air was thick with acrid smoke and the stench of death. The complete absence of laughter, of the cheery sounds of children at play, of chattering housewives, of yapping dogs, created a silence so palpable that it unhinged the mental faculties of some who had inexplicably survived.

Stooped and frail, the widow next door sat on a fragment of her front steps—all that remained of her home. Moaning softly, her head bowed and shrouded with a black shawl, she sat rocking, rocking as if thereby to find some comfort for herself. Heaped about her radiated mounds of rubble: the remains of her home, of a Gallo-Roman crypt, of the towers of the cathedral. An instant of thunderous chaos had reduced the village to heaps of debris; order, antiquity, and beauty devolving into crumbled heaps of stone, dust, and matchsticks.

The few buildings still standing looked as if a puff of wind would finish the job. Stones chiseled into columns and arches by master stonecutters of the Middle Ages now seemed to stagger and sway like drunken men. The tinkling of breaking glass broke the stillness; the old man shook his head in wonder: what glass could yet be unbroken after such a bombardment?

Enormous as the loss in buildings, the loss of human life far exceeded all other devastation. Though many had been instantaneously buried as their lives were crushed by hailing stones and molten shrapnel, yet were there many bodies undignified by such a burial. And as the April sun warmed the scene, grotesque corpses swelled in the heat. Others were so disfigured that they had ceased to affright, so inhuman had they become. Still others had

15

instantly been obliterated, their parts so ground up and mingled with the mud, stone, and earth that they no longer existed, or so it seemed. Hundreds of townsfolk—men, women, and children— had simply vanished without a trace, no mangled body, no dental work to compare with records.

There was a new sound that made the old man frown. Faintly at first: the rumbling of horse-drawn artillery, the clattering of hooves, the mechanical throttling of trucks and the grinding of gears—and the advance of men. German infantry soldiers in spiky helmets would be pouring in to the streets across the town, shoulder-to-shoulder, right arms swinging stiffly, their rifles over their left shoulders, their boots echoing with every tread more fearfully than their artillery had done before them. The old man had seen and heard it all before.

Grain Place had been reduced to a chaotic mound of rubble. Dazed at first, the old man and the boy picked through the debris that had been their home. It had been home to many families over the centuries, the family names obliterated by the forgetfulness of time, as were now its beams and stones by the relentless unforgetfulness of war.

Strewn amid the chaos were tufts of stuffing from a pillow, and there a mangled arm of a chair, here a broken leg of a table, and the battered head and foot of a bed frame. Unlike other mounds of debris that had once been the houses that made up the village, there were no human arms, legs, heads, and feet in the homey mound of rubble that had been Grain Place.

Recognition flashed across the old man's face as he discovered the final remains of his favorite chair, and here and there a page from the Bolsec book he had only the night before hurriedly laid aside to retire to the relative safety of the bomb shelter in the back garden. With a cry, the boy snatched up the shredded remains of his teddy bear, and a tear fell on the mangled creature's face as the boy clutched it, searching in the debris for an arm, a leg, an ear, the innards of its torso.

More familiar objects poked out of the rubbish: the old man's violin, never to be played again, and black and white keys from his piano, were scattered about the debris like the shrapnel of a melodic grenade.

Then, scowling, the old man let his eyes fall on an unfamiliar object. It puzzled him, because he could not remember having anything like it among his possessions, yet here it was in the rubble that had been his home and his things. Carefully picking his way to it, he bent low, with a hand clearing aside gravel and powder that had so late been solid stone. It was a battered metal chest, the same length and somewhat wider than an ammunition case for the .303 caliber rounds the British soldiers had used in their Enfield rifles.

Lifting it from the debris, the old man blew the remaining mortar dust away and studied the metalwork on the case more closely.

"Grand-père, qu'avez-vous trouvé?" called the boy.

"Je ne sais pas," he replied with a shrug.

He had no idea what it was, what it contained, but clearly it was very ancient. The rumbling, grinding, and trampling grew louder. The old man, tucking the chest under his arm, gripped the boy's hand in his own and scrambled through the wreckage back to the bomb shelter, now their only home.

Once underground, he took up a pry bar and worked at the lid of the chest. As he worked, so did his imagination. Perhaps inside there would be something of value, something of antiquity: bank notes from the sixteenth century would be nice, family

17

gemstones or gold jewelry better still, the title to a vast estate best of all. Food ration coupons would do, he thought grimly. With a sudden crack, the lid gave way. The man's heart raced as he lifted it and gazed inside.

Disappointed, he lifted a large sheaf of paper, yellowed with age. He looked more closely within. Underneath the pages, nest-like, were the decaying remains of a piece of cloth, silk it felt like, at one time perhaps a shade of blue. The cloth was fragile with age, and as he turned it carefully in his hands, he decided it had long ago been a *chapeau* for the head.

Again he looked within. There was a small leather-bound book. Opening it tenderly, he saw that it was a French Bible, hundreds of years old it must have been, and perhaps of some value. Indifferently he closed the book, though cautiously so as not to devalue it. He turned his attention back to the sheaves of paper, clearly some kind of manuscript, written in a hasty, agitated scrawl, but legible for all that, and in French. The writer had used both sides of each sheet of paper, and had allowed no room for margins, as if he feared he might run out of paper, as if he had much to say and little time or space in which to say it.

Who had written these words? the old man mused, thumbing the yellow pages pensively. It was eerie to think that a man long dead had penned them. And the old man, whose emotions had been dulled by the numbing years of war, felt a flickering of excitement at it all. *Why had the ancient writer walled this manuscript up in this house?* There would be no better way to find out than to read the pages, perhaps aloud to the boy.

So he did.

2

The Confession

AT THE LAST, they will discover me. I am as certain of the fact as I am horrified at it. No one is as intimate with their stratagems as I, Jean-Louis Mourin. Even now, they draw ever closer.

Pressed to the wall in a benighted alleyway, they are never far from me now. In the corner of my eye, I have seen them lurking. They consider me among the Huguenots. They are remorseless with any who dare to dissent from the proud singularity of Holy Church, as they term it. Whether I am such or no, I am daily followed. Though I attempt to make myself hope, I fear they will arrest and accuse me. And to be accused is to be condemned. I fear it with a certainty.

Sounds in the night trouble my rest, if rest it may be termed. Startled to wakefulness, with my eyes I desperately scour the darkness. It may be merely a rat prowling in the street rubbish, a man staggering home after being too long at the wine bottle, or a woman of the night shuffling to her place after her harlotries. It matters not. At the slightest sound, with racing pulse, I clutch the bedclothes to my quivering chin and strain my ears, certain that in those night sounds I hear them approaching.

Them—I am tormented by the dreaded anticipation of their poundings at my door. But it is the knowledge of what follows that wraps itself around my churning innards like the cold clutching fingers of the scourge of God—but I must not dwell on what will follow.

I am not strong like some I have accused and thereby condemned in my time. Too well do I know their schemes. When I think of what they will do to me, of their relentless cruelty, of the horrific effectiveness of their methods, of my certain and painful end at their hands, I fear I may lose my nerve, and be a castaway. No, I must not dwell on such things.

In an effort to cleanse my tormented conscience and steel my will, I do now take up my quill and set down what I know—what I have done. As a penitent to his confessor, I set these words down. Though expert at the bloody art of wrenching confessions from others, I am unable as a chronicler of my own, yet do I vow that what follows is a true and faithful chronicle.

Knowing that the noose is drawn ever tighter about me, I am possessed with a fear that my ability to complete the account may be cut short. And so to my reader, if ever reader there be, I am compelled to beg indulgence for my hasty syntax and the all too likely inevitability of incompleteness. Yet fueled by this knowledge and my own guilt am I driven with greater urgency to write. And so do I.

3

The Accusative Case

SOME FIFTY-FIVE YEARS AGO, July 10, 1509, Jeanne Franc Calvin gave birth to a son here in Noyon-le-Sainte, Picardy, within the half-timbered walls of Grain Place, as it is known—in which I do attempt to pen these words—perhaps born in this room, the very room in which I now cower and shrink, gnawing at my quill. Though a native of the same village, I remember nothing of those days, for I would not come myself into this benighted world for another six months. That birth produced a son—termed famous by some and infamous by others—whose subsequent life has given rise to many fantastical stories.

A canon of the cathedral, for example, in later years alleged that while the boy's mother gasped and strained in labor, there issued from the birth canal a swarm of large flies. The worthy cleric eagerly interpreted the phenomenon as an indubitable presage that the boy would one day be an evil speaker and a calumniator. I heard him tell the tale with my own ears, and he would draw out the final word in his many retellings with prophetic flourish.

My first recollections of the son of Gerard Calvin left an unshakable impression on my mind. Unlike my own, the boy's father doted in the most obnoxious way on his beloved son. One would have thought that the man had brought some kind of saint into the world, the way he dressed him in the finest clothing he could manage to afford from his civic income and the stipend he received from his services rendered on behalf of the bishop, and from the manner in which he strutted him through the streets of our town.

At the time, I perceived the boy himself to walk aloof from the rest of his fellows from the village. Looking back, I fear it may have been far more the poisoned perception of an envious peer; nevertheless, I felt certain he looked down on me for my father's humble calling and my coarse dress and manners, and later for my comparatively sluggish intellect.

As we commenced our studies in the local grammar school together, I came very much to feel that he was far and away my superior in matters of the intellect. Though I was leagues from rivaling for top honors in matters of the mind, yet did I feel in good company with the brightest of my schoolfellows in comparison with the demigod who sprang from the loins of Gerard Calvin. One incident will suffice to illustrate.

Our schoolmaster was droning on about the constellations, mingling mythological notions with ones more firmly rooted in matters scientifically verifiable. During his incomprehensible ramblings, I had, I must confess to my shame, been scribbling drawings on my slate of one I had come to believe to be the prettiest maiden in Noyon-le-Sainte, nay, in all the world.

Something had in those days come over me, and I found it impossible to think of anything but my beloved Monique, perfect in form and feature beyond description, and certainly beyond my pathetic ability to render upon my slate. Alas, to my anguish, she was oblivious to my adorations. O, if she had only been oblivious. Oblivious is particularly difficult to misinterpret when the object resides under the roof of the house next door, a fact that made the pain of these days more acute. Yet is oblivious not quite accurate. It is more correct to say that she was indifferent, yet still more correct might it be said that she was scornful of my undying worship of herself. Yet do I digress.

While I was thus amusing myself with doodling on my slate, our schoolmaster spoke of heavenly bodies in this fashion: "By the merest chance these clusters of shimmering light restrain themselves from the urge to wander aimlessly throughout the fathomless universe exploring the vastness of space."

We had heard this all before. A man not unaffected by the spirit of the age, he considered himself sophisticated, skilled in many disciplines of art, a humanist, vast in worldly learning. He was never far from reminding us of these his attainments in both subtle and ubiquitous ways. Such reminders did not have the effect our schoolmaster desired. I wonder if they ever have.

Schoolmaster had turned from his diagram of the heavenly bodies and surveyed us, one can only imagine, awaiting gasps of astonishment and adulation, gasps that remained conspicuously absent.

Then my attention was averted by a scuffling of feet on the flagstone floor at my side. I glanced up from my crude rendering of Monique's lovely profile. Gerard's son at my side was about to speak, or so it seemed. Agitated, the boy stroked his lean cheek, a habit that I came to understand as a presage to astounding reflections.

"Magister, with respect," he said levelly. "There is no chance."

Storm clouds gathered on schoolmaster's brow, and his eyes narrowed at the speaker.

"Because causes are hidden from us," the boy continued, "it creeps into our minds that affairs turn and whirl at the blind urge of fortune, as if God were making sport of men by throwing them about like balls. Yet St. Augustine lamented his regret at having in some of his earlier writings used the term 'fortune,' a derivation of the goddess Fortuna. Though the specific reason and cause of an event be secret to our minds, nevertheless we do well not to ascribe any event, cosmic or human, to chance by the use of the terms *forte, forsan, forsitan, fortasse, fortuito.* Basil the Great referred to these and like terms as pagan words, unfit for Christian expression."

As Calvin paused for breath, tittering began in a back corner of the classroom. He looked confused by it but drew breath and continued. "It would appear that sluggish minds, Magister, unable to ascend the heights of God's providence, call chance what lies alone in his decree. In an ordered world, it must be that God's providence is the determinative principle of all events, large or small, that he sometimes works through an intermediary, sometimes without an intermediary, and sometimes contrary to every intermediary."

Magister opened and closed his mouth, looking very much like a gudgeon gasping for air on the banks of the Oise, but no sound came forth. When at last he recovered his composure, he sniffed and said, "High sounding words, indeed," he sniffed again, "for one so inexperienced in lofty matters," more sniffing, "and for one so all-inexpert in theological considerations."

None of us dared speak as Calvin had spoken to Magister, and so at times like these, our boyish loyalties shifted to young

Calvin's side. But, I confess, these times were fleeting and few. I render the following to illustrate both his brilliance and the resentment it excited in his schoolfellows.

Magister had posed a question to the class regarding our Latin grammar, something to do with declensions of nouns and the accusative case; ever dull as I am, I fail to remember the precise question.

"Who shall give answer?" he demanded of the class.

That peculiar scuffling of feet commenced at my side, and I glanced in expectation at young Calvin. Again the fingers of a thin hand stroked the pale flesh of his left cheek as he briefly pondered a reply. These mannerisms were so common and predictable with him, and so free of pretense, that I was constantly torn with envy at his apt replies and with something akin to admiration at his unpretentious candor when rendering those replies—if a twelve-year-old might be said to be capable of admiration on such a level.

"The accusative case of the Latin noun," he began as if reciting from a lexicon, yet was no book open before him, "is the grammatical case employed to indicate the direct object of a transitive verb. The accusative case is thus employed in sundry modern languages with the task of forming objects of many prepositions. Essentially the accusative case is indicative of a Latin noun having some action exerted upon it. Moreover, the said case is frequently joined with the nominative case."

Wiping his brow, he paused for breath.

"That is all?" said Magister, his eyelids engaged in a flutter of agitation.

"I believe there is more," said Calvin, eyes straying to the timbered beams on the ceiling as if reading from a lexicon inscribed on thin air. "A noun in the accusative case," he continued, "can be used as a direct object to indicate duration of time."

"You speak in theory," said Magister, tapping his cane slowly in his palm. "For sluggish minds in our midst, might you offer an illustration of what you affirm?"

"Examples of nouns used as direct objects to indicate duration of time would be *multos annos*, indicating many years, or *ducentos annos*, indicating a duration of 200 years. If I am not mistaken, this is termed 'the accusative case of duration of time.'"

He took a deep breath and continued.

"Moreover, the accusative case may be usefully employed to indicate direction toward some object or destination, as in *domum*, indicating a homeward direction, or *Romam*, indicative of one going to Rome. Furthermore, there is no preposition needed in such renderings. Again, if I am not mistaken, this usage is termed 'the accusative of place to which.'"

"Might I presume," said Magister, his cheeks flushed, "that in this *petit* recital you have spent your knowledge of the accusative case?"

Calvin blinked at the ceiling beams once again and recommenced.

"The accusative case exists in all the Indo-European languages, including Latin, Sanskrit, Greek, German, Russian, and in Semitic languages including Arabic. Perhaps it would be useful to note that several Northern European languages employ two cases to mark objects, the accusative under our present consideration, and the partitive case. In terms of morphosyntactic alignment, both accusative and partitive cases perform the accusative function, but the accusative object, however, is telic, whereas the partitive case is not."

Telic? Morphosyntactic? My jaw slack, I must have stared at the young man next to me as if gazing at an object from another world. For several moments no one dared speak. Not even Magister. Young Calvin seemed confused by that silence, a silence perhaps inevitably broken by the bursting forth of pent-up envy, expressing itself in derisive laughter. It came from more than one of the young scholar's classmates—I am ashamed to confess, it came from me all too heartily.

"I propose a new name for Master Calvin," I told my fellows later that afternoon. "He shall no longer be John Calvin." With that I drew out my clasp knife and began carving in a weathered oaken timber at the back of our schoolhouse—my epithet remains to this day—

> For thinking you know better than we
> And putting us all in our place,
> We dub you, O high and exalted one,
> The morphosyntactic "Accusative Case."

Though my verse was rough, the new name was an instant success, and thereby I gained influence with my fellows that day. Hereafter, I and all his schoolfellows gleefully taunted him as the "Accusative Case."

4

Shorn Head

AN EVENT OF GREAT SIGNIFICANCE transpired on May 21, 1521. I was there. The smoky sweetness of incense drifted like wisps of lingering spirits from the chancel of our cathedral church in Noyon-le-Sainte. In my youth, as is the way of youth, I appreciated little about that great edifice. To me, then it was merely a stout old building made of shabby old stones, wherein candles flickered and lecherous old men and tender boy choristers paraded about, chanting the gloomy *Miserere*.

I have since learned that our Cathedral of Notre Dame, as I then knew it, had been rebuilt after the great fire of 1131, coming to its completion, I'm told, nearly one hundred years later. Pilgrims from time to time would pass through our town to venerate the alleged relics of St. Eloi, seventh-century goldsmith turned bishop of Noyon, patron saint of workers in precious metals. I thought goldsmithing a fitting avocation for a bishop. Inexplicably, St. Eloi was taken up as the patron of blacksmiths and, adding another layer of mystification, local horse breeders in Picardy still swear by the power of St. Eloi's remains to superintend the emissions

29

of their prize stallions while engaged in their seasonal duties of covering the heated mares.

In the thirteenth century, I've come to learn, there occurred a feisty dust-up between monks of the local monastery of St. Eloi and the bishop. The monks claimed to have the venerable bones of the saint, and thereby gathered healthy revenue from pilgrims coming to venerate his moldering remains, a practice that has always eluded my dull understanding. The bishop claimed that the saint's bones belonged in the cathedral; the monks soundly disagreed. Not to be outdone by a pack of greedy monks, the bishop began excommunicating pilgrims for paying their saintly respects—and their not-so-saintly money—at the monastery. Eventually the bishop won out and the coveted bones were removed to the cathedral. Miffed at their loss, the monks sued the bishop in court for the loss of 3,000 gold marks in revenue per annum, a handsome sum, and I didn't blame them for smarting at its loss. It was as if St. Eloi was still smithing gold from his troubled grave.

Not coming from a family with the means to ever lay eyes on such sacred and wealth-demanding bones, I had a natural incredulity about their genuineness. After all, how was one to distinguish saints' bones from pigs' bones? I was no careless Christian, however, so I kept my cynicism to myself to avoid the sin of sacrilege, and dutifully genuflected toward the high altar where St. Eloi and his bones made such a fuss.

Bulging the seams of his gilded vestments, the portly bishop looked like a well-stuffed sausage, bedecked with a prelatical mitre atop its head, if it may be said that a sausage can have a head. All the while, he chanted some nonsense in Latin, no doubt liberally employing "the accusative case of objects to which."

Sunlight filtered through the reds, blues, and yellows of the Gothic stained glass window depicting the Holy Virgin, her hand raised in divine-like blessing on the faithful. Shafts of multicolored brilliant light mingled with the blue smoke of incense wafting heavenward from the censers.

Center stage on the chancel knelt young Calvin, the filtered light playing on his robe and making it mottled with color. In one such flash of light I was reminded, to my annoyance, of Joseph's coat that was his father Jacob's gift to his favorite child.

Meanwhile, the bishop, Charles de Hangest, droned on in Latin, snipping rhythmically at the young man's hair, the shorn locks piling up on the stone floor about the young man's feet, like wool at shearing time.

Thus, my spying on John Calvin began early in life. That morning I cowered behind one of the grand columns where the south transept of the cathedral converged with the nave. If I may say so myself, I had even by this early date in my career developed an uncanny ability to be invisible. It is beyond my understanding to explain, but it is no less a fact for its inexplicability. When I cared to, I could move without making candle flames flutter. I confess to taking great pride in this my chief ability, and I am compelled to confess my employing of it in devious ways as it suited my fancy. My schoolfellows wagered bets on how close I could approach undetected upon unsuspecting lovers making rendezvous on the banks of our river, lovers who in my longing mind's eye had now become the goddess Monique locked in an embrace with my own self. Betting against my success, new fellows in our town lost every trifle they owned.

For all my stealth, when the prelate barber had finished his work, I nearly gave myself away. Calvin's new coiffure nearly made me burst with laughter. His freshly shorn scalp, now configured as a monkish tonsure, was so white it was almost blue, and what remained of his head seemed so small, so insignificant, I wondered that I had ever sat in awe of what emanated from such a head. As I buried my face in the sleeve of my tunic to suppress my mirth, I wondered how such a pointy skull could possibly contain brain matter sufficient to make him such a scholar.

Though I delighted in finding reasons to laugh at Calvin even then, yet did I know in the depth of my being that I had never been more jealous of anyone in all my life. I ran my fingers through my wavy locks, yanking at them till tears sprang from my eyes. Even this ridiculous haircut of his set him above me. For I knew that the chaplain of La Gesine had only just resigned his post and that the bishop was sure to confer the vacant chaplaincy on the young scholar.

Yet did I despise him still more for what it all meant. He was being marked out for priesthood, and more to the point, for a handsome income, one that would now fill the purse of the favored young man—further setting him above me and my station, and further embittering my heart against him.

I had seen enough. Soundlessly I turned my back and left the cathedral, the chanting of the bishop fading as I went. From the eminence of the cathedral's situation, I surveyed the tile roofs of Noyon, fanning out, like my life, in a disordered and seemingly random jumble.

Surrounding the tile roofs of the half-timbered, clustered houses lay wooded hills of beech and oak. For all its unremarkableness to me then, Noyon is an appealing town with a long history. Since the Romans subjugated the Gauls, the fertile plain on which it rests, watered by the Verses and Oise rivers, has been home to untold generations of craftsmen, farmers, bakers, butchers, tanners—like my family—horse breeders, nobles, and of course the clergy. I mused on the infinite variety of human existence represented by that tumbling array of individual houses connected by the narrow cobbled streets that we called our village. It had been called that by many before my generation, and was likely to by called so by many more, so I then thought.

As I stood considering the array of life that stretched downhill before me, the boy choristers must have ascended to the heights of polyphonic grandeur with the *Ave Maria, ora pro nobis*, for they succeeded, aided by the deep-toned organ, in pulling my attention back up the hill to the cathedral.

It was the only cathedral I knew, but since then I have seen many. Ours was of the sturdier sort. Heavy, boxy towers, which cast their wide shadow across the red-brown roofs on sunny afternoons, stood square and unyielding, as if guarding the west entrance with twin might against heretics and infidels.

I now believe the east end of Notre Dame Cathedral Noyon to be one of the most grand of all. Its magnificent flying buttresses flange out in three broad terraces holding the bishop's seat immovably in its place. I wondered at such grand old churches, built, it would seem, so to impress the viewer as to make them unshakably committed to the lesser visible dimensions of religion.

My revelry through the centuries was interrupted by the clattering of cart wheels and the clip-clop of oxen, the chatter of women at the nearby bakeshop, the buttery aromas of freshly baked croissants, the shouts of men repairing the tiles on the blacksmith's shop, the clanging of the smith's hammer on steel, the wheezing of his bellows pumped by a timorous looking apprentice, wary of the blacksmith's next blows, the hissing of hot iron as it cooled in tubs filled with water drawn from the river.

Glancing again at the fearful-looking apprentice, I felt my cheeks grow hot. I was late again, and my father could be brutal with tardy apprentices, more so if they happened to be his own flesh and blood.

Quickening my pace, I set off down the narrow street toward my father's workshop. But as I strode toward my duties, an idea began forming in my mind.

"Jean-Louis!" a voice broke in on my brooding, and I heard the clattering of wooden shoes on the cobbles behind me. I turned.

"Jean-Louis, leave your apron," said my friend Martin, "and come a-fishing with me this day."

"You know it is not possible," I said irritably. "Why do you mock me?"

"I do not mock you," replied Martin with a pout in his tone. "I merely want you to accompany me in the fishing."

"One day, Martin," I said, making my voice sound patient with him, "you too will be bound as an apprentice, as I have been. Then there is no more time for fishing."

"Could you not ask?"

"It would be of no use," I replied.

His face brightened. "Could you not come away with me fishing, and invent a convincing excuse? Plead your father's mercy?"

I eyed him and snorted.

"You might try," he urged.

"Even now I shall be late," I said, "and will face the lash. But Martin, what if you were to meet me at the riverbank this night, after supper? I have a scheme, and I shall need your help with it."

"What scheme?" he asked, tugging my sleeve and leaning closer.

"Meet at our usual place, and I shall tell you."

I managed to slink into my apron and commence my work while my father was engaged in haggling with a customer over the price and configuration of a new leather jerkin. It was a busy morning in the workshop, and my father seemed either not to notice my tardiness, or to be too busy to do anything about it.

But he did take notice when I laid my thumb open nearly to the bone while carelessly trimming a leather harness, and he rebuked me for ill attention to my duties—and for soiling the leather with my blood.

"There's more hide to be laid bare and tanned in this shop," he said with something akin to a growl, "than beast hide. Attend to what you're doing, or I shall be forced to pause in my attentions to this pig's hide—and give all my attentions to yours."

The nerve endings in my buttocks quivered, for I knew it was no idle threat; there was always a conveniently supple leather strap nearby in a shop such as my father's. I resolved to give greater heed to my duties. Yet did I reserve some attention for my plan. When at last darkness began to fall, and I had completed my duties and my meager evening meal, I set out for the banks of the Oise but a mile from the village.

"Martin," I called into the gloom.

"Here," came the reply from the shadows. "What is your scheme?" he asked as I joined him.

"The sky is clear," I began, "and I believe that this evening will be one of those nights that the Accusative Case, newly shorn and made chaplain, shall come here for his meditations."

"Ah," said Martin knowingly. "And we shall make contribution to those meditations."

"So I had planned," I replied.

"Why do you hate him so?" asked Martin.

I was offended at his question, for I did not want to be known for hating young Calvin. I desired that my pranks and name-calling be thought more innocent than hatred.

"Hate him?" I replied dismissively. "I do not care enough about him to bother with hating him. I plague him merely for my amusement."

"And what amusement do you propose?"

"Shh!" I hissed, clamping my hand on his mouth. "He comes."

5

The Voice of God

I HAD NEARLY FORGOTTEN that Martin had not seen the clerical coiffure of young Calvin. The initial flourish of my mirth had passed, but Martin came close to howling with laughter at the sight of the bald-headed young priest in training. Again I was forced to clamp a firm hand on Martin's mouth. Emanations of his compressed breath threatened to explode around the edges of my hand, and I knew we would certainly be betrayed by such wind-breaking flatulence.

I held firm, Martin beginning to beat frantically at my arm, his eyes bulging as he struggled for air. I grinned at him, intoxicated to feel that I had the power to end this young imp's life. What would it feel like to ignore his frantic eyes and flailing arms and legs, to feel him go limp with death in my grip? Fearing that his rigors would escalate above the rippling and shying of the river sounds, and thereby give us away, I slowly eased the pressure of my hand, thus permitting him to gulp down drafts of air.

For what seemed like ages, Calvin merely stood on the banks, his hands clasped behind his back, his head thrown back as he gazed at the starlight. I followed his gaze, and, in spite of myself, I found the wonder of the heavenly constellations having their effect on my imagination. But mine was a fleeting revelry, whereas Calvin seemed more and more rapt as he feasted on the heavenly display above us.

So long did he remain in that posture that I nearly abandoned my scheme. Little amusement could be had if he merely stood there transfixed.

"The heavens declare your glory, O Lord," he began, his voice faint at the first, but gaining strength as he continued his recitation. It was precisely what I had hoped for. It was a recitation from the psalter, to be sure, but made more personal by his turning the divine syntax into something more like his own prayer of adoration.

I waited impatiently for him to lapse into silence before implementing my scheme. But I recollect the frustration with which I waited. My mind was torn. His words were so heartfelt and sincere, how could I plague him with my cruel deception? But I despised him and longed to make sport of him and, what is more, to boast of my jest to my fellows on the morrow.

When at last he did fall silent for a time, I had resolved my dilemma. Rolling a piece of leather selected for my purpose into the shape of a cone, I raised it to my lips, aiming my voice toward a broad backwater on the far side of the river.

"I have heard your sighings," I began, making my voice sound as far off and bishop-like as I could manage. I paused to view his reaction.

Young Calvin's freshly shorn head gleamed more brightly in the moonlight as he seemed to lift his head, searching the heavens for the speaker, or so I desperately wanted to imagine it.

I persisted. "You are a chosen vessel, set apart to serve me." Again I paused. It was of no good to me unless I could describe his reaction. By this time having recovered his breath, Martin was nearly bursting with mirth at my side. Fearing he would give me away, I aimed a kick in his direction, and continued. "You alone, shall turn the hearts of men to me." Again I strained to see his reaction, hoping beyond hope that he would make reply, a reply that I would make to live with lavish embellishments in the memory of my fellows forever. If none came, I had every intention of inventing what I considered to be an apt reply; whether or not he rendered one mattered not. Again I spoke through my improvised horn. "All will look to you, will render highest honor to you for your greatness."

Perhaps I miscalculated with this comment, for Calvin turned slowly and scanned the banks of the river, a look of mingled scorn, anger, and something harder to detect in the dim light, but I thought it was a look of pity on his face. But to my frustration, he uttered no reply. After looking steadily in our direction for an instant—I was certain he could not see me—Calvin turned and walked briskly down the pathway that led back to the village.

"That did not go so well," said Martin, his eyes following the disappearing figure. "I'm not sure that you got God's voice precisely as it is."

I turned on him. "And you know what God's voice sounds like?" I growled.

"I do not," he admitted. "But Calvin seems to."

Giving him another kick—harder than the first—without a word, I stomped back to the village and home.

6

The Scourge of God

SOME TWO YEARS PASSED, during which time both Calvin and I were removed from the grammar school, he to continue his studies under private tutelage alongside the sons of the noble and enormously wealthy family of Hangest de Montmor, I to the drudgery of slaughtering pigs and tanning leather in my father's shop.

I saw him but occasionally in those years, but when I did it always reignited something within me that I found hard to understand. Within me surged a tempest of resentment toward him that felt like the rising fury of the tides at Mont-Saint-Michel. Just as those tides engulfed the hapless pilgrim, so I longed to drag Calvin beneath the waves of my envy, and hold him under the flood until he could rise no more above me.

Imagine, therefore, the height of my resentment when I learned that through some finagling, Calvin's father managed to secure yet another clerical appointment for the boy, this a priesthood *in absentia* at the nearby village of Pont L'Eveque. For this I hated him the more. I hated him because I knew that he now possessed not one but two incomes from clerical appointments he was unable to fulfill. I felt certain he could not have deserved these appointments. We who were his fellows in town had a good laugh at Calvin's expense. But it was a putrid green laughter, laughter indulged to mask our envy.

It was rumored that after his new priestly appointment he wanted to visit the village that now owed him a living. While there he actually attempted to deliver a sermon. I wished I could have been there to hear his efforts. I envisioned the slight boy— for boy I considered him, though he was months my senior—a boy festooned in a clerical gown many sizes too large for his frame, tripping over the skirts as he made his way solemnly to the pulpit. In my cruel imagination, I added a bishop's mitre cocked on his head, falling down about his ears and eyes. But events soon unfolded about which not even I could find cause for laughter.

It began early in the summer of 1523. I shall never forget the horror of those days in that dreaded year. We in Noyon-le-Sainte had, of course, heard of the deadly pestilence. For more than 150 years, I am told, it had mysteriously appeared across Europe as if by stealth. Perhaps it is human nature to express hope by clutching at the delusion that such a scourge could never strike one's own village. But when the nagging uncertainty feeding the delusion is forced to give way to the horrific realities of the Black Death, the greater the delusion the more acute the terror that drives it away. So it seemed when the plague descended on our village.

I shall never forget the cries emanating from our neighbor's cottage that morning in June of the year 1523. The cries came from the doomed child's mother. I shall never forget them. "O God, O God," she wailed.

My blood ran cold. Had the dreaded death come upon Monique? I ran out to the street. Not cautious of my step, I set my foot ankle-deep in the foul night waste that putrefied in the gutter before our door.

Rising and falling with anguish, the wailing continued. "Not my precious Francine. Not she! Not she! Not she!"

The rest was buried in the incomprehensible depths of a mother's despair. I, however, breathed a long sigh of relief at what I had heard. Their youngest daughter, pretty little Francine—so like her elder sister in feature—must have been seven or eight years of age. But at least it was not Monique.

Word travels rapidly under such circumstances. The child had complained of pain under her armpits and in the region between her legs. It was when her mother stripped the girl and investigated that her wailing began. Egg-size swellings had formed out of nowhere, viciously attaching themselves to the child in these regions of her body. By next morning, the tumors had spread to other parts of her frail frame. And some of the grotesque buboes had achieved the size of apples. Within the next passage of the sun, black blotches, like deep bruises, spread over her pale skin from head to foot.

By the third morning the child was dead.

Her mother was inconsolable. I glimpsed Monique in the grim funeral procession that emanated from their door. Shrouded in a black veil, she shuffled behind her father who alone bore the frail limp form of Francine. I recall being bewildered at how small that swaddled form appeared in his arms.

Following hard on Francine's death, more tumors strangely materialized. Deep purple blotches followed. More anguished wailing shattered the unnatural silence that had come over the town. It was as if everyone held his breath, hoping thereby to escape the dreaded plague. Then when there was no escape and a loved one fell to the pestilence, all the pent-up, soul-churning dread broke forth in cries so despondent that they haunt me to this day.

Late in the week of Francine's death, more wailing was emitted from our neighbor's door. Again my blood faltered in my veins.

But it was Monique's mother who had come down with the deadly tumors. Rapidly she sickened. And as suddenly—she perished.

No one comprehended the cause of the disease, but as it descended on more villagers, a mob consensus emerged. The sick must be mysteriously transmitting the plague to the healthy.

I happened to overhear one of those who ranked as a physician in our midst put it this way: "Just so as fire catches and spreads without restraint onto anything dry or oily near it, so I have come to understand that anyone speaking to or going near the sick is caught up in the flames of the foul contamination of this scourge."

"Am I to understand," replied the magistrate of our town, clutching a fistful of rosemary and lavender, and burying his nose in the cluster of herbs as he spoke, "that by aiding the sick we become so ourselves?"

The physician seemed loathe to make reply.

"Speak, man!" cried the magistrate.

"The scourge is in many ways mysterious, Your Lordship. But in this regard there seems no longer any mystery. Anyone who comes near someone who has contracted the disease, shall contract the disease himself. Nothing seems more certain."

"How can you be so certain of this?" pressed the magistrate, his voice quavering and growing thinner.

"I have observed, Your Lordship, that mere touching of the clothing or bedding of the sick, and the person touching it, regardless of their compassion and goodwill, receives the disease for their pains."

"What foul evil has brought this scourge of God upon us?" moaned the magistrate.

"I am no divine, your Lordship," replied the physician. "Though I too am bewildered at the divine consideration, I must confine myself to the physical sufferings all about me."

The magistrate took a step back from the physician. "Are you not fearful of the contamination? For surely you are hourly in the precincts of those damned to perish in this dreaded pestilence." Convinced by his own words, he took a yet larger step backward as he spoke.

"It is my calling," said the physician simply.

"Perhaps God shall keep you from the contamination for your compassion."

"Perhaps," said the physician, but I detected in his face and tone that he had little hope of this.

"It is a perverse disease, indeed, that so meanly rewards those who relieve suffering and comfort the dying." Again, the magistrate retreated before the physician, his voice growing louder. "But what prevention? Surely there is something that shall end the spread of this dread evil."

As the physician formed his reply, the undulations of a woman's wailing rose and fell from an upstairs window nearby. "I believe there is only one thing that shall end the advance of this disease, Your Lordship." He paused, casting his eyes about the doors firmly shut, and the shrouded windows, and the filthy pavement of the village. "It is said that a fire will cease advancing," he paused, "when it has nothing left to consume."

"Speak not in riddles, man!" cried the magistrate.

"As with fire spent for lack of fuel," continued the physician, "I fear, that this Black Death shall end only when it has consumed all in its path."

I must confess to gut-wrenching revulsion at his words. Though I at the time felt little or nothing of compassion for the dying masses, I did feel a gnawing fear at what might befall Monique. But in truth, I feared more keenly, deep within the marrow of my bones, my own dying. I felt profoundly ill prepared for such a death.

For days the slightest irregularity in my breath, or twinge in my flesh, on the instant set my mind to incontrollable speculations about what I must inevitably feel next as I fell under the doleful power of the pestilence. I could eat but little, my stomach churned so. This too I divined as a first sign of my contagion, awaiting with dread the blows certain to follow.

7

The Plague Closes In

"THE GERM OF THIS SCOURGE is conceived in the guts of infected fleas, carried abroad on the backs of vermin." The speaker uttering these words had set up a box to stand on in the town square. He was a plump man, dressed in a parti-colored vesture, and seemed to style himself an expert on the plague. From atop his box, he thus confidently pontificated on the causes of the disease, great and small.

So it was the fleas. I could not help myself at his words to feel an itching sensation spreading instantly over my entire body. The nibble of a flea was a commonplace, and not to me alone. How I longed to take flight and be rid of this place of disease and death. But where might I go where there were no fleas? Fleas were everywhere: in the market, in my father's workshop, in our house, in my clothes, in my own straw-stuffed mattress. Nothing could be more common—except the rats, the chariots of these winged bearers of death, if the man's theory was to be believed.

"We see death coming into our midst like foul smoke," the man continued, his voice rising and falling, his eyes bulging. As I listened, I came to believe that he derived some perverse pleasure from his vocation.

"It is a plague which cuts off the young, a ruthless phantom who has no mercy. Great is its seething like a burning cinder; it is an ugly eruption like an unseemly haze. It is merciless. No one shall escape. The youngest, the poorest, those without means or resistance shall be taken first."

Though my feet remained rooted, I attempted to stop my ears.

"They shall die in violent fever and horrific pain. When the foul disease shall, alas, have reached the lungs, the most violent and painful coughing up of blood shall rack the bodies of the dying."

It was then that I discerned his true intent.

"Ah, but I alone have developed the cure," he said, his eyes bright with the enthusiasm of one who hopes to empty the pockets of another. Apparently he was an herbalist, for he proceeded to explain that by blending columbine, marigold, a raw egg—and a secret ingredient he claimed was in a tiny vial he held aloft as if it were the relic of a saint—

"Then lay the life-giving brew to the fire," he continued, "but do not burn it. Blend all with good ale. Then make the sore-afflicted one to drink it. If he holds it in his belly, he shall be cured. He shall live."

I had heard enough and turned on my heel and fled.

In the days of misery that followed I saw little of our neighbors, what remained of them. But others I observed in our village. I watched with little emotion as the healthy abandoned the infected to their fate. Fathers shunned their children and fled from their infected wives in a debasement of fear. There were even mothers who, in a frenzy of terror, ran from the bedsides of their screaming children. One such mother—I shall never forget the scene—staggered sobbing from her door, her hands clutching her ears in a vain attempt to block out the raving screams of a child, abandoned to its fate, left alone to die.

Worse still, the bishop and his priests fled for their lives, careless of their flock. No one remained to comfort the newly infected who had but days to live, none to administer last rites to the dying, none to bury the dead, none to pray over the remains of the deceased, none to enfold them in clay with ceremony and dignity.

Only those of means could afford to flee the town. My father had no money to enable us to flee, and nowhere to go if we had had the means. We were not alone. With the wealthy and the bishop and his priests gone, all that remained was the peasantry.

Some of the devout poor, bewildered as they were, bravely attempted to fill the void left by the departed clergy. In a pathetic parody, they did their best to mumble words of consolation, botching the Latin chants in their ignorance. Impious as I was, even I felt there was something perverse in it all: the flock abandoned by the shepherds in the evil hour, the hour of greatest need.

Scarcely a family was spared. I could not escape it. So many died, and in such a short span of time. Alone they died, panting, gasping, eyes lolling in their sockets, balefully groping in the darkness for some comfort. But none was to be found in the horror of the great death.

Among those yet well, some pled with God to deliver them if he would. These attempted to mend their licentious ways in hopes of appeasing God's wrath, certain that if they were good enough, God would be obligated to lift the deadly pestilence.

Others chose a different path. Determined to wring the marrow out of life until the clutches of the scourge at last enfolded their miserable lives in its clammy grip, many wealthy clerics and nobles cloistered themselves in remote manor houses, there to feast and revel until doomsday had fully come.

And who dared trundle the bodies off to burial? Few were well enough to do it, and those who were healthy recoiled at the prospect, fearful of infection. But to leave the dead unburied was unthinkably worse. With dozens dying daily, hastily dug mass pits became the final resting place of the mounds of bodies that littered the streets.

One late afternoon, as the sun set in the west, I watched in horror as the town horse mucker, Filthy Frank, a simple man, miraculously robust in the midst of the emaciation and decay all about him, used a pitchfork to toss the spent bodies into the gaping hole. I marveled at how he forked the bodies without ceremony or feeling, as if they were but mounds of horse dung, his usual freight. The only ritual conferred on the undignified dead was his monotone humming. He perhaps imagined it tuneful, but it was indistinguishable from the snoring of a weary peasant or the wheezing of a sow being delivered of her suckling young. Yet infinitely worse to my tormented imagination, his unadorned requiem became in my ears a sort of mournful echoing of the wailings and gnashings of hell.

Sickened by it all, I anticipated my own infection hourly. With every breath I drew, I felt certain that I was transporting the deadly miasma into my lungs, and would soon commence retching and coughing up of my life's blood. The buboes would attach themselves to my body, and my life would be snuffed out before it had scarcely begun.

All this while I would occasionally think of what had befallen Monique. I even wondered whether she and her father had died days ago and lay rotting in their beds under the roof tiles next door.

Then one morning I rounded a great stone buttress of the town hall—and before me was Monique. Her eyes were sunken and her fair cheeks pale, but it was she, and she was alive.

What transpired next came over me in an instant. Had I taken time to consider my words more carefully, I never would have ventured to utter them.

"Monique," I said, reaching for her hand. "You remain alive, as do I. But if we remain in this place," I said, gesturing with a hand at the cluttered streets and the half-timbered houses, their windows shuttered tightly as if by this alone they could escape the plague, "we two shall die."

She looked uncomprehendingly at me, as if she were at church. I persisted. "But I can save you, Monique."

There was a flicker of comprehension at these my words. And then she spoke. "You?"

It was all I was ever to have from her lips, though in my folly I did not then know this, so I blundered onward.

"Monique, flee, now, this hour. Escape this place." I paused, uncertain how to proceed, whether to proceed. Yet was I in earnest, so I persisted. "Flee and live," I said, mustering as much feeling as I then had. "We two shall live. Flee with me." I faltered, but stammered stupidly on, "and be my lover."

I wrote that I was to receive nothing more from her lips, but she did render to me one piercingly eloquent communication from her eyes that moment. "I should rather die in agony a hundred times over in this my place than flee with you and be your lover," so her steady eyes precisely articulated. There was to be no misunderstanding in her look, a look I shall remember to my grave.

The next morning, it was the second day of August of the year 1523, my mother did not rise from her bed. There was great shouting and panic in our hovel that morning. I shall never forget it. The scourge was upon her, and I knew, if I had ever doubted it, that it would soon be upon me. My life would be over. Horrified at the prospect, I knew there was but one thing to do if I was to live.

After hastily gathering my flea-infested bolster, a wool cap I wore in winter, and a coarse cloak that had been a neighbor's, I made my way to the edge of town and the river. That night I slept in the grasses under a beech tree along the banks of the Oise.

Stiff with cold, I arose next morning, and as if by some dreaded compulsion made my way back to my home and my father's workshop, only to discover that the dreaded buboes had attached themselves to my little sister. She did not rise that morning.

My father said not a word to me as we attempted to go about our duty in the shop. I remember nothing of what I accomplished, but I do recall my father breathing hard and collapsing on a stool, his face buried in his work-roughened hands. At first I thought it might be grieving, and I marveled to see such emotion in him. But then I saw the sweat pouring from his fevered brow, the blotching pallor of his skin.

That night again, I made my bed out in the open air along the riverbank. My stomach gnawed at my innards as blood-red hues illuminated the dusky sky. The massive towers of the cathedral stood like twin black memorial stones against the fading brilliance of the sky as the sun went to its place.

As darkness fell, I listened to the shying of the river, murmuring softly as it passed. A gentle night breeze whispered in the beech leaves overhead, lulling me for the short hours of the night into an inexplicable sense of calm. But then I awoke.

As I climbed the cobblestones to my home, I knew before I arrived that my life was about to change forever.

I received the news without betraying my feelings, though deep within there was a wrenching I could not explain. My mother lay pale and still on her straw mattress. I had seen death before, but not my own mother rigid in its inexorable grip. By the violent disarray of the bedclothes and her disheveled hair, her passing had not been without great struggle. The presence of her body and the unnatural eeriness of her complete absence sent a cold grimace throughout my frame.

Numb, I proceeded to the bedside of my little sister. I at first thought she too was dead, but there was something different from the appearance of my mother. My face buried in the sleeve of my tunic, I detected a frail hint of life in her eyes and in the irregular flutter of movement in her tiny bosom. I did not go near and take up her tiny hand in mine, or stroke her brow, or whisper words of comfort in her delicate ear. I let her be. Within moments she was still.

Cursing and raging like a wild boar cornered by the huntsman in our Picardy forest, my father's death throes awakened no sympathetic impulses in me. Expending such prodigious energy in his violent war with death as he was, I knew not how long he might last. It could be no more than hours, though agonizing hours they would most certainly be. In an instant, I felt a torrent of desire to be forever rid of what had afflicted him. Tumbling over myself, I could not pass out of our house and into the littered streets of Noyon quickly enough.

It was as I passed by Monique's house that I noticed the door ajar. Pausing, I listened. I heard the all-too-familiar sound of panting and of sobbing, as of someone in mortal pain. Too well I knew those sounds. I hesitated.

My mind was in torment. The plague must be of a certainty upon her. Or was it she alone? Should I go to her? Not all who fell ill died. There had been stories. She might recover. But would I not contract the disease if I entered. Yet was I not already destined to contract it? I thought of that final look she had given me. Was that all I was to know?

Helplessly carried on the swirling current of some vast river, I felt like my life was about to be plunged over some mighty precipice, there to end, un-mourned and forgotten.

If only I could save her. Over and again I longed to deliver her from the scourge. I held out hope that perhaps her beauty gave her a strength that would prove at the last resilient to the deadly horror afflicting her fair figure. In my mind, if someone deserved to survive, surely it was she.

My feet carried me back to the river's edge. I think that for a moment, as I gazed at its broad expanse, I considered what it would feel like to plunge myself into its depths and thereby end the anguish that had become my life.

As I thus mused, inexplicably, I recalled the night at this very bend in the river when Calvin, looking to the heavens, had prayed. I also recalled how it was I who had mocked that praying.

But for a fleeting moment, I too determined to pray. What else was I to do? But I was soon to realize that matters as high as praying required practice and study, things I had miserably neglected. So inexpert was I in such matters that when I did find my voice, odd, confused, and humiliating was that form of praying I then uttered.

Faltering and low, I began. "I have long loved you but from afar. If there is a God in heaven who hears, and if I pray and you are healed, will you then return my undying affection and be my lover? Say that you will. O, say, 'I am yours,' and then shall we be forever united in heart and body."

"Jean-Louis, I have always loved you. Since first I laid my azure eyes upon your sturdy features, I have loved you. With all my heart do I adore you."

"With all your heart? Why, dear Monique, have you never shown this heart to me? Why have you inflicted such scornful looks upon me, and such fetching looks upon another?"

"My Jean-Louis, there has never been another, nor ever shall be, my dearest love."

"Then let your body follow, my dearest one."

I blush deeply to pen these words, but I have sworn myself to confessing all in this my unable account of these years. Perhaps my attempts at praying turned so quickly into a delusional attempt at seduction in part because of the traumatic events of those days. So afflicted was my mind and so tormented were my affections by the plague that I delivered up my petitions to Monique rather than to God in heaven. May he forgive me.

When I, to a degree, came back to my senses, I snatched up a fistful of mud from the riverbank and hurled it with all my might at the mottled trunk of a beech tree. It collided with a sickening splat. I scoffed out loud at my fantasy. Attempting to harden myself, I determined to abandon all hope for Monique.

Yet did my own troubles remain. As night fell, I gazed up at the stars as I had witnessed Calvin doing that night two years ago. Calvin's praying had been so different. His had been adoring words, to be sure, but so very different.

Did God hear praying? I had witnessed many desperate prayers in those days of plague and death, and yet the pestilence raged on. What is more, many of the corpses whose lips had uttered those prayers now lay pale and silent in mass pits, rotting alongside corpses whose lips had uttered curses and not prayers. I thought of my father. He had not prayed. He was one of those who cursed. I wondered whether his end had come. It soon would, of that I was certain, and, prayers or curses, he would be tossed on the end of a pitchfork into a mass pit alongside all those who had troubled themselves to pray.

Determined to save my breath—I who had so mocked praying by attempting to feign God's voice, and in this very place—bitterly I dismissed the notion of praying.

Curling up like a water rat in the grasses along the riverbank, I attempted to sleep. The river noises that had seemed so peaceful before now rumbled in my ears like a great cataract of churning water. Batting at a mosquito persistently whining in my ear, I lay wakeful.

It was that night that I determined to flee Noyon. Where I would go, I had no idea. How I would eat, I had no better idea. Yet flee I must, if I was to survive. Of that much I was certain. Through the night, I desperately labored to form a plan, but none came. How was I, without money or connections, with nowhere to go, how was I to escape this wretched place?

Clammy with the morning dew, I rose stiffly to my feet. It was yet dark, with but a faint hint of dawn on the eastern horizon. After stretching my aching muscles, I stood irresolute on the banks of the Oise. It is one thing to resolve in a flight of terror to flee one's hometown; it is quite another matter to turn one's feet from the only home one has known and set off. My resolution was further crippled by my lack of means.

In the midst of such indecision, my feet, as if against my will, turned back toward the village, and I found myself feeling my way in the dark toward the place of loathsome contagion.

What occurred next happened so suddenly, and my mind was so distracted with my troubles, that I scarcely realized I was falling until my chin struck something unyielding and pain shot through my jaw and down my neck. Working my mouth in an effort to relieve the discomfort, I placed my hands at my sides, thereby to lift myself from the ground.

I shuddered with horror. My right hand had lit on a large lump, over which I must have stumbled, a mound that was taut and yet that gave way under the pressure of my hand. I jerked my hand away, crying out in my fright and scrambling backward, scuttling like a land crab in my desperation to be rid of the foul object.

A few yards off, breathing hard, I stopped and sat in the dirt, my eyes straining to discover what it was I had fallen over. Deep within I felt that I knew what it was, and I shuddered at the knowledge. I sat and stared in the direction of the object as the gray light of dawn dimly illuminated the path.

As I had feared, it was a corpse, a victim of the plague, no doubt, and recently dead. I had seen, of late, many such corpses, though I was not for that any less repelled at the sight. But this one was better dressed than most who had remained to die in Noyon. Burying my nose and mouth in the sleeve of my worn tunic, I drew closer, my eyes diverted from its features. It was clear to me that its tunic and britches were of fine linen and crafted by a tailor. It wore a fine linen blouse, with waistcoat of blue silk and a chapeau to match, though these latter lay crumpled a few feet from the dead man.

I turned away and gulped down a mouthful of air. Then drawing nearer still, I spied something at his belt that keenly interested me. My fear of contagion was in an instant overcome by my greed. Drawing out my knife, I knelt at his side and slit the thongs of his purse. Stuffing it in my tunic, I hesitated. Snatching up the blue waistcoat and chapeau and stuffing them inside my tunic, I then turned and ran. I ran as if the devil and all his demon horde slavered at my heels.

8

Frank Next Door

ODDLY I FOUND MYSELF not running from the village but toward it. I could not at first explain this to my own satisfaction and even wondered whether it meant that fate had doomed me, despite my apparent good fortune, to contract at last the dreaded plague.

Upon reflection I slowly came to understand some part of the cause of my return. Like a torrent, tears welled into my eyes and overflowed down my face. Though with envy, I had at times observed the phenomenon in other homes; mine had not been a particularly affectionate household. My mother had always seemed too weary for demonstrative tenderness. Toward the infant in her arms, insincere scolding was the closest she came to displaying her love. I say, "her love," for I was certain she must love her children; I simply had never been the recipient of any tangible parceling out of the commodity.

Of my father, it would require still more creative fabrication to call any emotion he might have had for his family "love." His gruff demeanor knew no boundaries. Moreover, his gruffness, unlike that of some laboring men I had met, was no façade to conceal a kind heart from a world that had decided peasant men ought not to have one. His was the authentic article beyond a doubt. And gruffness was the kindest expression I recall ever receiving from him.

I shall never forget hearing him speak soothingly to a panicked horse, stroking its neck as he intoned words of comfort. That horse heard words and felt a touch from my father that I have no recollection of ever hearing or feeling. I remain troubled by the fact that a four-legged beast fared better in the hands of my father than ever I did.

Hence it was that I found myself deeply puzzled by my inability to flee my home, once and for all time, to forget my family. It ought to have been a simple matter. My reticence made no sense to me, and I wiped the tears away in anger, resolving not to allow such weakness of sentiment in myself. Far too inexperienced was I at that time to observe the irony in my resolve. Only much later—perhaps far too much later—did it dawn on my affections that in the resolve I had determined to be precisely like my father had been: devoid in myself of precisely that which I had so deeply longed for in another, but had come to the conclusion I was destined never to have.

Nevertheless, did my feet carry me back, against all sense or feeling, to the doorstep of my origin. Seldom since have I felt so conflicted in mind. I longed to fling open the door and find that it had all been a nightmarish illusion, that my mother and sister were alive and well, and perhaps that even my father lived. I found myself deep in remorse that I had not been at my mother's side when she was dying, had not felt her hand in mine while life still pulsed in her sinews. I longed to hear her voice one last time. And so I felt drawn by inexplicable forces to the door of what had been my family's house.

But by one and the same impulse, I was repulsed at taking a single step nearer to a place where I would most certainly contract the dreaded plague. And then in my mind I saw Filthy Frank drawing near with his pitchfork. Had he already come for my family? He would come.

Humming like the damned, he would lunge his tool into my emaciated body and hoist my remains into that loathsome trench, peopled by the rotting dead. A tremor shook my frame at the thought.

While I stood thus ruminating before my family's house and shop, there came the rumbling of a carriage and the clatter of horses' hooves on the cobbles. The driver was muffled to the ears against the contagion. Flitting from left to right, his eyes peeped in fear from under his hat.

Before the plague, it was common for carriages to halt before my father's shop. There is a great deal of leather harness involved in horses and carriages, and my father's trade was frequently engaged to effect repairs. I recognized it instantly as one of the fine carriages of the House of Hangest and drew closer in hopes of learning who was within.

Hurling a chunk of stone at the shop door, the driver then gave a muffled yell through his scarf. I knew that no one would emerge from that door, and it would only be a matter of a few more impatient moments before the driver would crack his whip and take his offending harness across town to the only other craftsman who plied the same trade as my father had done. I stole nearer.

Several things happened, seemingly at one and the same instant, yet must I record them as if they happened in sequence.

While the carriage driver raged on impatiently, Filthy Frank and his reeking cart clattered to a stand before the door next to ours, thus blocking the way for the Hangest carriage.

Humming his insane dirge, Frank slowly descended his cart, tipped his filthy cap to the carriage driver, and without bothering to knock at the door, entered the house that had been Monique's.

My heart nearly froze with dread in my bosom as I awaited what would follow. Unable to back his horses and carriage, the enraged driver, fearful of such immediate contagion, refitted his scarf and lifted his collar higher about his neck and face. The horses, sensing his agitation, clopped their hooves and shook their great heads, the harness fastenings clattering, as it seemed to my feverish imagination, like the chains binding the dead in the underworld.

Numbingly few moments later, Filthy Frank hummed his way back through the doorway, a limp bundle carried effortlessly over his shoulder. I observed once-lovely auburn hair hanging low and swaying with Frank's limping gait as if she were moving and alive. But there was no hint of life in the transparent paleness of the lifeless arm and limp hand that dangled grotesquely against his rump with his every step.

Rigid, like the cold stone image of St. Eloi at the cathedral, I watched the scene unfolding before me. The air about me was seemingly replaced with millions of particles of dust, and when I attempted to draw in breath, the barren emptiness of that involuntary impulse seemed to clutch with relentless grip at the inside passageway of my throat. Without ceremony, Frank heaved her from his shoulder, tossing the rag-doll burden over the sideboards of his death cart, a dull thudding sound coming from within as he let her fall. With a toothless grin, as if he'd just delivered a crock full of fresh cream, and with another salute of his cap, he then took up his reins, gave a low whistle and was gone.

In bitterness I turned heavenward. I shall recall it to my dying hour. Then drawing in a deep and violent breath, I raised my fists at the steel gray clouds presiding overhead, and released from deep within my being a prolonged wail of anguish; whether audible or no, it was anguish that metamorphized quickly into bitter rage.

I said that several things happened seemingly at the same instant. And so it was. No sooner had I raised my defiant grief than I observed a face appearing in the window of the carriage, an unmistakable face to me.

"So you have, as yet, survived," I spoke thus inwardly.

Our eyes met. I had convinced myself to expect hauteur from him, but as recognition flitted in his face, he raised his hand in a feeble attempt at a waving salute. I thought I detected something akin to relief, perhaps even pity, in those eyes as he observed me out that window. I recall deeply resenting pity from him, and I am sure that I scowled in reply.

As the carriage had been loaded with trunks and assorted cases, it was clear to me that there must have been several more people within, though I saw no one else. From such an abundance of baggage, I deduced that they were equipped to be away for an extended time.

"So you are to be rid of the contagion," again I mused, "by taking flight." I resented the world upon worlds that separated me from that fortunate one, John Calvin. We had been born but months apart, in the same village, had even for a season attended the same grammar school. Why was he the one to be so privileged and I to be so destitute?

The sharp rapping of a whip handle and a loud hollering from the driver brought me back to the instant. I had to act quickly. It occurred to my mind that I, in all likelihood, might perform the service required to the harness. At this, my imagination took hold, and like a flood I began seeing an opportunity unfolding before me, a way of escape.

Though lowborn, I had come to know a thing or two about carriages, and I knew what many did not know about the underside of one such as this one. My pulse quickened. Could I effect the needed repair on the instant, for there was surely no more time than that, and then would it be possible to stall the impatient driver a moment or two after I had completed the work? I then contemplated whether or not my nascent plan would best work if I were to don my new waistcoat and chapeau.

But as I thus hesitated, my heart sank in my bosom. There was a harsh cracking of a whip, and the carriage lurched forward, the driver now standing at the reins as he drove his team down the street. In such haste was he that I believe the carriage took the first turn on but two wheels. I nearly slumped to the cobbles in tears as my hope of escape disappeared around that corner.

Then a thought struck me like a blow from my father's fist. Surely the driver goes to my father's rival—to Jacques the tanner, across town.

9

Carriage Ride

I COULD NOT BE SURE that the carriage hurtled toward Jacques the tanner's shop. But I had no other hope. Instantly was I on the run.

By my slinking ways, I had come to know Noyon and her back alleyways better than most. It was through these passageways that I then bolted in those next frantic moments, moments destined to forever determine the remainder of my life, so I then believed and do so to this day.

My lungs felt as if they would explode from within my body as I ran. As I plunged through the market square before the Hotel de Ville, I confess to overturning a table of finely made lace, now soiled in the street muck, the merchant decrying me and shaking her fists at my heels. Next, without intending to do so, as God is my judge, I clipped a stack of earthenware pots at the market and heard shattering and more raging behind me. Feinting in an effort to dodge the pot shards hurled at my back, I disappeared over an iron gate and into a dark alley.

Would I make it in time? The driver and his four horses, though ever so much faster than I, must of necessity stay to the streets, while I could weave my way through the hidden intricacies of the village. But would I make it?

"God help me," I heard myself gasp aloud, and I wondered whether it was genuine praying, the sort that God answers if he actually does heed praying, whether this qualified as the sort of praying he heeded. But I left off thinking of such things as I considered which of two shortcuts would get me across town most rapidly.

At last, my feet aching from pounding the cobbled streets, and my bosom aflame, I rounded a narrow corridor and halted before the workshop of Jacques the tanner, my father's chief rival. I groaned as I collapsed onto the pavement, leaning against the corner of the workshop.

There was no carriage. Had it come and already gone? It would have been a very minor repair, indeed, to have been accomplished in so short a time. But there was no carriage.

My heart sank within me. And there was no sign of Jacques. Perhaps he had been taken off by the plague as well. Perhaps the Hangest carriage had come, discovered there was no help to be had, and fled in a huff with harness unrepaired.

"The gods conspire against me," I murmured, heaving a bitter sigh of weariness and resignation.

But what was that? At first but a faint rumbling. Growing louder every instant. Suddenly, and unmistakably, I heard a mad clattering of hooves and carriage wheels. And with that racket, hope reawakened in my bosom.

I could not as yet see the carriage, but I knew it had to appear in an instant, and I speculated where it would make its stand, slinking into the shadows nearby. Jacques, who was in fact alive and appeared, by the bulbous redness of his cheeks and nose and his stagger, to have been drinking, had heard the approaching racket and had now stepped into the street. I supposed him eager for a wealthy customer.

Amid a spray of fine gravel and grime from the street, the carriage driver halted his team and demanded repairs and quick ones. I knew that now was my one and only opportunity.

Dropping low, I scrambled nearer, approaching the carriage from the rear and in a line that shielded me from the eyes of driver and occupants.

Not making a sound, I rolled underneath the rear axle. Gripping it tightly, I hoisted myself up. Rolling onto the top of the axle, I supported my weight with my buttocks, my legs spread wide and braced against the leaf springs. It was not to be comfortable transport, of that I was certain. But desperate men will do vastly uncomfortable things.

I admit in retrospect, that perched as I was on the under works of an immobile carriage, I had simply no notion of how uncomfortable it would become, a miscalculation soon to be corrected.

As Jacques grumbled with the harness and his tools, I waited in the dim shadows of the undercarriage. I saw his battered wooden shoes shuffling toward me and the lower portion of his coarse breeches approaching; I then heard the hasty exchange of few words and coins. Holding my breath in anticipation, I felt that my entire life depended on what happened in the next hours, hours I hoped would not be too long.

Suddenly, with a lurch, the horses began their work, and the wheels on either side of me began whirring round and round. The springs were there, to be sure, but I had no cushioning from them atop the rigid iron of the axle. I realized within moments that I had undertaken a position so bone-jarring as to precipitate premature death. It entered my mind that death by being chopped to pieces in the spokes of the wheels, or being trampled by following horses, might be yet grimmer still than the very death by pestilence that I was fleeing.

Within half a mile I was caked with mud, and road filth so clogged my breathing that I feared I would perish for lack of air. Violent as his wrath could be, my father had never pummeled me like this. My spine felt as if it would crack with the constant jolting of the axle against the small of my back. But I had no choice. I had to cling to the under works of that carriage. It was my salvation.

I said that I had experience of carriages, yet am I forced to admit that I had never ridden in one. I doubted that anyone had ever attempted to ride one in such a perilous fashion. Yet did it puzzle me that we could be going at such a rapid speed and yet be taking such a gruelingly long time getting wherever it was we were going.

I did wonder where we were going, but it mattered little, so I gave but little attention to it. Wherever it was, it must needs be far from the pestilence that plagued Noyon. I tried not to think of Noyon, of never seeing it again, as I then supposed, of never seeing my mother, my sister, or my father, or anyone from there. Perhaps there would be no one left alive to see when the plague had spent its ravages on the town.

Then I thought of John Calvin, perhaps seated directly above me on a plush leather cushion, reading Seneca, or reciting from his Latin grammar. Another thought occurred to me. I had taken nothing to eat since the day before, and as the day ground on, my stomach convulsed, no doubt as much from the violence of the jolting of the carriage as from lack of food. My stomach was far more accustomed to lack of food than to such joltings. Then I wondered whether Calvin lounged above me eating sausages and cheeses, or perhaps he had curled up on the leather seat and was dozing.

There was to be no dozing for me. I could not sleep for fear of loosening my grip and thereby risking a fall onto the road, where I was certain to be run down by the whirring wheels, or trampled by horses following close behind.

When feeling had long since quitted my limbs, and I felt certain I could hang on no longer, the carriage slowed. The horses' hooves took on a more hollow sound as they clopped onto the cobbles, and faint as I was, I managed to observe the feet of other horses, the wheels of other carriages, and the lower extremities of human beings strolling along the pavement beside the street.

I had never been to Paris, but I began to believe that this must be Paris. I desperately hoped that it was here we would at last halt. Whether I would be able to move, I doubted, but if we did not stop soon, I was now more certain than ever that I would fall onto the cobbles and be crushed by the next carriage.

To my great relief, the carriage at last came to a stand. I had not realized how deafening the racket had been underneath, but all fell comparatively silent as we stopped, a silence instantly broken by the ringing out of great bells from some nearby church.

As it rang out the hour—it must have been eleven or twelve; I was too distracted to be sure which—I heard the carriage doors open, and the squeaking of cushion springs above my head as bodies lifted themselves from their place of rest. Feet and stockings appeared, three or four sets of these, and I heard groans as the occupants complained of stiffness from their long ride. Again was I reminded of the vast difference between their world and mine.

Only with great determination was I able to make my limbs cooperate, but I knew I had little time to extricate myself from that horrid undercarriage. Even I was challenged to do, in my condition, all this with silence, and I fell to the cobbles with rather more of a thud than I care to admit. But I was here, wherever here was.

Painfully, I opened and closed my fingers, then rubbed feeling back into my arms and legs, knocking off the larger clods of mud and road debris from my clothing as I did so. I knew I must hurry. With relief, I felt in my tunic for my waistcoat, chapeau, and newly acquired purse. Miraculously, they were yet where I had hidden them. Even in my sorry condition, I felt a lightness within. I was free at last from the deadly pestilence.

Eyeing the street side of the carriage, I waited until there was a congestion of horse-drawn equipages, and then rolled along the back left wheel, and rose stiffly to my feet. Crossing away from the carriage, I ducked into the shadowed archway of the church from which the bells completed their final ringing out of the hour.

Blending in with the riffraff that hung about the entrance, I turned and watched as the coachman unlashed a trunk and set it with a thud on the pavement. Calvin took his leave of the Hangest brothers, the carriage clattered off, and he turned his attention to the bustling sights and sounds, and to his trunk.

Without entirely planning what I was about to do, I slipped my arms into the sleeves of my waistcoat and drew out my bonnet, setting it on my head, low and partly concealing my eyes. For a fleeting instant I thought of the contagion and worried that I might have brought it with me in the dead man's garments. But it could not now be helped, and so, brushing my hands over the wrinkles in the waistcoat, I strode, insofar as my stiff limbs allowed, over to where Calvin grunted with his trunk.

"Might I lend assistance, Monsieur?" I asked, lowering my voice.

"I would be grateful," he replied, giving no sign of recognition. I knew I was safe. Neither Calvin nor anyone else would ever expect such fine clothes on one from my coarse station.

Calvin looked slight and not a little lost as he gazed at the busy streets and the towering buildings of the city. Though a few months his junior, I had for some time grown taller than he, and from hard labor in my father's shop I had acquired physical strength he seemed not to possess. Feeling smugly in this way his superior, I hoisted his trunk with ease to my shoulder.

"Where would you like me to deposit it, Monsieur?"

"I am to follow this narrow street from the church of St. Germaine L'Auxerrois," he said as if reciting the directions from memory, "where it connects with the Rue Vallette to the house of Richard Calvin, my uncle. I am assured that it is not far."

As we set off, my mind raced. I felt I must develop a plan, and somehow in my mind that plan demanded that I stay near young Calvin. For what good reason I was so compelled to remain near one I had so come to loathe, I could not then begin to explain to my satisfaction, yet was I so compelled. I have since come to believe that for most if not all compulsions there is little rational justification, yet are they no less compelling for their lack of measurable means.

It was but two or three short blocks to the house of his uncle, a distance we covered in a few silent moments, the blood circulating more freely through my limbs as we walked. When I had deposited the trunk on the threshold, and as I turned to go, Calvin tugged at my sleeve.

"You must take this for your pains," he said, holding a shiny franc in his palm, "yet more as a token of my gratitude."

I knew little of the value of coinage, so inexperienced was I with money, yet did that first offering of money glitter handsomely and entice me. I felt in my tunic and wondered whether my pouch, as yet unexplored by me, contained more of the same. He thrust the coin closer. Though there was nothing in his manner to harden me against him, yet was I determined to despise him.

"I need not your money," I said shortly. But then thinking rapidly, I continued. "Rather might I attend you."

"Attend me?" he repeated.

"You come to Paris to study," I continued, not at all certain this was Paris, though guessing it must be so. "I have heard that it is common for the privileged few who learn from books," I groped in my mind, certain I had somewhere heard of such things, "to allow such a one as I to attend on their studies, to carry books, bring them refreshment, assist them."

"I am not of such lavish means," he said, "as to afford to retain you as a servant. I am not a rich man's son and bring with me but adequate means to commence my learning."

"I ask for nothing," I replied, "but the honor of attending upon you."

"I could not presume on your labors," he said, "without payment for those labors."

"But it would be payment, indeed," I said, "to attend upon you and, thereby, improve myself in some small fashion from the leavings of your studious pursuits." Before he could make reply, his uncle flung open the door and began fawning on Calvin.

"Bonne journée! Le fils de mon frère! Tu es le bienvenu!"

Hugs and kisses mingled with squeals of delight as Calvin's aunt and uncle and his cousins welcomed him. There was another there to greet Calvin, one I had seen in our younger days in Noyon, his elder cousin, one Pierre Robert Olivetan. On the instant, as they pulled him into the house, young Calvin grabbed my hand and thrust the coin into my palm, closing my fingers over it.

"I commence my studies at the College de la Marche," he called after me.

The door shut with a bang. I was alone. In a vast city where I knew not a living soul, I was alone. It was growing dark, and though it was the month of August, I felt in my bosom a steely coldness.

10

My New Gown

WITH THE THUD of that door and the clattering of the latch and lock, I felt suddenly alone in a strange world, barred from the glowing light within, shut out from the familial warmth enfolding my rival. While Calvin was being thus welcomed by his relations, I pondered the cruel blows fate had dealt my family. And now there was no one else to feel the bludgeoning of those blows—but I. I alone remained of what had been, for all its disappointment, my family. Infected with these thoughts, a bitterness I felt certain I was powerless to suppress descended on me.

Yet did I reason with myself: I had escaped the contagion. I was alive. But as I ruminated thus on my escape, my mind grew heavier. I wanted to blame another for my misfortunes, but the deepest pang of all came from within my own bosom. At root, I was no better than the bishop and his priests, than the nobles, than the wealthy merchants in their silk and ermine gowns. Had any of my family remained alive, I knew deep within me, I would have, nevertheless, abandoned them for a carriage ride to Paris and safety, or so I then thought it would afford me.

What was the crime in that? I had merely longed to live, I further reasoned with myself. Would it have been such a betrayal of my family to want life, to choose to live, rather than to die in such a plague-infested place? I could not have saved them. What could I have done? It was futile speculation, I knew. Nevertheless, I indulged myself in it with, perhaps, some notion of assuaging what remained of a rapidly tottering conscience. I desperately tried not to care about any of this. My family, my old life, it was all dead to me now.

But death is a persistent companion, I have learned, not so easy a one to appease by striking hands in a truce. My resolves produced for me no tangible degree of comfort. In my troubled state of mind, a part of me longed to pray. I was troubled to recall my cry as I ran through the streets of Noyon but hours ago—was that a praying that was answered? Perhaps I would have met the carriage in any event, by my own cleverness and swiftness of foot.

Privileged Calvin had every reason to pray and revel in God's kindnesses, but I, that night, looked heavenward with a scowl. I had delivered myself by myself, with no help from God, such were the assertions of an ungrateful mind. And in this frame of mind, I then, in a manner of speaking, prayed.

"God above, if you are there, you are most unkind to me." I am ashamed to recollect such praying, yet did I then persist in it. "Therefore, will I not serve you, will I not worship you, will I not obey you. Henceforth, I give of myself to those powers that most work against you, against your will and ways, and against your servants."

It was a prayer that invigorated me, made me feel emancipated from divine oppression and injustice, the master of myself and my fortunes, the bold possessor of new freedoms.

But when the first flush of my defiance began to fade, I felt cold and empty inside.

Alone I wandered the streets of that vast city, palatial buildings, grand churches, luxurious hotels lining the streets of its fashionable districts. Then my feet took me to the Petit Pont where from the lingering smells, I was to conclude that there street merchants must regularly sell fowls and eggs, perhaps other meats. From there I wandered into the Place Maubert where I gulped in the aromas of baked bread. Then I strode along the wall encircling the city, a wall sturdy and broad, sufficiently wide for a vender to drive his cart, or a defender to position his cannon.

From there I tread the cobbles of the Rue de la Huchette to the street Pavée, and from thence to the street of the Abbey of Saint Denis, Saint Germain, Saint André des Arts, Poupée, the Barre, the Poitevins, the Serpente, the Plâtrière, Haultefeuille, Champ Petit, of the Harpe, and the great street of Saint Severin, the crossings of Saint Jacques, the street where notaries and scribes made books, from there to the alley of Saint Severin, Bourc de Brie, and then a street that led me before the grand Church of the Mathurins, the cloister of Saint Benoit, and the Sorbonne itself.

They were all foreign places to me that night, and I was to learn their names only in later years. Broodingly did I plod the Paris alleyways of ill-repute that night, therein to find commoners of my station lining the streets. I walked as if in a dream or perhaps a nightmare. Leering at me from the shadows, hands reached for me, enticing me to join them, beckoning me as if in answer to my praying.

My affections were divided. These must be God's enemies, and so I felt I ought to want to throw in my lot with them. Yet did something within me, against my will, hold me aloof. Aroused as I was by their unlaced posture, the disheveled boudoir fashion of their clothing, and the frenetic disarray of their hairstyles, I was equally sickened by them.

Then something occurred to me that gave me relief. I was greatly weary and had eaten nothing all that day. Perhaps my reluctance and the heaving sensation churning my insides were but the aftereffects of my tumultuous journey, the bone-numbing weariness of my limbs, and the longings of an empty belly. So I determined to take my fill.

And take my fill I did. But it was not only food on which I feasted. A week passed wherein the dead man's money pouch grew lighter. Having no experience of working and accomplishing a task and then being proportionately paid with money, I was sorely devoid of the skills needed to retain what money I had so effortlessly acquired. What had seemed to my imagination to be a vast sum, was in that short week of revelry reduced to a pittance. Moreover, I had precious little to show for my expenditures. The friends I thought I had secured by my liberality were like phantoms, vanishing as rapidly as the coins in my purse.

Then one day in my wanderings, my feet strayed into the Latin Quarter, as it seemed rightly to be termed. No longer did I hear the Frankish intonation, the becoming inflections, the soft undulations of my native tongue. This was the district of the Sorbonne; the vast and mysterious university lay all about me. Its lofty spires and stone cloisters, peopled by men and boys in black robes and angular wool caps, was as a foreign land to me, a region apart, another world, an empire wherein lofty doctors and Latin ruled.

Frantically, I grappled with my mind, attempting to recollect the grammar lessons taught by the pompous magister what seemed so long ago in my few years of formal learning in Noyon. I cursed myself for not attending to my lessons in those bygone days. And then I began studying the faces of those boys who shouldered past me. He would be among them, I mused. Why did I care to think on it?

"*Bon Dieu,*" I cursed under my breath, sneering at any who caught my eye. So these boys are to be the next lot of priests that shall abandon their flock in their greatest hour of need, abandon them only after fleecing them of their last franc. And Calvin would be like all the rest. I was determined to believe thus.

Turning down a narrow passageway, my steps took me to— according to the characters chiseled in the stone archway above me—the College de la Marche. Immediately I recollected that name, and I studied the faces more keenly.

Slinking along the shadows of the cloister, I observed from without the variety of life. These were clearly younger students, and I later learned that La Marche was where most young men entered the vast University of Paris, here to be vigorously drilled in their mastery of Latin grammar, writing, and speaking in preparation for their future studies in philosophy or theology, these to be pursued at another college of the university. Yet at the time I did not know this, and I marveled at their youth. I felt myself their superior in stature, for I was tall and built more like a man than most my age. I was certain he must be among these young scholars.

It occurred to me that it was most difficult for me to be invisible among these robed scholars, for I wore not their habit. But I prided myself on my jaunty waistcoat and chapeau and on my resourcefulness, and began looking keenly about me. I had so suppressed my conscience by this time in my young life that I scrupled not in the least at the deeds that followed. Such deeds came to me as naturally as vultures to carrion.

It was a warm August afternoon, perfect for what my mind began immediately to scheme upon. At last I spied what I had been waiting for. A carefree boy of about my height and build flung aside his scholar's robe of black wool and tossed it indifferently onto the stone bench that ran along the outer confines of the cloister. I had observed that these robes were one and the same; there could be no distinguishing evidence to set one apart from another.

Stealthily, I glided toward the robe, watching the careless scholar closely. He turned as if to make jest with his fellows. As they threw their heads back in hilarity at his words, I sprang. In an instant my chapeau was off and I was a black-robed scholar of the Sorbonne; none could gainsay my status.

Now bold and confident in my disguise, I strode round the east end of the cloister, where my eyes lit upon a small gathering of black-clad youths seated on benches in the inner court surrounded by the stone-vaulted cloister. An aged man, sunlight reflecting through transparent white locks flowing from under his black scholar's cap, stood over the boys and was speaking to them. I drew near, concealing myself behind the tracery of a Gothic archway. This is what I heard.

"Telle est la douceur de cette nourriture divine, qu'il rend l'esprit insatiable: plus nous le goût de celui-ci, le plus long pour nous."

I recall being profoundly shocked at what I heard. Shocked because I understood what was said. The venerable fellow spoke not Latin to these young men, but French, else I would have understood but the merest rudiments of his words. I recollect being deeply puzzled by this fact. I even wondered whether it was permitted to speak thus in French within these hallowed corridors.

But not only did he speak in the language of the common man, he spoke as if to the common man, with clarity, and with something else, something I had never heard before in my entire life. His words enchanted me.

"Such is the sweetness of this divine food," he had said, "that it makes the mind insatiable: the more we taste of it, the more we long for it."

In these words, he spoke with a conviction that was no less contagious than the bubonic plague had been in Noyon. And for a few fleeting moments I felt myself drawn in by that contagion. I longed to sit among those boys and feast on his words.

He now seemed to be moving to some weighty truth, if the flashing of his deep blue eyes was any indicator. And he seemed to warm with a sense of wonder at his own words, though he was no pedantic, and there was nothing of the pompous magister in his manner. It was not his oratory that transported his visage. It must be the things about which he was speaking that so animated his delivery. I pressed my face closer to the stone tracery so as not to miss a word.

"Ineffable exchange, the Innocent one is condemned and the criminal acquitted; the Blessing is cursed, and he who is cursed is blessed; the Life dies, and the dead live; the Glory is covered with shame, and He who was put to shame is covered with glory."

My bosom swelled with longing as I listened. Was it merely his craft, his eloquent oratory that so thrilled me? It seemed it must be something more. I understood the meaning of the individual words the elderly one spoke, yet did they confuse me, dizzy me with their paradoxes, and I wondered whether he was but playing word games with them—and so with me.

I listened intently for a time, and then his speech proceeded down yet another path.

"Those who are saved," he continued, stretching his hands as if to encompass the huddle of boys who listened. "Those who are saved are saved by election, by grace, by the will of God, not by their own. Our own election, will, and work, are of no avail: the election of God alone is profitable. When we are converted it is not our conversion that makes us the elect of God, but the grace, will, and election of God which convert us."

I studied his face more closely. This was clearly no word game. His conviction, his passion was too complete, too genuine for any mere game playing with words. Hungrily I listened on. He spoke of redemption, of forgiveness, of repentance and faith, of peace with God. He spoke like no bishop or priest I had ever heard before.

"Religion has but one foundation, one object, one Head, Jesus Christ, blessed forevermore. The cross of Christ alone openeth the gates of heaven and shutteth the gates of hell."

At this point in his speaking, a change came over the man. I thought I detected a glancing across the courtyard and a flicker of recognition in his eyes—or was it fear? He paused, his eyes returning to the faces turned toward him. Then abruptly he shifted to Latin, the majority of which was lost to me.

It was as I turned to go that I saw him. He had been in the back row listening to the man, and he was scowling deeply when he turned my way. So distracted was Calvin that he, at first, gave no evidence of recognizing me. I was mystified by my internal feelings. I wanted him to see me. For what reason, I was not then certain. I stepped more boldly into his path as he drew near. Still a frown furrowed his brow, and then he saw me, recognition spreading across his face.

"We have met?" he said.

"*Oui,*" I replied. "I carried your baggage."

He halted and stared more deeply into my eyes. "Jean-Louis? Of Noyon, our beleaguered home? How have you come to Paris?" He glanced at my stolen robe. "Are you to study?"

I resented his last question. The bewilderment I felt sure I had detected in his tone hardened me, and I chose to despise him the more for his candor.

"I am as you see me," I replied evasively.

He eyed me with what I feared was a look of incredulity, for which I resented him further. I observed in his keen eyes a hint of what I feared would be a barrage of cross-examination about which college I attended, where my room was, how I supported myself. But at the headwaters of the torrent, he seemed to check himself.

"Have you found another to attend?" he asked instead.

I was at first taken aback by his query. He was clever enough to have connected me with my previous disguise. The growling of my empty stomach acted as a check to what might have been a surly reply. Fingering my nearly empty purse beneath my gown, I felt I needed to answer with care and that a great deal depended on how I did so.

"I have by this means," I said, indicating my robe, and all the while feigning my most servile expression, "determined to make myself at your disposal."

It was by this seemingly chance encounter that I became a servant scholar to John Calvin at the College de la Marche. I told myself that he owed this to me; after all, he was a youth with not one but two benefices to support him. I took pains not to convey such feelings to him. There was no bed for me at his uncle's home, but he did see to providing me with an ample supply of daily bread, which I ate hungrily and, I must confess, resentfully.

Though I found it at times intensely wearisome, I was at his side as he was tutored in Latin. Dull and incomprehensible as the Latin tutor was, Calvin was transfixed by his magister and often spoke thus of the man: "Mathurin Cordier is an instructor sent by God. If ever I happen someday to write anything by which anyone might find profit," he spoke thus with glowing countenance, "it will be as a result of this singular kindness of God. Mathurin Cordier, like no other has done, is teaching me the true method of learning." Such superlative language more than bewildered me, yet did I remain at Calvin's side through arduous tutorials and lectures.

I knew not yet what precise advantage to take of my new situation, but I recollect being rather proud of my achievement and of my new status. Forgetful of my all-too-rapidly squandered means, I congratulated myself on my cleverness at thereby providing food for my belly. Best of all, or so I then considered it, when the wearisome day at the college concluded, I was free to wander about Paris for my amusement. And I did.

It is astonishing to consider how seemingly chance encounters, and what men term insignificant interchanges, produce profound and life-altering effects. Such was my new life, though I confess I then had nothing but scorn and contempt for such contemplations. Nothing then did I realize of the high intrigue into which my new situation would embroil my life.

11

The Price of Learning

CALVIN WAS A SLAVE to learning. There is nothing else to say of it. I have never seen his like. When I would join him at break of day, he had already been at his studies for some time.

Often he spoke not at all to me, for he was deep in meditation and recitation on some obtuse grammatical contemplation. His preoccupation I seized upon as yet another illustration of his superior attitude; his ignoring me was yet another expression of his determination to rise above me, to keep me low and insignificant.

On the rare occasion when he gave heed to me, it was to decry my amusements, of which he, by some inner divination, seemed to be keenly aware.

"Jean-Louis, you have been too long at the wine bottle," he said one gray morning.

At my denial, he would reply, "Your face and eyes, Jean-Louis, betray you." At my further protest, he would chide with a sniff, "As does your breath." He would say all this as a father scolds a child. I took pains to suppress my urge to rail at him, to curse him, and to taunt him as the Accusative Case. It would not do to let on the degree to which I despised him, and yet more so for his rebukes.

Oddly, I did take some pride in his achievements. In but a short time he had so outstripped his fellows in Latin that he was elevated from College de la Marche to the nearby College de Montaigu to pursue logic and the liberal arts. As I aided him with his books and papers, I sneered at his inferiors as if they were mine, and I swaggered in my duties at Calvin's heels as if his extraordinary achievements were equally mine.

Calvin was no longer to live with his Uncle Richard and family. Again, it was I who carried his trunk. He was now to be in strict cloistered life in preparation for his calling, as it was then supposed, to the priesthood.

The rigors of that life at College de Montaigu nearly unhinged me. I was in no way inclined or suited to Calvin's noble ideas about the priesthood, yet was I somehow to accompany him in this torturous chamber of self-denial. It nearly broke me.

I was not made for rising at 4:00 of a morning, nor for enduring Latin dirge chanting at such an hour, or any hour. Immediately following that first service of the day came a pedantic lecture that ground on until 6:00, though so dull was it that it felt to me as if it went on for hours. Promptly after the lecture we paraded back into the chapel for the Mass. What followed was termed "breakfast" but was food of the foulest sort, my stomach often revolting under the abuse; I seldom had much appetite after the first bite, and I'm loathe to attempt a description of the pasty gruel and stagnant water they termed our *petit dejeuner*. For the next three hours came the main class and discussion of the day. It was during these that I did my best to prop myself up and escape into the bliss of sleep.

We were then marched into the spartan meal hall, and while we attempted to sup on a morsel of dry bread one of our superiors droned out a reading on the life of St. Denis or some other saint. Another hour of discussion and questions followed, Calvin often posing questions that appeared to stump the exalted doctor, much to my enjoyment, though I was rarely aware of any of the substantive intricacies of these discussions. Next followed a time referred to as a rest period, though I never found the monotonous chanting out of the life of some medieval monk particularly what one would term restful. From 3:00 to 5:00 in the afternoon came the interminable lectures on Scholastic philosophy, clearly a favorite topic to the doctors of the Sorbonne. At last came evening prayers, more discussion, more bad food, more questions, more discussion, and finally bed at 9:00 in the evening.

As I said, such a schedule was nearly my undoing. But I might have endured all had more edible victuals been set before us. Never the merest scrap of meat did the scholars eat, and the best morsels of nourishment ever given these priests in training were stale eggs, eggs so fetid that they might lie within rats' reach for hours without fear of the foulest vermin attempting so much as a nibble.

Worse still, and more frightening, were the master's ideas of self-denial and pain. I witnessed the master uncoil his lash for the slightest provocation—or none at all. "The servant is not above his master," I heard him growl as he readied his whip with a stinging snap at the air. "Your master felt the lash, and so shall you. Now bare your back." What followed was pathetic and cruel, though, for one apprenticed to my late father as I had been, not particularly unusual. Cruelty, after all, was as ubiquitous as fleas.

One young scholar, when privileged to follow his Lord to the lash, was so weakened by sickness, so trembling and frail from lack of nourishment, that scarce three furrows had been laid on when the color fled from his features and he collapsed senseless to the flagstones. Within two days the poor creature expired. I was sobered by this, for a time, and I wondered what that scrawny cast-off boy might have become, what he might have discovered. I then mused, though still more fleetingly, on where he now dwelt, if a corpse can be said to dwell anywhere.

In my hours of leisure when not attending Calvin, I gorged on what meat and wine I could acquire. My appetite for meat and for the unencumbered life drew me to forgo sleep. On one such night I stole from my straw-filled mat, donned my satin waistcoat and chapeau, and stealthily made my way from the damp, oppressive dormitory of the Sorbonne into the light and revelry of the Rue St. Martin.

Calvin was ever dull in entertainment. In fact, I never observed anything worthy of the name beyond an occasional visit with his uncle and family on the Rue Vallette. He did from time to time engage in lengthy conversation with his passionate elder cousin, one Pierre Robert Olivetan. Their words were ever dreary to my ears, and often they spoke in what must have been Greek. It was ever such to me.

I had little money, for Calvin, knowing how easily I parted with money, compensated me for my service by paying me in bread, or a new tunic, or new sandals for my feet. "I'll not be party to your drunkenness," he would say as he handed me a new pair of socks or a muffler for my neck.

And so after pawning my newest garment for meat or wine or pleasures, I stole. The penalty for theft in Paris was stiff. Hands were not uncommonly hacked off the arms of thieves. But one had first to be discovered to be thus punished. And I felt myself invincible to discovery. So I freely stole.

Perhaps never before had two young men so entirely different from one another found themselves so constantly in one another's society. I have often mused on how different my life would have been if I had then and there parted with Calvin, as I often berated myself for failing to do. What would have become of me if I had had no more to do with his fasts and vigils, with his interminable hours of study, with the rank and meager food he was allowed, and with his sleepless nights? Why I stayed at his side, I cannot to my satisfaction explain, yet did I remain, after my sulky fashion, in attendance on this odd freak of a man, as I then was determined to think of him.

When I dutifully followed Calvin's heels into a lecture hall or the chambers of a learned doctor for several grueling hours of instruction, I folded my hands and feigned a servile sobriety, but inside I was bursting with anticipation. While Calvin filled his mind with knowledge, I unobtrusively curled up in the warmest corner of the room to recover the sleep I had forgone in my previous nighttime revelries.

On one occasion, however, as I stretched and yawned myself to wakefulness, I caught the sound of words expressed so differently from the dry thesis and antithesis of the Sorbonne. The tall lecturer was speaking not unlike the venerable speaker at La Marche that first day when I had stolen my gown. With curiosity, if not interest, I listened in.

"How scandalous it is," the tall man began in Latin, which I had somehow made sufficient progress in comprehending—I can only imagine—merely by constant hearing of it, for I studied little and ill. I wondered at his criticism as he proceeded. "How scandalous it is to see a bishop asking persons to drink with him, gambling, rattling the dice, spending his time in hunting, hallooing after rooks and deer, and frequenting houses of ill-fame."

89

At the time, this sort of talk greatly confused me. Such behavior on the part of clerics was so commonplace that criticism of it was incomprehensible to me. I had long accepted the sporting debauchery of the clergy as the luxury of their calling. It was what bishops did. Perhaps I envied them and inwardly aspired to just such a life of easy recklessness. But while I was, for my reasons, bewildered by such railings against the clergy, Calvin, after his fashion, appeared more deeply conflicted at what he heard.

I knew him well enough to know that it was for no sensual inclination that he disapproved of such railings. While I inwardly grinned in envy at the cavortings of the privileged clergy, he seemed at first determined to blind himself to the ubiquitous display of priestly philandering. I now know that he was truly grieved by the debased way of life so common to monks and friars, priests and bishops, and the high esteem he had for their priestly office deepened the pain he felt at their low behavior. This I now understand, but at the time I was devoid of comprehending any notion requiring the slightest degree of nuanced attention and consideration.

I was fascinated by the violence of the conservative reactions to such criticisms. "Like a nascent adder in the shell, we must crush heresy in the egg!" I overheard one red-faced doctor of the Sorbonne fulminate. The influential priests at the university seemed to agree. For my part, intriguing as it all was, I intended to watch what direction the political winds blew on the matter. Though Catholic in religion, King Francis I was known to be no political friend of the papacy, so it was by no means certain for a time on whose side of this question he would cast his royal frown.

Word was that his own sister, Marguerite of Valois, also known as Marguerite of Angouleme, and later as Queen of Navarre, was coming under the sway of the critics. I overheard whisperings that in her brother the king's very own court she was known to read from portions of the Bible translated into the French, and that she her very own self set quill to paper with devotional verses, these also written in the vulgar tongue. Moreover, she acted as unofficial patron to court poet Clement Marot who, it is widely reported, had created by versification Psalm poetry for singing.

All this to the king's great frustration, I am certain of it. What is a king to do when, against his wishes, his sister busies herself reading the Bible, writing devotional poetry in the vulgar tongue, and writing stories of Christian heroes for all to read? What is a king to do whose political theory demands uniformity of religion in his realm, but whose own family is perniciously out of accord with that uniformity?

And there was the matter of the king's mother. Louisa of Savoy was immoral, vicious, and a staunch hater of reformation or anything of true piety, and it was generally agreed that no one wielded more influence over the king than his mother. I learned of these things from my skill at listening in on the street gossip in the Latin Quarter. I must confess that the chief motive propelling what meager progress I had made in Latin—I cared little for Aquinas, still less for Augustine—was the intense desire not to miss out on any of the Parisian scuttlebutt. I was titillated by the latest word of Louisa's sexual life, and I must not have been alone, for her latest philanderings were discussed at every cafe in Paris.

Her latest favorite, one Anthony Duprat, now chancellor of France, was made so in exchange for his driveling attentions. It was pathetic, though I did not see it as such then. When not fulfilling his obligatory fawning on the queen mother, he was known by his foes and by honest friends as "the most vicious of all bipeds."

Then one drizzly afternoon in the cloister of the college, I listened in on a conversation that was to ignite in me the most monstrous schemes imaginable. I had learned by this time to stand in a servile manner with an appearance of indifference and at a sufficient distance, all of which had the effect of rendering me seemingly invisible to others. Yes, I was there, but I had learned to assume such a deaf-and-dumb posture—eyes glazed, head lolling to one side, lips slack and parted just so—that so unremarkable was I to those present that two men might pass the darkest secrets between them without the slightest fear of one such as I hearing or making any use of the intelligence that had passed between them. I confess that I took great pride in my ability.

By this my chief skill, I was privy to the fleshy underside of the back alleyways of Paris. I knew which silk handkerchiefs were snatched by which boys from which ladies. I knew which wine casks had been tapped, by whom, and what quantity of wine had been thereby siphoned and hastily consumed. I knew which friars visited which brothels and how often. I knew which prostitute emptied which priestly purse while her ten-minute lover dozed at her side, and precisely how many francs she gained from the whole of her enterprise.

But so astounded was I by what I heard that drizzly afternoon in the cloister that it demanded all my skill of concealment to veil my eagerness and remain unnoticed by Calvin and those with whom he spoke. The course of my life changed that day. So pernicious was that change that I fear my miserable life is forever beyond recovery.

12

Fleshed on the Prey

"The king carries on such a trade in bishoprics and abbeys," one young speaker remonstrated, his eyes flashing, "one would think France is Venice and the holy offices are pepper and cinnamon."

"And clerics so basely appointed," added another, "heed the charms of Paris far more than the pitiful bleating of their flocks."

"Which flocks after they have been thoroughly fleeced are ignored while their priests spend their takings on the wine shops of St. Antoine—"

"—Or the brothels of St. Martin's."

Calvin had thus far said nothing in this exchange, but leaned against a column gazing at the vaulting as he listened. There was nothing in the least remarkable in what had so far been spoken. It was what followed that riveted my attention so profoundly.

"What say the doctors of the Sorbonne?" asked one of Calvin's associates, Nicholas Cop, son of a physician from the city of Basel. Cop was the closest thing to a friend I thought Calvin then capable of having.

"They abhor the king's power to invest holy offices," replied another. "Yet must they exercise caution. One does not abhor a king or his policy without cost."

"Yet there are those," said Cop, "who are prepared to take the risk."

"Aye. The followers of Beda the inquisitor," continued the first speaker, "even now plot a scheme to restore the church to her former glories, a scheme by which they hope to win the king's approval."

"But what of the third faction?" were the first words that indicated Calvin had ventured in the conversation.

"The party of Luther?" said the one. "The reforming riffraff?"

"You term them so," said Calvin, "but what will become of them?"

"Recall when Martial Mazurier, the eloquent doctor of St. Michael's College, threw off restraint, not only decrying clerical abuses, declaring Holy Scripture to be above the pope and the traditions of the papal synods and councils—recall the virulence of the doctors of the university as they raged against him."

"Speak not merely of Mazurier," said Cop. "What of the white-haired doctor *d'Etaples*, Jacques Lefevre?"

"Him who labored to vulgarize the Holy Scriptures into the common tongue of the French mob?"

"The same. I have overheard the doctor of our College de Montaigu declare, 'If we tolerate these innovators they will invade the whole body, and it will be over with our teaching, our traditions, our places, and the respect felt toward us by France and all of Christendom.'"

"It is not an overstatement to speak thus," continued another, "and hence, the doctors of the Sorbonne have declared war on the advocates of the new doctrines. And so they ought to do."

"And the king?" This from Calvin again. "What is his royal attitude?"

"It is almost certain," began the first speaker, "that when the followers of the conservative party at the Sorbonne win the king's approval—and it is as good as accomplished—the king will join them in their war and strain every royal sinew in crushing the followers of the drunk Saxon."

"You speak as if this remains to be determined," said another. "The king has even now commissioned royal agents to ferret out the pernicious perpetrators of the reformed doctrines—agents he rewards handsomely for their efforts, I'm told."

I had, thus far, been ensconced in a niche on the inside wall of the cloister, farthest from the noisy drizzle wetting the inner courtyard, thereby more able to catch their words. "Handsome rewards," one had just said. It was those words that so intoxicated my imagination. With mounting eagerness I listened.

"Agents, spies? And all cloaked in forbidden secrecy, say you?" chimed in one who had heretofore been silent. "If such is true," he paused, grinning at his self-perceived cleverness, "how is it that anyone knows anything at all about it?"

"Yet it is true," continued the speaker. "There is just such a system of terror set afoot not only in Paris but throughout France. How else would the heretics, Lambert, Leclerc, Pavanne, and many others—how else would they have been discovered and condemned?"

"Those of the Reformed doctrines," continued the skeptic, "are known to be bold, even reckless in their fervor. Such men proclaim from the housetops their raving expositions, and therefore need not the services of spies and agents to expose their heresies. Their own zeal has done the deed."

"Indeed, some are as you have described them. But these are more often the zealous tradesman, the enthusiastic cobbler, the baker, giddy with new discoveries. They seldom are the theologian, the eloquent preacher, and the influential leaders. It is the latter who have the power to win over a vast following and, thereby, empty our churches. And so it is these who must be stopped; it is these who shall lead us to all the rest; and it is these men who are best ferreted out by clandestine agents."

"But it is not only the king who employs such agents," said another. "The spies of the Sorbonne, commissioned by the priests and doctors of the university, by cunning and stealth enter churches, colleges, and even private families to catch up any word of evangelical doctrine . . . ."

My mind was aflame. In an instant, I perceived my true calling. My skill, of which I was so proud, could be put to grand use, so I then believed it, and fill my purse with gold in the bargain. What could give more nobility to my wretched life? And not only would I be serving the grand interests of my king and country, and of religion, I would be growing rich all the while. My head spun with these reflections.

"It is certain," agreed one of them, "that these agents will, at the last, hunt down and trample underfoot the heretics of the Reformation."

I fear that had all those present not been so intent on the conversation, that my agitation would most surely have given me away. I stole a glance at Calvin. His pale brow was furrowed in thought. He was stroking his left cheek as if to speak, but no words came from his lips.

"But none of this need be merely in the realm of theory," spoke one who appeared to be the youngest. "We may shortly witness the effects of these efforts. There is to be one such heretic tried at the Place de la Gréve. He is one they call the hermit."

"And when is this hermit to be silenced?"

"I'm told," continued the young man, "at midday, on the morrow."

13

Paris Burning

ONE MIGHT EASILY have drawn flawed conclusions about what was imminently to transpire next morning in Paris. The atmosphere before l'Hotel de Ville was one of celebration and revelry, as if all Paris had been granted a special indulgence by the pope. People were giddy with expectation.

The narrow streets were choked with venders hawking everything from shimmering silk to roasted chestnuts, and merrymakers abounded as if it were to be a holiday. A parti-colored *jongleur* with bells dangling from the corners of his red-and-yellow hat entertained while standing knee-deep in the fountain. Amid shouting and cheering, he managed to keep simultaneously aloft a scent ball, a dagger, an apple, and a cobbler's awl. Without missing a catch, he nodded in the direction of a fine lady dressed in green satin. "Your diamond ring, Madam," cried he. "Throw in your diamond ring, and, for your pleasure, I shall juggle the lot."

The crowds roared, the peasants urging her to do it, the proud nobility sniffing in contempt at the base greed of the common hoard and passing on. Feigning a mortal wound from the dagger, the jongleur collapsed completely beneath the waters of the fountain. I was astounded at his ability to hold his breath, for he stayed facedown beneath the waters for such a time that many became alarmed and more than one fellow clambered into the murky water to rescue him. He appeared lifeless, limp as a drowned cat, as they hoisted him to the surface by the arms. Suddenly, a long arching spout of water emitted from his mouth, and his eyes popped open. Leaping to the rim of the fountain, with a grand flourish, he bowed. Looking hopefully at the delighted crowd, he extended his soggy hat for coins.

Whole families had gathered. One child of two or three, from atop her father's shoulders, squealed with delight at the jongleur, clapping her chubby palms together with glee.

Meanwhile, walking solemnly at Calvin's heels, I had been attempting to veil my enjoyment of it all. He, and I with him, had been persuaded to go to the Place de la Gréve that morning. I had needed no such persuading, but they had had considerable work to do winning Calvin over to the venture.

My attention was suddenly drawn by the smell of burning. In a medieval city one could never be overly cautious about fire. One spark could set alight an entire town, the raging flames leaping from rooftop to rooftop, from ancient half-timbered house to town hall, from parish church to grand cathedral. Such had happened in my own village of Noyon long ago. Again I sniffed the air. Smoke rose into the sky from near the center of the plaza.

Compelled forward by the jostling mob, Calvin, his friend Nicholas Cop, and the young scholars with him made their way to the center of the Place de la Gréve. I felt a surging of excitement as we drew closer. A mad expectancy came over me, and I groped forward through the masses like a man possessed.

When at last I could see what the source of that burning was, my heart deflated, and I confess my keen disappointment. Before us stood a half-circle of priests and monks, their hands piously folded and heads shrouded and bowed. In their midst was a mound aflame, fueled by what at first looked like chunks of wood, but on closer inspection I observed to be an array of books and pamphlets.

"Whose are these?" asked an indignant voice. Jostled by the mob close about me, it was impossible to be certain who spoke. I had observed, however, that somehow in the press of bodies, Calvin's cousin, one called Pierre Robert Olivetan, had joined him, and though I had heard him speak very little, I wondered whether it had been his voice that had posed the question.

"We shall soon know," replied another.

One of the priests then raised his head and lifted his arms toward the fire and the mob. "By decree of the holy doctors of the Sorbonne," he began, his voice ringing above the noise of the crowd and the hissing of the flames. The bonfire lay precisely between where I stood and the speaker, and the heat from the flames obscured his outline and made his vestments quaver like I imagined the souls damned in hell to writhe in their torment.

"By decree of the holy doctors of the university, these the heretical writings of Martin Luther and the pernicious translations of the Holy Scriptures into the vulgar tongue are hereby condemned."

So that was it, was it? I recall thinking to myself. I had heard Calvin speak of this Martin Luther fellow, and I had heard more than hints of the efforts to create a French translation of the Bible, but I had no clear understanding of why these books would so trouble the holy doctors of the Sorbonne. It occurred to my imagination that if these things were of so little worth, as the priests clearly believed, it might have been a better strategy not so to elevate the books by creating such a sensation with their destruction. The streets of Paris were blockaded, so vast was the mob come to witness their burning.

As more books were carelessly flung on the flames, I heard a sharp intake of breath close at my side. Glancing to my right, I observed Calvin gazing into the flames, yellow flickers reflecting on the watery orbs of his eyes as he stared. I could not quite discern the meaning of his looks. Was it merely his love of books and learning that made him appear to recoil at such wanton destruction of calf leather and rag paper? I studied him the more closely. *Or is there something more?*

Their eyes were wide with pity, Calvin and his cousin Pierre Robert Olivetan, who bent close to Calvin more than once and seemed to be speaking earnestly in the young man's ear. I believe this might have been the first time that I began to entertain thoughts that Calvin himself might be developing sentiments similar to those of the reformed party. It seemed odd indeed, and I had precious little evidence, to be sure, but the seed was planted that day in Paris, and I began to nurture it carefully.

We watched in silence as the fire burned lower. I remember feeling profoundly disappointed. *So that is all there is to be?* I mused with disgust.

But it was suddenly obvious that the conflagration of a few books was not, in fact, all there is to be. I had heretofore not noticed the charred stake protruding from a hole in the paving stones. But I was now compelled to notice it, for being led on either side by a hooded monk was one who must be the man they called the hermit.

His own clothes had been stripped from him, and in their place he had been forced to wear the cursed *sanbenito*, the loose tabard-like garment crudely decorated with devils howling in flames, part of the humiliation of the heretic condemned to die.

My attention was suddenly kindled, and I felt a quickening of my pulse at what was unfolding before me. We had had no burnings of heretics in Noyon. The odd witch now and then was drowned in the Oise River, but no burnings. I felt I was about to witness something that would be extraordinarily intriguing to me, and I could barely contain my eagerness.

I then observed two men wearing leather jerkins that extended to the knees, each with a coarse black hood pulled up over his head and rising to a stiff point. Except for their eyes, their faces were concealed behind black masks. I studied them at their work. With keen interest I watched them as they set some kind of steel implements into the glowing hot coals remaining from the fire of books.

"The holy doctors of the Holy Church," cried out the priest in charge of the unfolding scene, "have, in fair trial, deemed this miserable wretch to be an enemy of the Holy Church. He has defied the pope's supremacy, forbids prayers to the holy saints and Our Lady the Mother of God, and denies the transubstantiation of the Mass. Therefore, do we condemn his body to the flames of eternal damnation, commencing in this his death by slow burning."

I was never clear who commenced the cry, but one arose against the heretic, and soon many in the mob took up the chant. "Death, death, to the sacrilegious wretch!"

So absorbed in the frenzy of what was underway before my eyes, I was in no condition to notice details of Calvin's reaction to what followed. I do recollect his silence and that of his cousin pressed by the mob close at my side while I and all about me dutifully raised the cry against the condemned man.

Amid the yells and groans of the mob, one of the masked men took up a sword and hewed off the hermit's right hand. As if he had accomplished some heroic deed, he held high the man's mangled hand for the pleasure of the onlookers.

But I wanted to see the hermit's reaction to it all, so I studied the sufferer's face. I had hoped for blood-chilling cries of agony, eyes wide with horror, writhings and gnashings of teeth. I had hoped he would scream for mercy, blubber out a recantation of his errors, and then be forced to feel the torments of hell, nevertheless. So I had anticipated.

I looked more closely at his eyes and was profoundly disappointed at what I saw therein. He was clearly in a great deal of pain—who would not have been?—but he was bearing it far too well for what was then my chief pleasure. He bore a look that suggested none of this was coming as some great surprise to him. I have come since to know that if a victim's preconceived notion is that nothing so impossibly horrible could fall on him, he will descend more completely into that unmitigated horror that proves so entertaining at such burnings. But the hermit had clearly spent far too much time preparing himself, steeling his will, for what he now passed through. It is no exaggeration to say that there was a calmness and a fortitude about his features that not only bewildered me but increased my feelings of being cheated. I consoled myself that all was far from over with the hermit.

Then one of the executioners stripped off the sanbenito, and roughly lashed the man to the stake, but feigned difficulty with tying of the final knot.

"With the tying of this knot, man, will you not—" he broke off, looking for encouragement in his jest at the onlookers. "Will you not lend me a hand, man?" His fellow executioner laughed uproariously at the witticism, slapping his mate on the back and waggling the mangled hand before the hermit's face.

"I had forgotten, man," he said in his mirth. "You have already lent us your hand." Some in the crowd guffawed with laughter at his jest. I confess, I was among them.

Meanwhile, the other masked man had taken up the red-hot pincers from the coals, flourished the glowing iron tool before the crowd, who responded with *ahs* of expectation. Then slowly, steadily, he leveled the pincers at the hermit's face and moved toward him. The mob began crying out, "Eyes, eyes!" while others screamed, "Lips, lips!" and still others cried, "Ears, ears!" The hooded executioner waved off their cries, apparently having another preference.

As the red-hot iron came ever closer to his face, the hermit remained steady much longer than I thought any human would be able. That first stench of burning flesh wafted my way, and I inhaled it like incense.

The two masked men had clearly worked together at their grim business before, for no sooner was the man's nose burned off, than the other executioner began making menacingly cruel movements toward tender parts of his body with a sword. After tormenting the condemned man thus, with a flick of his wrist, he would effect a gash where it had not been expected. And then he would do it again, lacerating the hermit's arms until blood flowed freely. How I relished such acts of cruelty in those days.

Then as if by rehearsal, the other executioner came on, his pincer reheated while his fellow had been slashing with his sword.

This time after prolonged and feigned contemplations, and amid raucous yelling out of body parts from the mob, the executioner proceeded to clasp and gouge with the hot iron pincer the most tender region of the condemned man's breasts.

The hermit was in agony, but had not as yet cried out. So when I observed his mouth opening at this latest infliction, I readied myself for the screams of anguish that had thus far been lacking. Others must have been anticipating it too, for a hush fell over the mob. But what followed was then profoundly disappointing to me and to the priests and monks there attending.

With eyes lifted upward, the hermit spoke these words: "Our God is in the heavens: he hath done whatsoever he hath pleased. He will bless them that fear the Lord, both small and great. O my soul, trust thou in the Lord. O Lord, thou art mindful of me, thy child. Thou, O Christ, art my help and my shield. Thou wilt bless me."

I confess to being angry with the man. But from that moment onward there were no more raucous cries from the mob, no more taunts from the executioners. Even some of the priests and monks seemed moved to regard the hermit with a degree of compassion.

A degree, I say, but not a sufficient one to halt the proceedings. The faggots were lit, and amid the heated roaring of the consuming flames, the billowing of smoke, and the indescribably grotesque sights and sounds made as raw human flesh roasted before our eyes, the hermit expired in silence in the burning.

I was taken up in it all by something akin to an altered state of consciousness. I was intoxicated in a kind of frenzied madness, the details of which I cannot fully explain.

When at last the ordeal came to its charred and sinister end, I, who had been fit only to be observed, began more closely to observe Calvin's reactions. It was clear that he was moved, troubled, conflicted in mind and in body. He seemed hunched over as if in physical pain, and he said not a word, to me or to anyone, for the longest time. His aforementioned cousin, Olivetan, had now laid his arm in paternal fashion across the hunched shoulders of his younger relative. Tears streamed down the cheeks of his friend Nicholas Cop. I do believe this burning marked a significant turning point for Calvin, though he said at that time nothing that gave me a clearer notion of what direction that turning might take.

For my part, I could not stop thinking about the employment I had so lately learned of. Might not I serve my king and my church by using my talent to sniff out heretics like the hermit? Sickening as it all had been, was it not also heady and exhilarating? And was it not all effected in a high and noble cause? Would not my service in such purifying endeavors be a grand employment of my gifts? So I thus reasoned within my bosom. The chief and enduring effect that Paris burning had upon me was, henceforth, to give relentless determination to my nighttime revelries. With but one purpose, I would begin keenly listening, observing every hint. I was from that day unflinching in my resolution to find my true calling.

Hence, was I resolved. I would become one of those agents of the king or of the doctors of the Sorbonne. I cared little which.

14

My Chapeau

How my commissioning as a royal agent came about was so unlikely as to be incredible. Unbeknownst to myself, I had for nearly two years been carrying in my bosom that after which I was now so determined. How I thus discovered this depended so entirely, as I then understood such matters, on a mere and so very ordinary twist of fate, as to be comic.

"*Bon chance*," we glibly say. The events that next transpired in my life, a life against my will so inextricably entwined with that of John Calvin's as to drive me nearly mad, were seen by me as bon chance, good luck, anonymous good fortune, wealth, and even status, though of necessity a status entirely veiled from common view. But there was a goodness about these events to which I was then as one wholly deaf and dumb.

The year was 1528. I was then nineteen years of age, as was my countryman Calvin. We had little then in common save our age. Calvin had for the last two years been enamored of yet another instructor he considered a mentor. How he came to value such dull fellows as these, I shall never fully understand. I slept long and well through many of John Major's lectures. Major had returned to Paris from his native Scotland in 1526 and was renowned for his scholarship as much as for his defense of Roman Catholic doctrine.

Looking back on those days, I believe Calvin for a time found solace in Major's position on the Holy Church and on reformation. I once heard him say of his instructor, "His word is as an oracle on matters of religion." He often spoke thus of his favorites and termed Major, "a deeply knowledgeable man whose virtue is as great as his faith."

Yet did I hear this redoubtable professor condemn and criticize lazy clergymen who wantonly neglected their flocks, paying hirelings to do their duties while they pursued worldly pleasures with their takings. All of which seemed eminently obvious to any sane observer. "Grasping abbots," Major termed such fellows. I heard these things between blissful episodes of dozing during his lectures. He railed against bishops whose lustful offspring they had the gall to see installed as priests, and against other corruptions any man with eyes knew existed in the church. Major went so far as to state boldly, "They deceive themselves who think that the approval of even the supreme pontiff can reconcile such things to the dictates of conscience."

To suggest with words that even the pope could not approve of such licentious behavior among the clergy might have fooled some into concluding that Major was of the reforming party, a follower of Martin Luther or Jacques Lefevre. But in matters of orthodox medieval doctrine he was no evangelical reformer, or so I was forced to conclude after one discussion time where the man fell into a railing against "pernicious upstarts who would ruin the church by placing the Word of God in the soiled hands of the common man." I was ever dull, but I had come to understand that where a man stood on the church and reformation came down to what a man believed concerning translating the Bible into the common language of common folks. At the last, that made the difference.

Meanwhile, as Calvin distinguished himself at the University of Paris and neared the achieving of his degree from Montaigu, I had been busy, indeed.

It fell out after this fashion. One early morning as I attempted to make my way back to the dormitory of Montaigu from my night revels in St. Antoine, one of my companions, so I then believed it, shouted out a challenge. After a night of drinking and carousing about Paris, and with the river so near and sounds so oddly projected by its waters and the stone walls confining its course, I could not be sure from where the voice of that challenge came.

Nevertheless, challenge it was, and I staggered up on the ledge of Pont Neuf, the bridge hard by the grand Cathedral of Notre Dame. Sober, I would have had little difficulty striding along the barrier erected to keep fools such as I from tumbling into the black waters of the River Seine. Sober, however, I was not.

Though early morning, it was still pitchy black nighttime. As occurs in minds benumbed by excessive wine, many of the details are hazy in my recollection, but I recall that the stone ledge appeared to be growing narrower and seemed to quaver before my sight. Yet did I boldly march forward, one foot before the other. I then made the fatal error of looking below my feet to the shimmering blackness of the Seine far below.

As I so tilted my head, at precisely the same instant a gust of wind lifted my chapeau from atop my head. Like the fool that I was, I lunged in an insane attempt to catch up in my grasp the dead man's chapeau. Teetering now on but one foot, I watched with sinking heart as my beloved chapeau, kept and cherished by me for these five years, disappeared into the river. Arms wheeling, I desperately attempted to regain my balance and check my fall, but to no avail.

Absurd details imprint themselves on one's mind in times such as these, and I recall catching a glimpse of the blue silk of my chapeau as I fell rapidly closer to the surface of the water. The current had snatched it downriver so that it was some yards ahead of me when I heard my own splashing and felt the cold waters of the river enfold me.

If ever there is one reading this account who happens to have that exceptional skill called swimming, such a reader may be inclined to think this a rather mundane predicament, not worthy of such excessive narrative attentions. For one such as I, however, who swims after the fashion of a weighty sack of bricks, it was a fatal predicament indeed.

I thrashed in panic, wrestling, as it were, with the ubiquitous substance surrounding me, pulling me downward in its icy clutches, but my efforts, prodigious though they were, were to no avail. As the Seine closed in over my head, and just as, in horror, I expected my hapless life to be at its end, I felt myself lifted by some inexplicable phenomenon. To my momentary relief, my head had returned to the surface, but no sooner had it done so than I felt a downward tugging at my flinching limbs, an irrepressible ebbing of my being into oneness with the muddy depths. Filling my sodden lungs with air, I screamed for aid. It was no ordinary scream released into the early morning mists; it was one I intended to be sufficient to awaken all Paris, so desperate was I to be rescued from my watery grave.

But no aid came, and I felt myself drawn again into the greedy maw of death. Was such a death reserved but for wretches such as I had become? Was this some kind of cosmic mockery of my life, a cruel prolonging of suffering, an elongating of my existence for the sole purpose of snatching life from me, but only after toying with me, making me suffer the torments of hope three times over? Just when my being felt as if it would burst in protest, when it appeared that all hope was delusion and my miserable life was at last to be smothered into nothingness, I felt a sharp pain clawing, as it were, at my back.

Was this some new torment? But no. The clawing stopped and I felt myself now lifted, clearly a lifting sensation, and oh, the relief I felt in that elevation. A tightness increased at my back and encircling my torso. The next thing I remembered was hacking, choking, my stomach revolting, and being sick, my face pressed hard against the paving stones.

"I've, at long last, landed the big fish," I heard a man saying. His words came to my ears as laughing words, and I recall feeling that there was little matter for laughter in my mind.

"Gulp down a bit of air," he continued. "Then follow it up with a bit of this."

The passageway in my throat was ill disposed for much that could be termed gulping in those moments, but I did manage to wheeze down sufficient breath to restore my senses. Rolling onto my side, I took hold of the wine bottle he held out to me.

"Now, the question is," he continued, and it was then that I began to have my doubts about my rescuer, "how am I to prepare you?"

With those words, he poked at my ribs and squeezed my arms and legs. At first I thought he was making a morbid jest. Then

I began to sense that the poor old fellow was not entirely sane. Next I realized that he was in earnest.

"You may be *al dente* and so *a la Newburg* may be best, or perhaps *a la Provencale*, with the garlic and oil." He paused, musing and nodding as he pinched my forearm until it hurt. "Perhaps *flambeau a la broche* would suit best. Tough things taste so much better cooked in flames on a stick."

For the first time in my life I began to comprehend the meaning of the adage, "out of the frying pan into the fire," and I staggered to my feet, not genuinely afraid of the old man, nevertheless determined to be away from the odd fellow.

"I am grateful for your having rescued me," I said, backing away from him and making an attempt at a bow. "Indeed, I am, but I have no intention of being your breakfast, your lunch, or your dinner. Prepare me how you will; however great your skill as a chef, I am far too tough for your palate, I assure you."

His face fell, and for an instant I felt sorry for the old fellow and wondered whether it had all been in fun and he had simply overdone it. Perhaps, lonely old man that he was, all he wanted were a few moments of conversation and companionship. I hesitated, and as I did, I noticed in his catch basket my blue chapeau. He must have fished it from the drink before catching me.

"And now, with undying gratitude, I'll just have my chapeau and be on my way." With that, I snatched it up, gave it a quick shake to free some of the water out of it, turned on my heel, and set off. It was getting late, and I might find it difficult to reenter Montaigu if I didn't hurry.

The old man began chuckling as I set off, and I became more convinced of his madness as it escalated into full laughter. Suddenly, and to my utter surprise, I felt my chapeau yanked from my head. Clutching after it, I turned. It was hopping across the pavement toward the old fisherman like a rabbit in the Picardy forest. The old man laughed so hard that tears came down his cheeks. Hand over hand, he gathered in his fishing line, my chapeau lurching with his every pull on the line.

Late as I was, and though my entire body ached from my ordeal, I too managed to laugh at the sight. I followed my chapeau back to the fellow and sat down. Teeth missing, he grinned at me, thumping me on the back companionably at his joke. I pieced it together. He must have caught the chapeau with a fishing hook, but I came along before he could take the hook from it, so he had simply tossed it into his catch basket to attend to later. It all made sense. Still grinning, with a yank he extracted his fishing hook and handed me my tattered chapeau.

"We could share a dish of chapeau a la mode for petit dejeuner," he called after me, still laughing. I doffed my chapeau at him and, in spite of the misery I felt in my every joint, took off at a run.

I narrate this episode because it would prove to have the profoundest implication in what follows, though it would be some hours before I was to know just how significant these events were.

15

My License

NEXT DAY, I FELT myself slipping off into sleep during the afternoon lecture of John Major; he had been droning on about how precisely Aristotle and the Holy Church were in agreement. I heard many such declarations while at the University of Paris. Though I had slept not at all the night before, and from my near-drowning ordeal was in desperate need of rest, it was to prove to be a short and fitful rest.

For some reason this particular day the man would halt in his Latin lecture and digress into what must have been an anecdote told in his native Scots tongue. Some said they reckoned the man was wearying of Paris and longing for his native moorlands and heather, whatever those might be. All but one or two in the room would have understood nothing of what the man said in such a tongue. It was all rolling of the "r" sounds, lilting undulations, and guttural ejaculations to my ears. But that was precisely the problem. So unaccustomed were the sounds to my ears that I could not get my proper sleep during the lecture. I wondered whether there was some recourse to which a student, a servant student, that is, might appeal to have his rights.

Awake now, I listened as Master Major, resuming the Latin tongue, turned his discourse to what he termed "the new learning." I had heard it called this before, most generally by those who seemed to have a strong distaste for such learning. "Do not these advocates of the new learning recommend that all men read the Scriptures? Small and great, and in the vulgar tongue? Does not the pernicious Jacques Lefevre d'Etaples and his followers declare therein that whoever loves not Christ's Word is not a Christian, and that the Word of God alone is sufficient to lead to eternal life?"

At these words, I observed in Calvin, at my side, a conflicted blinking of his clear eyes, and his hand strayed to his cheek, as was his custom when thinking deeply or longing to express those thoughts.

"Yet does this Lefevre, this royal favorite, publish his Psalms of David, his New Testament, and now most recently his Pentateuch, and all from Jerome and into the vulgar tongue, the common French spoken by the street urchin."

"Is not he, Magister," ventured a particularly attentive young man seated squarely in the front and center, "is not he the royal librarian of Blois, made such by the king's own hand?"

Major reddened before answering. Though from Scotland, he knew the dangerous shoals into which answering such a question might launch him in these French waters. "Indeed, he is," was his terse reply.

"I have heard," continued the intent young man, "that although his works have been condemned by a commission of the parliament, it is the king's excellent sister Marguerite d'Angouleme who protects the ancient doctor d'Etaples. Is this not so, Magister?"

"Indeed, while others have been burned for much less, it is she who favors the man," replied Major. "It is to be noted, merely as a fact, that her royal highness Marguerite's own devotional poetry is so flavored, shall we say, by the new learning that the same parliamentary commission that condemned Lefevre's pernicious translations of Holy Scripture," his eyes blazed, and he brought his fist down into his open palm with his final words, "that same commission also censured her evangelical verses."

"I have heard the Excellent His Supremacy the Doctor Noel Beda here of the university declare—if I may have liberty to render a recitation of his words?"

Major nodded approvingly.

The earnest young man cleared his throat and continued. "His words were precisely as follows. 'What! Lefevre affirms that whoever places his salvation in himself will surely perish, while the man that lays aside all strength of his own, and throws himself entirely into the arms of Jesus Christ, will be saved! Oh, what heresy! To teach the inefficacy of meritorious works! What a hellish error! What a deceitful snare of the devil! Let us oppose it with all our might.' So declared Magister Beda."

"It is indeed a great error," said Major, scowling as he said it.

"And so we must oppose it with all our might. Do you not agree, Magister?" continued the young man.

Major affirmed his agreement, but with a degree of caution that seemed not to satisfy the enquirer.

At this exchange, I gave my attention to Calvin's pensive looks, the luster in his eyes becoming brighter as he listened to the words. I wondered whether the young man's railings were having the same effect on Calvin as they did on the speaker, who had recounted them with such relish.

The young zealot was now carrying on about some connection between Lefevre and one Guilliame Briconnet, Bishop of Meaux, accused of having sympathies with the reforming faction.

Still I studied Calvin's face. By the furrowing of his brow and the intensity of his eyes alone I was unable to interpret to my satisfaction whether Calvin was scowling as an indication of his agreement with Beda's condemnation of Lefevre, or whether his troubled looks were an indication of his agreeing with the evangelical assertions for which Lefevre was, herein, being railed against. It was too bewildering, and so I attempted to resume my napping, only to be intruded upon again by the earnest young man.

"There is one more thing I heard the distinguished Noel Beda declare on the subject at hand, Magister, and this in dialogue with the exalted doctors Duchesne, and Lecouturier, and offered without equivocation, Magister."

Again Major nodded, giving leave for the boy to speak on.

"They concluded their discussion, all rendering vehement agreement with Doctor Beda's words in summation of the whole. 'Let us banish from France this hateful doctrine of grace.' So did they all agree, Magister."

There was more said, but I had heard enough of such intellectual wrangling, and so in my frustration and loss of sleep, stealthily I pulled out my chapeau from within my breast. I did so merely with the notion of inspecting damages, for I felt certain the old fisherman's hook had done it no good. As I turned it over in my hands, with a sinking of my heart, I discovered that the hook had laid open a frightful tear on the inside, and part of the insides of the thing were trying to come out. It struck me like a blow from a fist; I knew of such blows.

Odd as it might seem, that filched chapeau had come to represent bigger things in my mind than I was entirely able to comprehend, much less explain. It had done so against my will, but nevertheless it had achieved some greater significance to me. Perhaps it was because I had discovered it in my own town of Noyon and so it felt like my only link to my past, to the place of my birth. But I vaguely felt it must be more than that. It had come to me as an important part of the string of events that had led to my escape from the dreaded plague. It had acted as a covering for me, enabling me to go places and do things I would never have been able to do without it, or so I imagined. It had served as the means of reprieve from the otherwise intolerable life John Calvin and the rest lived in this miserable college of self-denial. Without it, so I told myself, I would be forever trapped within these oppressive walls. In some convoluted and inexplicable way it had, to me in any event, become considerably more than a blue chapeau.

Brooding thus, I picked away at the threads frayed by the offending fishhook, calculating its prospects for repair. It was then that I discovered it. What I had at first thought to be merely some inner lining stitched in place by the tailor to give shape to the chapeau and comfort to the wearer, I then discovered to be entirely other than this.

Cautiously, I lifted my eyes to make certain I was, as was my studied practice, invisible to those about me. All eyes were on Master Major as he now resumed his lecture on the subject of the supremacy of papal interpretation of Scripture; as near as I can recollect, this was his subject. I saw rapt attentiveness on Calvin's face and realized that he had not so much as glanced in my direction for more than an hour and a half. Though he was often thus, I resented him for it. Here I was at his side, and so careless was he of my very existence that I could be preparing to slit his throat and he would never have seen the knife coming. I was chilled and invigorated by the fact, for fact I knew it to be.

Slowly did I then pull out the object of my fascination. It was a piece of pale linen, finely woven, about the size of a book they call a quarto, and folded double. My hands trembled slightly with expectancy as I unfolded the cloth. What met my eager eyes looked very much like a letter written on rag paper. My heart thundered in my bosom as I commenced reading the words. They were few and without equivocation.

"Maurice de Picard, commissioned agent of his Majesty Francis I, by this license is hereby and in perpetuity granted impunity for his services rendered to his royal Majesty, the King of France, in the honorable pursuit of enemies of the royal personage, of the realm of France, and of most particularly those who wage war against the Holy Church by their heretical preaching, writing, placard posting, desecration of sacred images, lecture and speech delivering, or by gathering in private homes or other unconsecrated locations there to presumptively conduct heretical religious services. Such persons engaging in such activities, or any other subversive religious behaviors, are deemed enemies of the King of France. This license, hereby, grants royal authority for its holder to search out by every and all reasonable means such pernicious persons, and guarantees impunity from prosecution for all such reasonable means engaged in the honorable employment of delivering up all traitors and heretics over to royal authority for punishment.

"This license, furthermore, may be presented by its holder for the procurement of all means necessary, including financial moneys to be drawn from the royal coffers through the several ministries of his Majesty, King Francis I, upon demand and throughout the said king's realm."

Hastily, I reread the words. It was signed by the hand of the royal minister of finance and had the impression of the royal seal pressed into the cloth in bold ink. I read it a third time, this time more slowly. Could it be? Had I been carrying about my person so carelessly such a license and for these five years? I shuddered as I recalled how I nearly lost the chapeau in the Seine, and gripped the linen page more tightly with the recollection. It was beyond belief, and I confess, I read the letter once again, as I was to do perhaps a hundred times over the next weeks.

While John Major droned on about the primacy of the papal see, my mind was awhirl with my discovery. What had Beda declared? "Let us banish from France this hateful doctrine of grace." And I held in my two hands such a license that called me to be an instrument to effect such a banishment. I gave no thought at this point to the fact that I was not Maurice de Picard. It was my license, and mine was a royal commission, one that granted me wide-sweeping privileges, for which I might be paid large sums of royal money.

As I thus mused on my good fortune—I recollected with scorn how long ago Calvin had decried the term "fortune" as a pagan one—I came to venerate that linen document as if it were a relic of the Virgin's veil. It represented a divine summons, one providentially or by fortune delivered to my very own person, an honorable mission, to which I alone had been called. Term it providence, term it fortune—I had no intention of quibbling over the verbiage.

16

Changes Afoot

WITH HIGHEST HONORS, Calvin achieved his theological degree in 1528 from the University of Paris, that grand monolith of Renaissance learning. For me it was a time to draw near, to suspend for a few moments my surly resentment of him; rather did I come close so better to share in my brilliant young master's accomplishments. I hoped, thereby, to elevate myself to a vantage point from which I might look down with scorn on the lesser capable fellows; a category, it is no exaggeration to declare, into which all other students fell next to my John Calvin. Basking in borrowed glories, I thus, for a brief time, feigned a more attentive posture toward him.

Some months after his graduation, he received a letter from his father that had the effect of troubling him. I was no personal confidant of Calvin's troubles, to be sure, but I had come to be a master at reading his moods, at knowing, so I thought, his inmost self by careful, and I believed astute, observation of his brow and eyes.

Where this was deficient, I yet more accurately gained my knowledge of him by intercepting his correspondence. It was never difficult for me to read his letters, for he often had me deliver those he wrote, and I had become a master at opening them without notice and reading their contents. Rarely, however, did I find anything of interest to me: no secret *amore* with some lovely girl across town, as I had long given up hope in the man; no letters from or to debtors for bills unpaid; no court summons for even the most mundane of infractions. Really, the man was a total bore in such matters. Nevertheless, did I regularly read his mail.

The letter in question from his father, one I had read before he did—by often doing this I fueled my scorn for him—came in heavy bold strokes, as if the man were angry as he wrote it. Without elaboration, his father hinted at a dust-up of some proportion with the bishop of Noyon, Charles Hangest. What was clear was that Gerard Calvin had new plans for his son. That was bluntly stated. Reading the nuance between the lines, however, as I so enjoyed doing, I concluded that Calvin's father's new plans for his brilliant son were an expression of spite for the bishop. The long and short of it was, Calvin was no longer to study theology. His father had arranged for him to matriculate at the University of Orleans and commence study of law. Further parsing the subtleties of the white space betwixt the lines, I divined that Gerard had some notion that Calvin's great scholarly gifts might be more profitably employed in the practice of civil law. To put it bluntly, I believe the father thought he might enrich himself more expansively by putting his son's academic prowess to use in legal transactions.

In that same year of 1528, Calvin's cousin and native of Noyon, Pierre Robert Olivetan, was forced to flee Paris. I knew these things for I had intercepted a communiqué penned by a secretary of the university and signed by Noel Beda himself, wherein

Olivetan was denounced and condemned, not only for preaching the new learning, but for "pernicious plans to translate Holy Scripture from the original Hebrew and Greek into French." So the letter had read.

I mused a good deal about Olivetan. So one could be denounced and condemned merely for planning to effect such a translation. One need not actually do the deed to fall under the condemnation of the Roman authorities of the university. And I mused at length about Olivetan's familial relationship with Calvin. Though I was forced to admit, I had seen no clear outward identifying on Calvin's part with Olivetan and his ideas, yet did I wonder whether his elder cousin might prove to exert influence over the young scholar. I thought of my commission and was determined to observe this more closely.

When I learned of our departure soon from Paris for the city of Orleans, I fell into a panic regarding my royal commission. How was I to make formal my new status? I confess, my concern lay far more with how I was to present my commission and thereby have royal money laid into my hands than with how I was to honorably denounce those deemed heretics by both church and state. Surely Paris was the city in which to make good my new status. But how to set about it? That was what troubled me so greatly.

I rather liked my name, Jean-Louis, and was loathe to give it up for one such as Maurice. Nevertheless, it would be foolish, indeed, to retain a name that would require me to forego such status and profit. Whatever the discomfort, assuming the name Maurice might not be such a bad thing.

Though one would never know it from Calvin's iron self-discipline, after earning his degree from the university, our life was less dominated by the rigid authoritarian rule of the master of the College de Montaigu. Yet one such as Calvin needed no imposed structure. The morning after the solemn celebration during which his degree was conferred on his head, he lay in bed for two hours, but not sleeping. He was rehearsing some lengthy passage he had read, and by the sounds of it, memorized from St. Augustine, I believe it was—a saint growing to be a favorite of his, I had begun to observe. Two hours of recitation, and that after having earned highest honors. Was there to be no relaxing of his self-imposed rigors? Such labors after learning were beyond my comprehension in the extreme.

But my time was far more my own, a reality I comprehended and appreciated well. One evening while strolling along the Rue de la Monnaie, as I passed under the narrow arch of Pont des Arts, whom should I happen upon but my fisherman.

He was whistling to himself a French folk song I vaguely recollected hearing before, and sat rocking back and forth on a herring barrel set on its side. As I drew nearer, he looked up, and broke into a wide grin.

"It is my friend with the blue chapeau," he said, motioning for me to sit at his side on the wooden barrel.

"And the fishing?" I said, sitting down and attempting as I spoke to match his odd rocking on the barrel.

"The fishing has improved," he said, eyeing me closely. "It has just improved greatly, my friend," he added, winking significantly, though I had no notion of what was supposed to be so significant.

"Your meaning, sir?" I asked.

"You of the blue chapeau," he said, "I have often seen you on your night revels. Often, indeed, have I seen you."

I felt disconcerted by his words and still more indignant at his tone. "You have been spying on me, then?" I said, attempting to effect lightness and unconcern by my tone.

"Ah, spying," he said, tugging gently on his fishing line. "Now we come to our topic, do we not?"

"Our topic?" said I. "I did not know it was to be our topic, my friend. You rescued me from drowning, was it two weeks past? And we meet again to speak of spying. I do not understand your meaning, sir."

"You shall, you shall," he replied with one of his knowing chuckles. Then growing suddenly serious, he seized my chin and drew me close to his face. "You have newly discovered something?" It was a question, but rendered in the tone of a declarative statement of fact.

There was to be no deceiving of this fellow, that much was clear to me, especially not with his green watery eyes but inches from my own. I attempted to pull away, but his grip was firm.

"What does it mean?" I asked.

"So you have discovered it," he said, nodding knowingly. "Its meaning is for you to find out."

"But how?" I asked. I had no other plan, so I determined to question this fellow, but I also determined to be guarded. In times such as these, one could not be too careful. I had learned that much about Paris these years. "Where do I go to commence my work, to set in motion my new commission?"

"Ah, these are good questions, my boy," he said. "Tonight, at midnight Mass. St. Germaine l'Auxerrois, near the Palace of the Louvre."

"I know the place," I said. Though I had never been inside its walls, it was the church before which I had extracted myself from

129

under the carriage, when first I arrived in Paris five long years ago. "I am to attend midnight Mass. That is all?"

"You must do so with stealth and shrewdness," he said. "And you must wear your blue waistcoat and chapeau—and you must have the newly discovered article on your person. You will be asked to present it, of course. Everything depends upon your having it. Everything."

With these words he released my chin. I felt that I would wear a bruise for life from his iron grip. Rubbing my chin, I strode away, the fisherman humming the old folk tune after me.

I was more than mystified by what had just transpired. Was that voice I had heard daring me to attempt to balance atop the Pont Neuf that night, was that the old man's voice? And how did he know of my commission? Was there something in the cut of the chapeau or of the waistcoat, or of them both together that gave me away? Was I going to be accused of stealing these articles, stealing or worse? I felt my wrists and remembered the hermit's hand severed from his wrist before his burning. Or was this all to be somehow part of my new vocation? Was I hereby to enter into my new calling?

As I puzzled over all these questions, in my musings I found that my feet had of their own accord taken me to Rue Vallette, whose narrow cobblestones I had first tread, bearing Calvin's trunk on my shoulder, five years ago.

Down the narrow street I walked, half-timbered houses leaning over me, pressing down on me from either side, their gables appearing to meet in the night sky far above me. Their windows were shuttered tightly against the night noises and the vaporous cold, and as if against the sinister forces lurking in the alleyways of Paris.

I wondered whether I was one of those sinister forces, or whether I was about to become a legitimate agent of his royal Majesty, the king of France. I thrilled at the thought. My life would have significance, importance, and I would be doing something grand and important for Holy Church and for France. I had been over this ground before in my troubled conscience, and it bothered me that I felt so compelled, yet again, to justify my scheme. Nevertheless did my feet take me to the west entrance of the royal church of St. Germaine l'Auxerrois.

I shuddered as I drew near. The night was chilly, and mists from the Seine crept about the ancient church. Glaring down at me were rigid gargoyles, mouths unendingly agape in hellish screams. Again a shudder went down my spine at these nightmarish creations of the stonecutters of the Middle Ages. Specter-like, the mists entwined their vapors in and through the flying buttresses, encircling the Romanesque bell tower and growing thicker as they rose ever higher on the spire.

Suddenly from the bell tower came a single clear tolling of the half hour. Thirty minutes before midnight Mass. Thirty minutes to concoct a scheme, to ready myself for this mysterious encounter, one that I anticipated with equal proportions of eagerness and of dread.

With that tolling came a new dread in my bosom. What if I was discovered in this my deception? What if it was known I was not Maurice de Picard? What if I was to be accused of murdering the man and seizing his commission? If I were thus accused, there was enough truth in the accusation as to render me without defense. What was I to do? I even entertained the unlikely notion that perhaps the truth in its entirety might prove to be my best defense, and the sure path to making Maurice's commission my own. Fleeting, indeed, were such thoughts. So divergent then was the path of honesty to my own that I dismissed any truth telling as out of the question.

Flickers of candlelight shone through the yellow and blood-red images enshrined in the stained glass of the rose window above the west door. The door was ajar. Making not a sound, I peered through the opening. I sensed as much as saw in the dimness a figure. My senses were at full alert. He had not observed me, and I faintly heard his footfalls as he paced to the right of the nave.

Knowing that for an instant longer his back would be to me, I soundlessly made my way through the door, ducking into the shadows at the cold-stone base of a column on the far left of the nave. All in a fraction of time and all inaudible.

Slowly the man returned to the door, peered out into the night, then moved with little sound my way. His footfalls came to my ears as those of a man who was good at being stealthy, but who was forced by nature to work very hard at it. Moreover, I concluded that, perhaps from an old injury or perhaps from a minor deformity from his birth, he placed slightly more weight on his right leg than his left when he walked, thus creating a minute rhythm, one that delivered to the air about him a distinctive character, discernable to my ears though perhaps to few others.

While drawing these conclusions, my mind was equally employed in searching out a safe vantage point from which I could view my surroundings and see whoever was to meet me, see him before he saw me. Such was always my plan. To see and not be seen. I lived by this.

The scent of burning candles and the lingering aroma of incense filled my nostrils. Candlelight illuminated the center aisle of the nave, and still more shimmered farther away, on the high altar of the chancel. I was at first irritated by the sounds of the flames burning the wicks on the candles, faint though those hissings were. Within moments, however, my mind found a place for them and they no longer distracted me from my attentiveness to sounds that demanded my acute attention.

Along the north corridor into which I now moved, only the dimmest emanations of candlelight illumined my steps. Treading the ancient flagstones of the church so as not to disturb so much as the dust, past the cold and silent remains of once-proud knights and nobles now entombed and moldering beneath pious effigies, with stealth I made my way farther into the sanctuary. I was determined not to be caught unawares, and I marshaled all my skill.

It was then that I saw them. Perhaps "saw them" is not quite accurate. I sensed their presence and froze in my stride, my ears groping the silence to identify and categorize what I had sensed. Their breathing betrayed them, and then as I studied the shadows across the nave from which that breathing had come to my ears, I did see them: two men. One was seated on the bottom step of the pulpit stair, and the other stood nearby, his arm resting on the pulpit stair rail.

"It was nothing," I heard one faintly conclude, following this with a long emanation of breath as if he had been holding his for a time. Also in a hushed whisper, the other man spoke, but I could not discern his words. Determined to hear all their counsel, I made my way closer. It would be difficult, for to draw nearer the speakers would require me to pass across the center aisle of the nave, and this was illuminated with candlelight far in excess of the shadows in which I now lurked. Yet was I determined to hear their words.

Crawling as close as I dared, I waited for developments. Suddenly I heard footfalls, steps made without stealth or pretense. It must be one of the monks preparing for the Mass, I concluded. I knew that the two watchers at the pulpit would be instantaneously distracted by the monk and so, silently but boldly, I bolted across the aisle, immediately hunkering in the shadows, now on the north side of the nave, near the pulpit. I heard the faint rustling of their garments as they turned back from looking after the monk. There was no outcry. I had not been seen. In their husky whispering voices, they continued speaking.

"The time is short," said one.

"Indeed, it is," replied the other.

"I fear we shall not this night find our man."

"Fear, indeed. You choose the correct word."

"We need no more bunglers. Street riffraff looking for a royal handout make worthless agents. Worse yet, we get blamed for their stupidity."

There was suddenly a ruckus at the west door.

"Jacques has discovered another one, and good riddance to him."

"Soldiers looking for a new commission are not much better."

"Yes. They know nothing of stealth and resourcefulness. Want to march shoulder to shoulder, charge into the fray, blow trumpets, render volley fire at their enemies. They have no patience, no subtlety."

"Indeed, they do not. Now give me a fellow who is silent as the grave, who has nothing to live for, nothing to lose, who is devoid of that faculty called conscience, can act without scruple, is unencumbered by principle, who is barren of all human kindness, yet is clever enough to feign duty and kindness when such is required—now there's a fellow who would be worthy of his royal commission."

"You have neglected to mention an all-important quality, my friend."

"Have I? What quality?"

"Cruelty. Direst cruelty is demanded of such a fellow. He must be one who would, unflinching, deliver up his own frail, shrieking mother to the pyre."

As they thus spoke, I had made my way to within arm's reach of the fellows, they oblivious to my presence. In their fine satin attire, on which I observed flickers of candlelight to shimmer as they moved, I deduced that they were in fact in royal service, perhaps pages here on an errand for some ranking minister of the court. Lowborn, I was little familiar with court life and so was only able to surmise, but this seemed logical to my mind. But I was unclear how I ought to proceed, and Mass would commence in less than a quarter of an hour. Yet how to do so?

Suddenly an idea occurred. As they next spoke, I pulled my chapeau from my head, lifting out the linen commission. When they next paused and silence lay all about us, I tossed my chapeau at the feet of the one seated on the pulpit stair.

"What have we here!" cried the seated fellow, recoiling from the chapeau as if it were an adder about to strike.

"The blue chapeau," said the other. "From where did it come in this light-deprived place?"

"It is mine," I said, sliding from my place and standing before them.

They looked at me as if looking at a dead man.

"And I have heard all your counsel. I am the man you are seeking." Deeply grateful for the darkness of midnight and the dim candlelight, I plunged onward. "I am Maurice de Picard, royal agent of his Majesty King Francis I."

"How did you get here?" stammered one of them. "How did you get past Jacques guarding the door?"

"How did you appear so suddenly here before us?" asked the other. "And why did we not observe you?" He sounded genuinely frightened at his own question, as if I were a ghoul arisen from deep within one of the stone tombs that lay all about us.

"How I did these things is my business," I said, affecting as bold a manner as I dared. "That I did them, and am able to do them and more again and again, should be proof enough that I am no bungler, no street riffraff here to sponge a royal commission. I am the man you seek."

They stared mutely at me. I picked up my chapeau and placed it on my head as if to leave.

"You seek a royal commission, then?" asked the shorter of the two, the one who had sat on the step through all.

"I seek not what I already possess," I said, a hint of scorn and condescension in my tone. Pulling out my linen commission, I unfolded and turned it toward the nearest candle.

Silently they scanned its contents. When I felt I had given them sufficient time to read it, I continued.

"I merely ask for the honor of my commission," I said, "for late instructions in the fulfillment, thereof, and—" Here I paused, significantly, eyeing them. "—and for royal means to carry out my duties without hindrance or scruple."

Here they appeared to be recovering themselves and glanced at one another before making reply.

"So it is money that you seek?" said one, attempting, as it seemed, to sound condescending. "And you presume to imagine that we will simply, because you have asked for it, hand you a purse full of the king's gold? Is that it?"

"No," I said firmly. "And I shall not prevaricate about it with you. I seek it because I have his Majesty the King of France's royal guarantee that I shall have it, his royal seal hereon affixed as my surety." I held up the linen paper as I spoke. "But if that is not good enough for you, I shall now depart your company and resume my royal duties with your faces clearly imprinted in my mind. I do, in fact, have all of the qualities aforementioned in your conversation—most especially am I skilled in the latter of them."

At these words a bulging sack of gold coins appeared and was placed within the palm of my right hand. With prodigious self-control, I refused even to look at that purse, so fearful was I that my greed might betray me. With studied indifference, I closed my fingers about the smooth calfskin folds of that laden purse and slowly thrust it inside my bosom.

"We must report on where you now work," said the short one. "And the king is most anxious to see the results of your labors."

"I am implanted within the very walls of the Sorbonne," I began, my mind racing as I proceeded, "and I have, by my skill, ingratiated myself into the inner circle of the principal proponents of the new learning. His Majesty shall see my results. But I pursue not the zealous tradesman, or the eager young student of the Saxon heretic Martin Luther. No, my pursuits require skill, and patience, and the greatest care. My objects are the influential leaders of the new doctrine. Without a doubt, I will, by my wit and skill, deliver them up to His Majesty, but it shall take time." Here I patted the money purse in my bosom. "But I assure you, my prize shall be worth a great deal to His Majesty."

They assured me that if it was not, His Majesty would have my head for it, and then they proceeded to give me the details of making contact and precisely how, where, and when I was to render my denunciations.

"It is most critical," the short one concluded, "that you follow these instructions. If you do not, as you denounce one of His Majesty's enemies, you denounce yourself. Lose your covert status, make yourself known for what you really are—" I did not like the manner in which he said this. "—And you are of no future good to the crown."

It was not until I had quitted the church and had ducked into an alleyway off the Rue de Rivoli that I felt I could breathe again. My charade had demanded so much energy that I nearly collapsed in a heap. Yet could I not help smiling at my cleverness. It had worked. I had achieved a royal commission from the King of France. I felt that whole new worlds lay before me.

I did not then have a moment of remorse, no thought of what it would all cost me in the months and years that lay ahead. I was as one intoxicated by my own importance. Surely I would still be required to demure, to feign servile attentions on John Calvin, but with what high purpose did I now engage in the duties of my calling, with what a grand and honorable object in view.

17

Orleans

GERARD CALVIN WAS NOT a man to be put off. His son would leave off the formal study of theology and study law, and he would quit Paris and take up residence in Orleans. That much was certain.

Torn as I was at leaving my beloved Paris and all her charms and diversions, I felt as if by an inner compulsion that I ought to stay close to Calvin. As the day approached for our journey south to Orleans, I briefly entertained, with scorn for him, the notion that I no longer needed his paltry allowance of food and clothing. I was a king's agent and could attach myself with ease to another in Paris. Yet, inexplicably, did my nerve fail me, and I remained in his service.

On arrival in Orleans, however, I felt a sinking in my bosom at the place. To be sure, Francis I, my king and patron, had commissioned the building of a new palace, ostensibly to house his royal governor, and I found some diversion in watching the masons as they created mosaic patterns on its façade with varied colored bricks, and the stonecutters as they crafted luxurious balconies and soaring gables. Thrilling, indeed, if one is thrilled by such things, but I found Orleans to be prodigiously deficient of the charms of Paris.

If I had had an appreciation for the architecture of the Renaissance I might have found diversion enough in the place. The local bishop had apparently thought the cherished remains of St. Aignan worthy of a new transept and quire built in the chiseled symmetry of the Renaissance, and completed only a few decades before our arrival.

Dull to the finer artistic elements no doubt worthily executed there, I fairly drooled at the lavish gold gilding on the shrine containing the bones of St. Aignan, housed within the new church. New, I say; however, an old fishwife in the market told me with religious fervor of how his venerable bones had been bringing blessings on Orleans since the time of Attila the Hun. She spoke with such certainty of these things that I marveled at her age.

I found myself yawning often in Orleans. Far too quiet did I find the place, and I often daydreamed of my revelries in St. Antoine and the steamy nightlife in the wine shops and brothels along the River Seine. I puzzled over how I was to discover anything sinister in such a dull place, and I felt I'd better use my gold coins with care, though there was little to spend them on, little that I valued, in any event.

Ironically, as my life felt more austere, Calvin's life altered in quite the other direction. Gone were the vigils and torments of the College de Montaigu. No longer in priestly training, he began to appear in another light to me, and I was forced to admit, this light revealed a human side I had, heretofore, refused to see in him. To be sure, his iron self-discipline in the pursuit of knowledge had not altered a jot. He had become no slacker. Nevertheless, he had many more hours at his disposal for vigorous conversations, companionable strolls through the town, or meeting with friends over bread, cheese, a bottle of Chenin Blanc, and a book. Indeed, he read far more, if that were possible, and, I was to discover, he read more widely.

Ever obedient to his father's wishes, Calvin here set himself with determination to master his studies of civil law. After remaining in his bed for upwards of two whole hours reciting with precision the lessons he had somehow memorized verbatim from the previous day's lecture of Pierre Taisan de l'Etoile, "the most distinguished professor of jurisprudence of the day," as he often termed the man, Calvin would rise and be off to another lecture.

What astonished me the most in Orleans was how Calvin made friends. To be sure, he had acquired in Nicholas Cop something of a friend, and he did continue to exchange letters with Cop while in Orleans. But combine these new friends with the comfort and liberty afforded by his own rooms and it was astonishing to behold. With these new companions Calvin spoke, dined, read, and yes, even laughed. It was astonishing to me then that he had acquired an ability for laughter.

Perhaps it was because of Calvin's love of books and reading that he became, within the first weeks of our time in Orleans, fast friends with the librarian of the university, Philippe Laurent. Fellow students Francis Daniel and Nicolas Duchemin would often accompany Calvin back to our lodgings for discussion after attending de l'Etoile's daily lecture. These men were a world apart from me. What they found so fascinating about all this learning and inquiry ever eluded me. They were as excitable about discussing Plato's *Republic* as I had been about carousing the streets of Paris. Odd, indeed.

One evening after dinner, Laurent, the librarian, produced a large leather-bound volume.

"What have we here, my friend?" asked Calvin, eagerly taking up the book and opening its ponderous boards to the title page. "The New Testament, Philippe," he said, eyeing the man, "and in Greek."

That was all I am able to record about the evening's discussion. I trimmed candles as evening fell, and uncorked another bottle of wine. But hours passed where Greek was read out from the book's pages, discussion was engaged, largely in Greek, with snatches in Latin, and an occasional jest rendered in French, but all so disjointed by lengthy Greek speaking, of which I understood absolutely nothing, that I have nothing herein to record of the evening.

Nothing, that is, about their actual words. But perhaps because I understood so little of what they said, I observed all the more closely how they said it. There was a growing animation that came over the friends as they read and spoke with one another. I felt profoundly left out of those readings, and there were to be many such to be left out of. My resentment, never far from my brow, simmered those many nights. I angered my own self with my feelings. I felt, much to my consternation, a hint of a desire to be in on what made them so enthusiastic, so animated, so enthralled. Yet did I feel a man apart from their words, and their friendship.

One such night, after clearing away the remains of the evening meal, as I settled down to brood over my miserable life, they continued speaking in French.

"I have only recently acquired," said Laurent, "a copy of a most intriguing letter."

"So this night we are to read that which was intended for another," said Duchemin. His words were delivered in a playfully rebuking tone.

"Have you stolen the letter?" asked Francis Daniel. "Thou shalt not steal, my good friend."

"It is not like that," said Laurent. "It is a letter penned by Her Highness, Marguerite, sister of the king, for her own children, but freely circulating throughout France."

"Freely, Laurent?" said Calvin.

"Well, not as freely as many would like, but freely, may I say, if acquired through the proper channels."

"Channels to which you as librarian," said Daniel, "the illustrious keeper of the university's vast collection of written materials, to which you have free access. Am I correct?"

"You are, indeed," said Laurent, rendering a bow of acknowledgement. "These are dangerous times in France. Hence, this letter must be read with discretion."

I made no move, no sign that might betray the fact that there was to be no discretion with me in the room.

"You are among the best of friends," said Duchemin, waving a hand about the table. "Read the letter, man."

"So I shall read it," said Laurent.

Unfolding the parchment, the librarian began reading. This is what I heard that evening in Orleans.

"You ask me, my children, to do a very difficult thing—to invent a diversion that will drive away your *ennui*."

My ennui? She knows of my boredom? I felt at her opening words that she had penned the words for me. The librarian continued.

"I have been seeking all my life to effect this, but I have found only one true and perfect remedy, which is, reading the Holy Scriptures. In perusing them, my mind experiences its true and perfect joy; and from this pleasure of the mind, proceed the repose and health of the body. If you desire me to tell you what I do, to be so joyful and so well, in the midst of the trials of life, it is because as soon as I awaken, I read from this sacred book.

"Therein I see and contemplate the will of God, who sent his Son to us on earth, to preach that Holy Word, and to announce the sweet tidings, that he promises to pardon our sins and extinguish our debts, by giving us his Son, who loved us, and who suffered and died for our sakes.

"This idea so delights me that I take up the Psalms and sing them with my heart, and pronounce with my tongue the fine hymns with which the Holy Spirit inspired David, and the sacred authors. The pleasure I receive from this exercise, so transports me, that I consider all the evils that may happen to me in the day, to be real blessings, for I place alone Christ in my heart, by faith, who endured far more misery for me.

"Before I sup, I retire in the same manner, to give my soul a congenial lesson. At night, I review all that I have done in the day; I implore pardon for my faults; I thank my God for his favors; and I lie down in his love, in his fear, and in his peace, my soul being free from every worldly anxiety. Behold, my dear children, what has, for a long while, made me so happy."

Looking about the room at his friends, Laurent slowly folded the document. Against my will, I found myself charmed by her words, and wondered at how beautiful a woman must be, of necessity, who was thus so happy.

"Does the king's sister," asked Calvin, slowly weighing his words as he spoke, "read Latin?"

"She does," replied Duchemin. "She is extraordinarily well tutored in languages."

"Am I to assume, then," continued Calvin, measuring his words, "that she reads from Jerome's Latin Bible, the Vulgate?"

"She does not," said Duchemin.

"So in what tongue does she read the Holy Scriptures?" asked Calvin.

"French," said Laurent, simply. "She reads from Lefevre's French translation of the Psalms and the New Testament. The good doctor gave her a copy with his own hand."

"Is it not, my friends, a practice strictly forbidden," said Calvin, "by the Holy Church?"

"Indeed," said Daniel. "Queen Marguerite of Angouleme well knows that it is, and she knows what it is to be suspected and hated for doing so. Montmorency, the king's premier, boldly declared before his Majesty that if he wished to be rid of reformation heresy, he must begin within his own house, within the royal court itself, especially among his sister, Marguerite, Queen of Navarre, and all her court. I'm told he reserved choice invectives for her court poet, Clement Marot, for his heretical Psalm versifications into the French."

"Heresy," said Laurent, musingly. "They term it heresy to commune daily with Christ as Marguerite does, and to restore the devotions of the psalmist to the common man? Such seems odd, to my mind."

I felt confused at their words. If I could trust what these men were saying, I would need to tread most carefully in fulfilling my commission. It was rather confusing to my dull mind. How was I to deliver over enemies of the Holy Church and thus of His Majesty the King of France, if that king protected in his own court, nay, within his own family such bold proponents of reformation doctrine? I was deeply troubled by these things, and determined to be cautious, more so than I had, heretofore, thought necessary. It would be baffling intelligence such as I had just heard that would so enervate my ability to perform with greater effectiveness my calling in the years ahead.

Another brief episode of note transpired during our time in Orleans. After attending Mass one evening in the new cathedral of Notre Dame de Recouvrance, the four friends, and I with them, retired to Calvin's rooms for a late supper.

"That was too much for my taste," said Duchemin, breaking off a hunk of cheese.

"But it was as things have always been," said Laurent. "So why too much?"

Duchemin chewed slowly before replying. "I do not entirely understand myself," he said with a frown. "But of what worth is a service all in a tongue that common men understand not, and all so full of slavish superstition?"

"Perhaps it is reading Paul that had done it," said Daniel. "There is surely nothing of all this sacramental pomp in Paul's epistles."

"Sacramental pomp?" said Duchemin. "Call it what it is. It is base idolatry."

"Truly the artists of the age have outdone themselves with making graven images to saints and the Virgin," said Laurent. "I wonder that I have never observed so many poor misguided sheep prostrating themselves before the glittering splendor of some image of a saint."

"It is, however, no recent development." These were the first words I observed from Calvin that night.

"No indeed!" said Daniel. "But for that reason all the more reprehensible as more generations have been so seduced thereby."

"We know how detestable a thing idolatry is in the sight of God," said Laurent, "and history abounds with narratives of the dreadful punishments with which he visited it, both upon the Israelites and upon other nations."

"Even your beloved pagan Seneca," said Duchemin, turning to Calvin. "Even a pagan such as he knew enough to rail against idolatry. Render it again. You recited it to me from your own lips not two days ago."

Calvin looked awkward, almost defensive, but he dutifully commenced a brief recitation. It was a wonder to see his ability in doing this without consulting any written material with his eyes.

"This from Seneca against Latin idolatrous superstition. 'They establish the holy immortal and inviolable gods in the most vile ignoble matter, and invest them with the appearance of men and wild beasts; some fashion them with sexes confused and with incongruous bodies, and call them divinities; if these received breath, and confronted us, they would be considered monsters.'"

"Astonishing, my friend," said Daniel, nodding in wonder. "It is no lengthy passage, but how is it that you do call them so precisely upon demand to your memory? It is truly astonishing."

Calvin looked bewildered at his words and dismissed them with a slight wave of a hand.

"Seneca, indeed," said Laurent. "But how much the more from God's own mouth, do we hear vengeance denounced against all ages. He swears by his holy name, that he will not suffer his glory to be transferred to idols, and he declares that he is a jealous God, taking vengeance upon all sins, and more especially on this one."

"Truly, indeed," said Duchemin. "This is the sin on account of which Moses, who was otherwise of so meek a temper, being inflamed by the Spirit of God, ordered the Levites to avenge God's right." Here he broke off, and looked at Calvin. "How does it read, my friend?"

Calvin blinked, eyed the rafters for but an instant—I render these things without exaggeration—and recited the following:

"Moses gave the command 'to go in and out from gate to gate throughout the camp, and slay every man his brother, and every man his companion, and every man his neighbor.' Thus, we read in the Book of Exodus; I believe it is late in chapter thirty-two."

"Elaborate, thereupon, my good friend," urged Duchemin.

"Idolatry is the sin on account of which God so often punished his chosen people, afflicting them with sword, pestilence, and famine, and, in short, all kinds of calamity; the sin on account of which, especially, the kingdom, first of Israel, and then of Judah, was laid waste, Jerusalem the holy city destroyed, the temple of God laid in ruins, and the people whom he had selected out of all the nations of the earth to be peculiarly his own, entering into covenant with them, that they alone might bear his standard, and live under his rule and protection? The people, in short, from whom Christ was to spring were doomed to all kinds of disaster, stripped of all dignity, driven into exile, and brought to the brink of destruction. It would require far too lengthy a recitation to detail all, for there is not a page in the prophets which does not proclaim aloud that there is nothing which more provokes the divine indignation than idolatry."

"What then, my friend?" urged Laurent. "When we see idolatry openly and everywhere stalking abroad, what then are we to do? Be silent at such idolatry because it has for so long been the corrupt practice of the church? Surely you do not advocate such silence, such a rocking of the world in the sleep of death from which it might not awake."

"Is not this like the defection of Judah with foreign gods?" asked Daniel. "It seems precisely so to me. Does it not to you, Calvin?"

Never did a man seem so conflicted, so reluctant to speak and so very much compelled to do so as did Calvin that night.

"Divine honors have long been paid to images, and prayers everywhere offered to them, under the pretence that the power and deity of God resided in them. So too, dead saints are worshiped exactly in the manner in which of old the Israelites worshiped Baal. And by the artifice of Satan, numerous other modes have been devised by which the glory of God is, herein, torn to pieces.

"A mere superficial reading of Holy Scripture reveals that the Lord burns with jealousy when any idol is erected, and Paul demonstrates, by his own example, that his servants should be zealous in asserting God's glory alone. This I believe you will find in the book of Acts and chapter seventeen, if I am not mistaken, midway in the said chapter."

Calvin paused for breath but now needed no encouragement to continue.

"It is no common zeal for the house of God which ought to penetrate and engross the hearts of believers. When, therefore, the divine glory is polluted, or rather lacerated, in so many ways, as we this night have observed, would it not have been perfidy if we now wink or are silent? A dog, seeing any violence offered to his master, will instantly bark. Can we, in silence, see the sacred name of God dishonored so blasphemously? In such a case, how could it have been said, 'The reproaches of them that reproached thee are fallen upon me?'

"The mockery which worships God with naught but external gestures and absurd human fictions, how can we, without sin, allow to pass uncorrected? We know how much God hates hypocrisy, and yet in such a fictitious worship as we have not

149

only observed this night, but, alas, to our shame, participated in, hypocrisy reigned supreme.

"We hear how bitterly the prophets inveigh against all worship fabricated by man, but in this entire body of worship which has been established, there is scarcely a single observance which has an authoritative sanction from the Word of God."

"But what of the authority of popes and councils over worship?" interjected Laurent. "Are not their judgments to be considered?"

"We are not in this matter," said Calvin, his eyes now ablaze as he spoke, "to stand either by our own or by other men's judgments, be they popes or councils. We must listen to the voice of God, and hear in what estimation he holds that profanation of worship which is displayed when men, overleaping the boundaries of his Word, run riot in their own inventions.

"The reasons which he assigns for punishing the Israelites with blindness, after they had lost the pious and holy discipline of the church, are two: namely, the prevalence of hypocrisy and practicing a form of worship contrived by man.

"'Forasmuch,' says the prophet, 'as the people draw near me with their mouth, and with their lips do honor me, but have removed their heart far from me, and their fear toward me is taught by the precept of men; therefore I will proceed to do a marvelous work among this people, even a marvelous work and a wonder: for the wisdom of their wise men shall perish, and the understanding of their prudent men shall be hid.' This from the prophet Isaiah midway in the twenty-ninth chapter."

He wiped his brow and looked around the table at the faces of his friends gazing back at him, their mouths silent and their eyes wide at the words that had been uttered.

"May that marvelous work begin," said Laurent at last.

150

"And may the pretended wisdom of such bishops as we have observed this night," added Daniel, "forever perish."

For my part, I too was astonished at what I had heard. If I had been in Paris that night, I believe I would have put on my blue chapeau and made my way on the run to St. Germaine at midnight. For surely enough had been uttered against our Roman worship, against saints and the Virgin, against popes and councils to render him guilty of heresy. But how was I to prove this? Still more, had not others, even John Major, spoken against superstitious corruptions in the church? How was one such as I to sort out what was raillery against corruption safely within the boundaries permitted by the prevailing spirit of inquiry, and what crossed those boundaries into unmitigated and unadulterated heresy?

18

Light in Bourges

"I would gladly die if by my death I might see all such offending images ground to powder." The words were uttered three weeks later by Calvin's cousin Pierre Robert Olivetan, who had in these last days appeared in Orleans from his exile in Strasbourg. I knew he had been denounced in Paris for plans to translate a more complete version of the Bible into French. But why he had now come to Orleans and his cousin's side I had yet to learn.

Olivetan had taken up lodging with Calvin, and thus with me, and so I was to see and hear a great deal from him in the immediate future, and he often spoke thus unguardedly about religious matters. I knew him to be part of the new learning and, therefore, one whose influence over Calvin I must carefully observe. And so I did.

Meanwhile, it had transpired in the lectures at the university that Calvin had so distinguished himself that several of the professors in civil law invited him to teach in their stead. His legal studies, as near as I could determine from observing him in study and listening to his recitations, demanded less of his mind and energies than had his religious studies. So did he seem freed to engage in other pursuits. I observed him writing some sort of theological polemic against what he termed the ancient error of soul sleep, some obtuse debate, it seemed to me, over the relationship of the body and the soul upon death. As near as I could tell, none of this was required study by his professors. I marveled that a man of his youth found such motivation within himself to occupy his leisure upon such considerations.

Looking back on those days, it was inevitable what next transpired. One day it happened that the distinguished civil law professor Pierre de l'Etoile graciously deferred his lecture to Calvin's expertise. Whereupon the university, amid an extravagant chorus of adulations, conferred the office of civil doctor, without cost or obligation, on brilliant young Calvin.

After the solemn ceremony conferring the degree on Calvin we repaired to his lodgings.

"You, my cousin," cried Olivetan, "have achieved at the age of twenty years that after which most scholars labor unceasingly throughout more than half of their natural lives. These coveted degrees, my cousin—they are not awarded lightly!"

"In an age of new learning and brilliant men," said Laurent, "you, John, are foremost."

As the others chimed in their agreement, Calvin, with a gesture of his slender hand, put their words aside. "You are all too kind," he said, "if not scrupulous in your honesty."

"It is yours to be modest," said Laurent. "And we honor you the more for it."

"And for your unprecedented achievement," said Daniel, uncorking a bottle, "from the Loire valley, I have contributed this fine Cabernet Franc in honor of our good friend."

"And I this camembert," said Duchemin, placing a cheese wheel on the table as he spoke.

"And I this loaf," said Laurent.

It was a cheerful repast, and Daniel handed me a glass of wine, including me in the several toasts offered to the young doctor of law, John Calvin. When all had eaten and drank, Olivetan rose and turned to his cousin. I anticipated another toast.

"And I, herewith, contribute," he said, taking something from his satchel, "this."

It was a beautifully calf-bound volume. With feeling, Calvin expressed his gratitude and took it in hand. Opening to the title page, he read aloud. "A faithful translation of the Four Gospels from the Latin Vulgate into the French. Jacques Lefevre d'Etaples, 1522."

"It is a book for which some have died," said Olivetan, "and more are like to die. Yet for all who feed upon it, live or die, it is the book of life. Make it yours, my dearest cousin."

"A fine gift, indeed," said Laurent.

"Read from its pages," urged Duchemin.

"Yes, you must," said Daniel.

For several moments Calvin thumbed its pages. I wasn't sure whether he was actually looking for a particular passage or whether he was waging a war in his own bosom at the prospect of reading from a prohibited book such as he knew it to be.

"Might I suggest that you read from John's Gospel," said his cousin, "and chapter one."

Dutifully, Calvin turned the pages of the little volume with purpose and began reading.

"Au commencement était la Parole, et la Parole était avec Dieu, et la Parole était Dieu. Il en va de même était au commencement avec Dieu. Toutes les choses ont été faites par lui et sans lui n'était pas fait toute chose qui a été fait. En lui était la vie et la vie était la lumière des hommes. Et la lumière brille dans les ténèbres et les ténèbres-il pas compris."

"What I would not give," said Laurent when Calvin had finished, "to have whole shelves of such books in my library."

In all this, I felt that heretical things had just transpired, but I felt equally incapable of doing anything about it. I confess that for a fleeting moment I delighted in Calvin's reading of those French words far more than any man faithful to Rome, and still more a royal agent, ought to have delighted. But I did swear myself to honesty in this my account, so honest I must be.

More bread and cheese and wine were consumed, and conversation turned to the future.

"And what lies ahead for Doctor John Calvin?" asked Duchemin.

"Yes, for one who has so displaced the scholars of Orleans," said Daniel, "what new pursuit lies next on your horizon?"

"Your father set you to the study of law," said Laurent with a laugh, "which you have mastered in so short a space of time as to astonish all the scholars of jurisprudence in the realm of France."

"It is certain that de l'Etoile is the finest legal mind France has produced," said Olivetan. "And by his own declaration you have mastered his learning. So to what inquiry do you now give yourself, my cousin?"

As was ever his custom, Calvin mused silently for a moment before making reply. "There is now in France, my good friend Nicholas Cop informs me, the finest civilian of the age. I'm told that Andrew Alciat of Italy has been persuaded to take the chair of law at the University of Bourges."

"Where Melchior Wolmar is public professor of Greek!" cried Olivetan. "He is the finest there is, and it has long been on my mind to master Greek under his tutelage."

"My comprehension of Greek is so meager," said Calvin, "as to be nonexistent. And so might I benefit from the great Wolmar's tutelage. That is, if he will have me."

His companions broke into laughter at his words, while Calvin blinked in unfeigned confusion.

"If Doctor John Calvin will away to Bourges," said Duchemin and Daniel together, "so shall we."

"O to be young and unencumbered with base employment," said Laurent the librarian with mock offense.

"We shall not be so far from you, good Laurent," said Calvin. "And shall ever remain in your debt for the many books you have lent us these months."

So it was that I found myself yet farther away from Paris, some one hundred and fifty miles and many days of weary travel from that fair city and her delights.

I must confess regarding Bourges that I was immediately awestruck by her cathedral. Those of the high culture who tell us what we are to value in the new art would term St. Etienne of Bourges a barbaric structure conceived in the Dark Age. "Gothic" they derisively term such places, presumably in reference to the uncivilized Goths of the great invasion.

Yet was I awed by the prodigious length of the nave, uninterrupted by the transepts that extended north and south in most churches to form a cross shape. St. Etienne had none. A vast network of flying buttresses support what must be massive weight combined in the great walls and high stone-vaulted ceilings. Even for one as crude as I, it was, indeed, a sight at which to marvel.

We had been but a week in Bourges when a discussion ensued among Calvin and his cousin and friends regarding the church and her services. It later proved of such significance that I herein include a summary of that discussion.

"So great is the contagion of her error," declared Duchemin one day as we stood gazing at the vast stone edifice of St. Etienne, "that I wonder at our drawing near such a place."

"So idolatrous has she become," said Daniel, "as to produce but bastard children. Hence, I shall not enter."

"I would see all such offending images," said Olivetan, making a great sweep with his arm at the church, "ground to powder."

Calvin said not a word, and his friends took note of his silence, as did I.

"Do you not agree, cousin?" asked Olivetan.

"I do not," said Calvin, making determined strides toward the west entrance.

Passing through the central doorway of the five elaborately carved west entrances, with an unusual degree of sobriety did I consider the writhings of the damned carved in graphic stone relief above the ponderous oaken doors.

"But, it is all idolatry," said Olivetan, yet following his cousin. "Whorish error, false doctrine, base corruptions and inventions in defiance of the true worship of God. Do you not agree?"

"You have said the same yourself, Calvin," said Duchemin.

We passed into the cool silence within the great edifice. I had been inside many cathedrals by this time in my life, seldom for holy purposes. Yet was I struck with how vast a distance separated the west entrance through which we had just passed and the high altar on the chancel. It was a nave of greater length than any I had ever seen. Still more was I smitten by the transcendent height of the side aisles, the weighty perspective of their grand columns, and the seeming infinity of their length. It was, to me, as a world apart from that which we had only just left behind in the town.

Gone were the street sounds, the clatter of wooden shoes, the laughter of children, the rasp of the carpenter, the rhythmic hammering of the blacksmith, the gossip of housewives as they did their shopping in the market square, the clopping of horses' hooves and the thudding tread of oxen, the rattling of cartwheels, the droning of honeybees, and the yapping of dogs.

All that was gone, and herein was silence.

And gone were the smells of human life, the appealing aromas of baking bread, of crepes warming on the griddle, of fresh fruits and herbs, of lavender and rosemary, and the overpowering odors of laboring sweat, rotting turnips, cattle dung, charred wood, and human excrement.

In their place were silence and the smell of stone made fragrant with incense. My eyes, moreover, feasted on the impossible splendor of the place.

While I, thus, adored the church, Calvin and his comrades engaged in heated debate over the very object of my adoring contemplations.

"But, I say, it is the product of base error," said Daniel.

"Most pernicious error," added Olivetan. "Surely you have come to see it as error?"

"Of course, much of it is error," said Calvin.

"See, there," said Olivetan. "But if you agree, thus, with us, why are we attending on this place?"

Their voices had begun to disturb the silence of the cathedral, and three hooded monks came and stood about us, herding us without a word. Their meaning was obvious, and so did we retrace our steps, exiting the north-aisle entrance.

Sprawling at the foot of one of the flying buttresses, on the shady side of the church, they recommenced their discussion, Calvin now taking the lead.

"But how is there being error in the church unlike that of any other era in the history of God's relationship with his people?"

"What is your meaning?" asked Duchemin.

"Observe Adam and Eve in the garden, Abraham and his cowardice in Egypt, the conniving patriarchs, Moses and complaining Israel in the wilderness, the prophets raised up to denounce gross errors, and what of the Pharisees in the apostolic age? In none of these times of obvious error were the faithful, be they few, instructed to defect from the church.

"The prophets neither raised themselves new churches, nor built new altars for the oblation of separate sacrifices, but whatever were the errors of the people, yet because the prophets considered that God had deposited his Word among that nation, and instituted the ceremonies in which he was there worshiped, they lifted up pure hands to him even in the congregation of the impious. If they had thought that they contracted any contagion from these services, surely they would have suffered a hundred deaths rather than have permitted themselves to be dragged to them. There was nothing, therefore, to prevent their departure from them, but the desire of preserving the unity of the church."

"But can you declare," said Duchemin, "that God has instituted these popish ceremonies?"

"And you speak of the unity of the church?" cried Daniel. "There is but one thing around which the Roman Church is unified: error!"

"But hear me, Daniel," continued Calvin. "If the holy prophets were restrained by a sense of duty from forsaking the church on account of the numerous and enormous crimes which were practiced, not by a few individuals, but almost by the whole nation, it is extreme arrogance in us, if we presume immediately to withdraw from the communion of a church where the conduct of all the members is not compatible either with our judgment or even with the Christian profession."

"But what are we to do?" asked Duchemin.

"St. Cyprian and the early church fathers," said Calvin, "well did they comprehend what the faithful are to do in every generation."

And then Calvin proceeded into another one of his remarkable recitations, he with no book before him, and I here, likewise, to render as faithfully as I am able.

"'Although tares, or impure vessels, are found in the church, yet this is not a reason why we should withdraw from it. It only behooves us to labor that we may be the wheat, and to use our utmost endeavors and exertions that we may be vessels of gold or of silver. But to break in pieces the vessels of earth belongs to the Lord alone, to whom a rod of iron is also given. Nor let anyone arrogate to himself what is the exclusive province of the Son of God, by pretending to fan the floor, clear away the chaff, and separate all the tares by the judgment of man. This is proud obstinacy, and sacrilegious presumption, originating in a corrupt frenzy.'"

"Cousin, you astonish me," said Olivetan.

Calvin ignored the comment and proceeded.

"Yet with all her errors we may learn from the title of the visible church, 'mother.' How useful and even necessary it is for us to know her, since there is no other way of entrance into life, unless we are conceived by her, born of her, nourished at her breast, and continually preserved under her care and government till we are divested of this mortal flesh and enter into glory. However ill she may be, she is our mother, our school from which we must not dismiss ourselves. We must continue under her instruction and discipline to the end of our lives. It is also to be remarked that outside of her bosom there can be no hope of remission of sins, or any salvation, according to the testimony of Isaiah and Joel, which is confirmed by Ezekiel—I can render references if you wish—when he denounces that those whom God excludes from the heavenly life shall not be enrolled among his people. So, on the contrary, those who devote themselves to the service of God are said to inscribe their names among the citizens of Jerusalem."

"But is she our mother," said Duchemin, "when she has so defected from doctrinal truth as to be unrecognizable any longer as the visible church. Is name alone sufficient to make her the church?"

"Indeed, does not 'faith come by the Word of God'?" said Olivetan. "It does not say that faith comes from a mother church who has defected from the Word of God."

"He makes a point, Calvin," said Daniel. "You must address this in your argument, my friend."

Calvin was silent for a moment and then he said, "A holy unity exists among us, when, consenting in pure doctrine, we are united in Christ alone."

"'Pure doctrine.' *Solus Christus*. There," said Olivetan with triumph. "You have said it your own self."

"Indeed, if concurrence in false doctrine were sufficient," said Calvin, "in what possible way could the church of God be distinguished from the impious factions of the wicked?"

"Calvin, man, you defend not yours but our argument," said Duchemin.

"I care not for mine or yours," he said soberly. "But for the truth. And the truth, according to the apostle Paul in his letter to the Ephesians, chapter four, I believe it is, when he declares that the ministry of the church was instituted, 'for the edifying of the body of Christ: till we all come in the unity of the faith, and of the knowledge of the Son of God: that we be no more children, tossed to and fro, and carried about with every wind of doctrine, but speaking the truth in love, may grow up into him in all things, who is the Head, even Christ.' So it reads."

"So it does, indeed, cousin," said Olivetan, his hand resting on his cousin's shoulder.

Calvin grew more agitated during the time we spent in Bourges. He often met with Olivetan and with his new Greek professor, Wolmar, about whom he could not speak highly enough. Their conversation agitated him, as I have said, but it invigorated him as well. Such was evidenced on his features from day to day. And he often read in the French Gospels given him by his cousin, yet more often still in a Greek New Testament that he acquired, at no little cost to his purse.

Meanwhile, did I attend on his needs, wondering to myself all the while whether I had sufficient evidence to denounce him. False and disloyal as it must sound to any who might read this account; nevertheless did I spend many hours musing over how and when I would betray the man, and on what I would do with all of the wealth I would receive for doing so.

Then one afternoon, as I tidied up goose quills, ink pots, and papers about his writing desk, light from the window fell on a page on which he had been most recently writing. I considered it an important part of my duty to read anything he had written, though I am sure had I no royal commission to justify the deed, I would have just as readily read what lay before me that day. By the scrawling character of the words, I concluded that Calvin had been in haste or perhaps agitation of mind when he penned these words.

"Like a flash of light, I now realize in what an abyss of errors, in what chaos I have been. Though I have, heretofore, been so obstinately devoted to the superstitions of popery, God by a sudden conversion has subdued and brought my mind to a teachable frame. He has, by the secret guidance of his providence, given a different direction to my course. Having now, thus, received some taste and knowledge of true godliness I am immediately inflamed with so intense a desire to make progress therein, that although I will not altogether leave off my legal studies, yet will I pursue them with less ardor."

I was astonished at what I read. In this was Calvin converting to the evangelical doctrines? I considered what I was to do about the matter. I had even snatched up the page and was preparing to enfold it in my tunic, when it occurred to me that, by that single act, I would give my subterfuge entirely away. This could not be good, so I then assumed, carefully placing the page back where I had found it.

Sunday was but two days away, as I recollect, and as if to make good on his confession, Calvin announced that he would travel to a nearby village where a fellow student of Wolmar lived and had invited him to come.

I was unprepared for what would transpire in the village of Ligniers in the Province of Berri that Sunday morning. The faithful had gathered in a large barn, yes, with cattle lowing, goats bleating, and chickens scratching and clucking about. I suddenly felt smug, more the high-church Romanist in that base environment, so debased a place next to the pomp and grandeur of Catholic worship.

Then, to my astonishment, Calvin, with his Greek New Testament in hand, shuffled through the hay to the pulpit. Pulpit, I say, but in fact it was fabricated by upturning a rough and creature-besmeared feeding trough, upon which he opened his book. He then declared that he would read out a passage from Paul's Epistle to the Romans. It occurs to me now, though it eluded me then, that he must have been translating from the Greek into French as he read, an exercise, I suspect, not easily done. And then he commenced to preach. From which sermon I shall attempt a faithful summation, though I must confess that these my recollections of this particular sermon may be mingled with later sermons I heard him deliver on the Epistle to the Romans and on this theme.

"We shall presently show how men become holy, but first it must be established how miserably exempt is mankind universally from that condition. Paul, herein, reveals to us what all men are when left to themselves: lost in sin and deprived of God's glory.

"Furthermore, this depravity is not determined by the judgment of men, but by the judgment of God, before whom no man is counted righteous. God justly demands perfect and absolute obedience to his law, which is everywhere clear from both his promises and threatenings. No one of us in this place dares to claim such a perfect measure of holiness, without which holiness no man is right before God. Hence, it follows that all are in themselves destitute of righteousness.

"Were there indeed such a thing as half righteousness, nevertheless would the sinner be by his half unrighteousness therein condemned. Hereby is the figment of partial righteousness, as they call it, sufficiently confuted, for if it were true that we are justified in part by works, and in part by grace, this argument of Paul that all are deprived of the glory of God because they are sinners would be of no force.

"Nevertheless, you may rise in your own defense and attempt to excuse your sins by your good works. But the apostle Paul stops every mouth, cuts off every evasion and every occasion for excuse. He employs in his Greek a metaphor taken from the courts of law, where the accused, if he has anything to plead as a lawful defense, demands leave to speak, that he might clear himself from the things laid to his charge. But for us there is no plea, no defense. Our crimes are too great, our offence against God's holiness too expansive for our words to deliver us. We must, with Job, lay our hands on our mouths.

"Paul expressly excludes the sufficiency of our works to make us right with God, and makes clear that our justification comes by faith alone. But many of the priests in the present day deny the sole sufficiency of faith when they attempt to blend faith with the merits of works. They indeed allow that man is justified by faith, but not by faith alone. But Paul herein affirms that justification is so gratuitous, that he makes it quite evident that it can by no means be associated with the merit of works.

"It is the righteousness of God, the origin and founder of this justification which is found alone in Christ and is apprehended by faith. It is necessary that Christ should come to our aid, who, being alone righteous, can render us just by transferring to us his own righteousness. Dear people, do you now see how the righteousness of faith is the righteousness of Christ? When, therefore, we are justified, the efficient cause is the mercy of God, the meritorious cause is Christ, the instrumental cause is the Word embraced by faith. Hence, faith is said to justify, because it is the instrument by which we receive Christ, whose righteousness is conveyed to us.

"Having been made partakers of Christ, we ourselves are not only just, but our works also are counted just before God, and for this reason, whatever imperfections there may be in them are obliterated by the blood of Christ, for God rewards our works as perfect, inasmuch as their defects are covered by his free and gracious pardon.

"Moreover, Paul urges on all, without exception, the necessity of seeking righteousness in Christ. There is no other way of attaining righteousness; for some cannot be justified in this and others in that way; but all must alike be justified by faith, because all are sinners, and therefore have nothing for which they can glory before God.

"There remains nothing for you to do; there is no work for you but to perish, to be smitten by the just judgment of God. If you, any of you, are to be justified before God, you must be justified freely through his mercy, for Christ alone comes to the aid of the truly miserable, and communicates himself to all who believe, so that they find in him alone all those things in which they are lacking. Paul here illustrates in a striking manner the efficacy of Christ's righteousness. He shows that God's mercy is the efficient cause, that Christ with his blood is the meritorious cause, that the formal or the instrumental cause is faith in the Word, and that moreover, the final cause is the glory of divine justice and goodness.

"With regard to the efficient cause, he says that we are justified freely by his grace, repeating the words to show that the whole is from God, and nothing from us. Lest we should imagine a half kind of grace, he affirms more strongly what he means by a repetition, and claims for God's mercy alone the whole glory of our righteousness.

"Alas, in our day the sophists divide into parts and mutilate this justification, that they may not be constrained to confess their own poverty. They deny that this Christ by his efficacious redemption, by his perfect obedience has satisfied the Father's justice, and by undertaking our cause has liberated us from the tyranny of death, by which we were held captive. By his sacrifice alone is our guilt removed. Here again is fully confuted the gloss of those who make righteousness, in any degree, a work of man, for if we are counted righteous before God, because we are redeemed by a price, we certainly derive entirely from another what is not in us. And Paul immediately explains more clearly what this redemption is, and what is its object, which is to reconcile us to God; for he calls Christ a propitiation, by which he means that we are not otherwise just than through Christ propitiating the Father for us.

"And when did God set such a propitiation forth? The Greek verb, herein employed by the divine writer means to determine beforehand and to set forth. Paul, herein, refers to the gratuitous mercy of God, in having determined to appoint beforehand Christ as our Mediator, that he might appease the Father by the sacrifice of his death. It is no small commendation of God's grace that he beforehand, of his own good will, sought out a way by which he might remove our curse and pronounce us justified.

"But how are we declared justified? It is by imputation of Christ's righteousness that we are so. Thus, we more clearly understand that in this saving righteousness there is no merit of ours; the remission of our sins is not from ourselves, and since remission itself is an act of God's bounty alone, every merit falls to the ground.

"It is by faith alone; there is nothing that we can claim for ourselves; for faith receives all from God, and brings nothing except a humble confession of need. Come, then to Christ, in whom alone is found the perfect righteousness of the law, which becomes ours by imputation."

There was indeed much more, but to me at that time it was as if he had been for the last three quarters of an hour speaking Greek. I comprehended nothing of his words, though oddly I found myself groping to do so. It troubled me a good deal. How was I, an agent of His Majesty the King of France, how was I to know heresy when I heard it if I was ever so dull of hearing, if I so little comprehended theological matters? I berated myself for my inattention to such things, and resolved to give greater heed to theological instruction so as to be better equipped to fulfill my calling.

Over the next weeks, Calvin occupied himself with attending the lectures of Alciat and Wolmar, and with his writing about the error of soul sleep, and with some translation work he seemed hard at, I believe it was, from Seneca. Simply recounting it with my pen, I weary of such a rigorous schedule of work. Yet did Calvin manage still more to spend long hours with his Greek New Testament, and he often preached, as I have recorded above. Meanwhile, I pined for Paris.

While thus pining, a letter arrived for Calvin. I had made it a habit to read all of Cop's letters sent from Paris, but there was never anything therein that satisfied my appetite. This letter, however, had been posted from Noyon. Such being not only

Calvin's but my birthplace as well, my curiosity was piqued. As had become my custom, carefully I opened it and read therein. It needs no elaboration. A summation will suffice. Calvin's father Gerard was dying. The letter not only announced this, but it served as a request from his brother Charles that Calvin return to Noyon as soon as possible to attend his father in what must be certainly his fatal illness, and, in the all too likely event of his death, to assist in closing his father's accounts and distributing his effects.

I felt at these words a dread deep within my bosom, and at one and the same time a longing thrill at the prospect of returning to my home. What had it then been since I had been there? Six eventful years had elapsed. Yet did I sorely dread the painful memories of the place.

19

Seeking Calvin

IT WAS MAY 1531, springtime in Noyon, when we arrived there for Calvin's grim duty. It was the first time I had ever been inside the Calvin house, oddly called Grain Place, and I was given a small corner bed in the garret. Yet more odd is the fact that I sit in that very house as I pen these words and render my account.

The first morning I had leisure to move about the village, I noticed many changes, and few familiar faces. There was a decided lack of gray hairs among the sellers of lace in the market, or among the tradesmen at their tools. A new tanner tended his vats where once my father had stooped at his labors. And among the new occupants of the village there was a gaiety that offended me. I felt they were not sufficiently somber considering all that had transpired in the plague-infested place that I had last known Noyon to be. I resented them, and felt a man displaced and eager to be away from it all.

Meanwhile, Calvin attended with earnestness on his father, and I observed him frequently at prayer for the man, even with tears. I wondered whether I could have found such prayers and tears in my bosom for my father, so unlike Calvin's had he been. One evening Calvin said, not so much to me as to himself, "There remains no hope of recovery. The approach of death is certain." With those words Calvin began reluctantly to lay aside that deceitful commodity hope, and in its place came the cathartic commodity grief, and so in a torrent.

Not willing to trespass on that grief, I left him, walking the streets of Noyon in my melancholy state of mind. Thus, I brooded over the ruins of my family's house, and the ruins of the fantastic dreams I had once entertained about my neighbor, the lovely Monique. I shed no tears, and the dullness of my inner feelings disturbed me, but only somewhat, and only because I still entertained some notion that such things ought so to disturb a human being.

After pausing on the banks of the Oise, recollecting many things, but chief among them my discovery of the dead man, Maurice de Picard, and my later discovery of his commission which I had taken up as my own, I halted at a broad, low mound on the edge of town, extravagantly alive with white and yellow daisies and with a coverlet of petit French primroses. I breathed in the air perfumed with the sweet scent of hawthorn and lilac blossoms. How warm and beautiful it all now seemed. How different from when I last stood in that same place when it was a wasteland of death, and I had been forced to bury my nose in my sleeve.

I passed a mournful hour at that grotesque mound where I could only assume Filthy Frank had pitchforked the spent husks of my family along with hundreds of others. No doubt Maurice de Picard's remains now mingled with those of my family, of Monique, and of a numberless spectral host.

Though lavishly festooned with spring flowers, it appeared to my imagination as a mocking panoply of unfulfilled dreams, a mass grave of unrequited affections, a bewildering monument to the teetering vanity of earthly existence. I wondered precisely what human souls did do while their bodies commingled with the entombed generations that had been laid hold of by the clammy grasp of death.

After a weeklong vigil, Gerard Calvin passed from this life. Unlike my father, he was laid to rest in the consecrated ground of the churchyard, all holy rites properly chanted, sprinkled, and conferred by the priest and paid for by Calvin and his diminished family. I observed a change in him, and I connected that change to the closing-in sense of mortality that hovers ever nearer when a child loses one who had given him life in this world. I felt superior to him in this, for I had long ago been forced to embark into the swirling blackness of those waters, and I felt smugly that I understood their chilly encirclement better than he.

We remained in Noyon for but a week and a day longer and then, at long last, we were away to Paris. This time I rode with Calvin, not under him. But I did find myself wincing at every pothole in the road, at every lurching of the horses, and at every tremor that passed through the structural materials of that carriage. I wondered whether Calvin had any knowledge of how it was that I had first come to the city. Surely I would not tell him.

Calvin had previously arranged through letters to lodge in an upper room of the College de Fortret, to continue his study of Greek with one Pierre Danes of the College Royale. But at first to my bewilderment, I had observed him making odd scribbles on paper in these weeks, and so clever had I become that I prided myself in knowing them not to be Greek. During this short stay in Paris, as it would prove to be, he simultaneously commenced, and in earnest, the study of ancient Hebrew with Francois Vatable.

Again, it wearies me simply to recount it with my pen, but while vigorously studying Greek and now relentless in his pursuit of Hebrew, he also found time to complete and publish a commentary on Seneca's celebrated *De Clementia*. This he managed to accomplish in less than one year, in the month of April 1532, and out of his own purse did he pay for the printing. He duly dedicated it to Claude Hangest, now abbot of St. Eloi in Noyon, his childhood companion and friend.

"Well, at length the die is cast," I managed to read in a letter Calvin wrote to his friend Francis Daniel on April 22, 1532. "My commentary on the book of Seneca, *On Mercy*, has been printed, but at my own expense, and has drawn from me more money than you can well suppose. At present, I am using every endeavor to collect some of it back. I have stirred up some of the professors of this city to make use of it in lecturing. In Bourges I have induced a friend to do this from the pulpit by a public lecture. You can also help me not a little, if you will not take it amiss, if you will do so on the score of our old friendship, especially as, without any damage to your reputation, you may do me this service, which will also tend to the public good. Should you determine to oblige me by this benefit, I will send you a hundred copies, or as many as you please. Meanwhile, accept this copy for yourself, while you are not to suppose that by acceptance of it, I hold you engaged to do what I ask. It is my wish that all may be free and unconstrained between us. *Adieu*, and let me soon hear from you. He who will give Le Roy his copy will dutifully salute him."

It occurred to me as my eyes passed over his words that engaging in writing scholarly commentary on a work by pagan Seneca would not afford much material for denouncing him, should it come to that. I had figured out a thing or two: the Romanists held pagans in high regard, and many of the new learning did not—or not for the same things. Yet here was Calvin expending his energies writing commentary on a pagan. It bewildered me.

But as if to awaken me from any such complacency regarding his true views, Calvin's rooms at College de Fortret became as if a public house of inquiry. Rarely were we at peace in that year in Paris, which makes it all the more difficult to comprehend how it was that Calvin accomplished so much in such a short time.

Austere as I was determined to believe Calvin to be, I was again astounded to observe him making what could be called nothing short of deep friendships with some of these inquirers. One such was a man named Etienne de la Forge, a man of considerable means, a drapery merchant I believe him to have been. I was immediately suspicious of the fellow. Unlike other merchants I had observed, he appeared openhanded and generous to a fault, and I wondered what he had in mind. Surely he intended to gain by his pretense of friendship with Calvin, who was neither poor nor wealthy. Fueled by my suspicions, I persuaded myself to develop another theory. I concluded that this Etienne fellow knew Calvin for a great scholar, a genius, and so intended to bring him into his home as one might acquire a painting by Leonardo da Vinci and display it on the wall, thereby flaunting one's own wealth and good taste. I was convinced this was his intention with Calvin.

Then one evening we were invited to dine at the home of Etienne de la Forge, the House of the Pelican, as it was called, a house to me so extravagant that it left my jaw slack. Trading in draperies had clearly enriched the fellow, and that in a lavish manner. But more than the gilded mirrors, the finest harpsichord, the latest design in furniture, the most intricate window treatments I'd ever seen, I was astounded at his manner when he greeted us.

"I must apologize for this," he said, reddening at the cheeks as he spoke. "I am ashamed of the vanity of my former life, and I am painfully aware that all this stands as a monument to that vanity. Do forgive me. I am another man now than the one who by honest industry acquired all of this."

He said the latter while scowling at the silken furnishings, and he bit his lower lip as he directed Calvin to a chaise lounge fit for royalty. I dutifully found a stool in a corner and took in the scene. Two more men were announced and entered the room moments later.

"Ah, my good Roussel," said Etienne, rising and grasping the man's hand. "And Nicholas. You are well acquainted with John Calvin, no doubt," he said, gesturing toward Calvin, who had risen to his feet.

I listened intently as they spoke. Roussel, Gerard Roussel, from what I gathered was under the patronage of Marguerite of Angouleme and Navarre, sister to Francis I. He had first expounded reformation doctrine before his patroness under the very nose of the king at his palace the Louvre. And Calvin's eloquent friend Cop was a rising star at the Sorbonne.

"You are in line for high things at the university," said Etienne.

"Perhaps," said Cop.

"It is your oratory, my friend," said Roussel. "And I am convinced that you shall one day be rector."

"It is by no means certain," said Cop.

"And when you are," said Etienne, "you will use your gift to proclaim the grace of Christ alone, will you not?"

"I can envision it now," said Calvin. "What will you speak to convene the university?"

"Let us praise the sciences," said Cop with a flourish of his hand.

They all laughed.

"And therewith commence your speech as every other rector for three hundred years has done so?" said Etienne. "Surely not, good Nicholas!"

Their conversation meandered for a few moments and then turned toward the Paris burnings, now so common as to attract far fewer spectators. My attention was piqued.

"They have become more frequent of late," said Roussel, "and I fear for my patroness. One court official had the audacity to declare that for her support of reformation of the church she deserved, as he termed it, to be tied in a sack and hurled into the Seine. Imagine such words about her Highness."

"Her brother, the king, is now resolved," said Cop. "He has set afoot throughout his realm such a bloody system of terror—we must be cautious."

"True, but we must be faithful," said Etienne.

"The spies of the Sorbonne," said Roussel, "and of the monks creep by stealth into churches, colleges, and even into private families to catch up any word of evangelical doctrine."

"Indeed, the king's soldiers arrest on the highways," said Etienne, "hunting down and treading underfoot everything that seems to bear the stamp of reformation."

I suddenly felt as a young boy does who has just been outleaped by his playfellow. Burnings in Paris may have increased, but not as a result of any overt activity on my part. When I had been in Orleans and then Bourges I explained my inactivity to myself on the basis of logistics, my distance from the capital. Yet here I had been in Paris these months and not one man had I denounced. Mine had not, heretofore, been an empathetic existence, and so I was bewildered by my laxity in the fulfillment of my commission.

Inwardly, I attempted to stir my will to do what I knew I must do if I was to make good on my new calling.

It was not as if I lacked opportunity. Perhaps there was no agent more capable of denouncing more people, and that with very little effort. After all, they came to my very door. And they came in droves. Yet here I sat.

Students from the university came, often at night, cloaked and as if on some secret mission, to inquire of Calvin. Conflicted in mind as I was, rather than denouncing them or Calvin, I oddly began to assume the curt role of a gatekeeper, or more accurately the handler of some exotic subspecies of baboon from a far-off land. Strange as it was, I became determined to protect my personal genius from these intruders. Yet did they come on. Like an irrepressible tide did they come on.

I shall record a summation of one such conversation, this from an earnest youth, a student as it happened, of the College de Montaigu where Calvin himself had studied.

"I am disturbed by the violence of my fellow student," he began after introducing himself and exchanging pleasantries, "one we call the Limping Basque."

"Violence, you say?" replied Calvin.

"He is an extreme ascetic and clothes himself very carefully in beggar's rags."

"Clothing oneself in beggar's rags," observed Calvin, "does not make one violent."

"Indeed, it does not," continued the youth. "But the man is fanatical, I say. He is blind to the corruptions rampant in the church and speaks with violence against the new learning."

"Speaking violence," said Calvin, "and doing violence are not one and the same."

"True, but there is something in his eyes, and in the manner of his speaking against those who speak against the supremacy of the pope. What is more, he becomes especially violent when he speaks of those who translate the Scriptures into the vulgar tongue."

"There is that word again," said Calvin. "What are they teaching you at Montaigu these days? You insist on describing words as if they were deeds. Against whom does he turn his rhetoric?"

"Jacques Lefevre d'Etaples," replied the young man, "for his translations from the Vulgate, but even more virulently does the Limping Basque rail against the one who labors to translate from the Greek and Hebrew, Pierre Robert Olivetan."

Calvin made no immediate reply at his words.

"There is a sort of madness about the fellow," continued the student. "I am convinced that though he has done no violence yet himself, he is capable of greater violence against the new learning than we have heretofore seen in Paris, and we are seeing more burnings than ever before."

"And what think you of the church and her authority to pronounce judgment on those she terms heretics," asked Calvin, "and to burn them?"

"It is my opinion," he began, "that the church has granted herself an authority that is pure fabrication. There. I have said it. No man ought to be burned for his opinions. The authority of popes and councils have so often disagreed with one another that it is a wonder anyone seriously believes that the church is infallible in her authority."

"And whose authority," asked Calvin slowly, "would you place above the authority of Holy Church?"

"The opinion and will of the individual," said the youth boldly. "Aided by the light of nature, each man can discover truth and walk, therein, according to his individual conscience. That is my opinion."

Calvin looked closely at the young man, and then posed a question. "You are, no doubt, aware of the anecdote of Cicero concerning Simonides' reply to the tyrant Hiero when asked what God was? Simonides asked for a day to ponder the mystery. When Hiero asked what God was on the second day, Simonides asked for two days to ponder the mystery, and so forth doubling the duration of time for his considerations until he finally concluded, 'The longer I consider this, the more obscure it seems to me.'"

"Yes, yes. I do remember that one," replied the student. "What is your point in recollecting it?"

"It is precisely this. If you and your opinions about God are informed only by nature you will hold to nothing certain or solid or clear-cut. You vainly and foolishly worship an unknown God and bring torments upon yourself and all who hear you when you corrupt pure religion by granting to each man the madness of his own opinion. Such will only serve to separate men from God, to make him more obscure to us."

"But the church is so hopelessly corrupted by—"

Calvin cut him off. "—by the opinions of popes and councils. Yes, in that you are correct. But you go from a bad to a far worse if you render each man the master of his own opinions about God. Socrates praised the oracle of Apollo for commanding that every man worship the gods after the manner of his forefathers and according to the custom of his own city. But whence comes this law to mortals that they may by their own authority define what far surpasses the world? At the last, each man will stand on the vanity of his own judgment about what God is. Fatal error results. Hence, wise men must reject all base cults contrived

180

through the will and opinions of individual men. Surely you must see this."

"But what of the pure light of nature?" asked the youth.

"In one sense it may be said that if man is ever to know God, God himself must give witness of himself from heaven."

"There. From heaven," said the young man. "Surely God can be known from the heavens."

"A tempting conclusion, indeed," said Calvin. "But men who presume to find God in the starry heavens shall conversely blind themselves to all heavenly mysteries. The most illustrious lamps of nature burning in the universe cannot show forth the pure glory of their Author. Although they bathe us wholly in their radiance, yet they can of themselves in no way lead us into the right path. Surely, they strike some sparks, but before their fuller light shines forth these are smothered. For this reason, the apostle, in the very passage where he calls the worlds the images of things invisible, adds that through faith we understand that they have been fashioned by God's Word. He means by this that the invisible divinity is made manifest in such spectacles, but that we have not the eyes to see this unless they be illuminated by the inner revelation of God through faith. All else is fatal error."

"And so what am I to do?" said the young student.

"Cease exulting in your own vanity, my son, and apply yourself teachably to God's Word alone. In order that true religion might shine upon us, it must take its beginning from heavenly doctrine. No one can get even the slightest taste of right and sound doctrine unless he be a pupil of Scripture.

"Errors abound, my son, but they shall abound still more if each man is left to his own opinions. Errors can never be uprooted from human hearts until true knowledge of God is planted therein.

Moreover, it is God alone by his lawful sovereignty who plants saving knowledge in our hearts."

They spoke for some time longer, but I have herein recorded the best summation of that conversation. There was, however, one final exchange that would later prove significant. When the young man rose to go, seemingly as in afterthought, Calvin asked, "By what proper name is this man of violence, as you term him, this Limping Basque known?"

"He is Ignatius Loyola."

20

Cost of Quietude

AND SO IT WENT, day after day. Clop, clop, clop, forever clopping on our doorstep. And all so earnest and serious-minded. I wondered what was becoming of young men in those days. Did none of them know anything about having pleasures and diversions? All reading, studying, reciting, and writing. Yet, I'm forced to confess, did they find great stimulation in their pursuit of—I suppose they would term it—truth, so lively and spirited were their conversations, Calvin entering in with his usual restraint. It is a wonder that the man did not work himself to death with his Greek, with his Hebrew, with his writing, and with all these hangers-on.

Yet would I be misrepresenting Calvin's growing entourage to say that they were all students and scholars. One Pointent, a surgeon of Savoy and an outspoken man, often sought out Calvin's company.

"The monks and priests are the worst!" I overheard him declare one day in a conversation with Calvin after supper. "And they have the gall to come to me for relief from their shameful

diseases, the cause of which every man in Paris knows. Celibacy—
it has become the jest of France."

"And what do you propose as a solution?" asked Calvin.

"Marriage," said Pointent, bluntly, bringing his fist down on
the table between them with a crash. "You are the scholar, the
theologian. Where in Holy Scripture are Christ's shepherds forbidden to marry? Though I refuse to name these frauds among
Christ's shepherds."

There were many others, cobblers, lawyers—these seemed
particularly drawn to Calvin—and others, brick masons, stonecutters. There was no explaining his appeal. Why young and old alike
followed him, hanging on his every word, completely mystified
me, but there it was.

As the months passed, I observed a growing change in the
man. In the midst of all this activity, Calvin was clearly restless.
Perhaps it was lingering grief at the death of his father that made
him so, yet do I have another theory. Theory, I say, but I have it
on better authority than the theoretical. Nothing of Calvin's was
sacred to me. I considered it my duty, my commissioned obligation, and thus high virtue in myself to read his mail and peruse
the scattered and occasional entries he made in his journal. It was
while reading one of these entries that the reason for his restlessness was disclosed to me.

"I am quite surprised to discover in this past year that all
who have a desire after purer doctrine are continually coming to
learn of me, me a mere novice in true Christian faith. What is
more, I am of a disposition somewhat unpolished and bashful.
Hence, I love the shade and places of quiet retirement. I am now
resolved to seek some secluded corner where I might withdraw
from the public view."

And so it was that I was not entirely surprised when a week or so later Calvin announced to me that we would be away to Orleans for a time. Inwardly I groaned, while dutifully I packed his things and prepared for another journey.

Orleans was as I had remembered it. Yet was Calvin not to find here the solitude he so longed for. It was as if a bird had flown ahead of us, announcing our arrival. Within hours, Calvin was consulted on a point of corruption in the church, or on his interpretation of Holy Scripture as it illuminated the relationship between law and grace, or human freedom and divine sovereignty, or imputed righteousness and sanctification, or the proper understanding of the sacraments, or any other of what they termed "the pure doctrines." And he was often called on to preach there, and as often he did so.

Nor was he to find peace and quiet in the library of his friend Philippe Laurent, who excitedly welcomed him, introducing him to many of the young scholars who came to him for books.

"They prefer Augustine to Cicero," said Laurent. "But still more do they prefer the Greek New Testament of Erasmus to the Ethics of Aristotle. You must come and deliver an address to them."

One week later, on a Sunday evening, Calvin was escorted by his friend Laurent into the library of the university.

I was astounded at how many earnest young students there were here in Orleans. Seated about the stout oaken tables, flanked by walls of leather-bound tomes, some of the young men had large books open, three or four of them crowded about the pages. I had come to expect this in Paris, but it was here too. Calvin read out a text from the Acts of the Apostles, something about a man named Simon who desired to purchase from the apostles with money the ability to heal the sick. Then he commenced his address, which I shall herein summarize.

"In the courts of princes one may see today youths having three abbacies, two bishoprics, and one archbishopric. Indeed, it is common to find canons laden with five, six, or seven benefices, for which they have absolutely no care except to receive their revenues."

He paused significantly, his brow furrowed, and then, his voice lower, he recommenced.

"I shall not urge as an objection that God's Word everywhere cries out against the abominable foulness of this practice, for the Word has long ceased to be of the slightest significance to them. These are monstrous abuses, which are utterly contrary to God, nature, and church government. What is more, amid such villainy they boast of the holy succession of church offices. Such is an open mockery of God when men hire out their priestly duties and, turning things upside down, confer abbacies and priories upon mere boys."

Again he paused, wiping a thin hand across his forehead before continuing.

"A few examples of this nefarious infamy shall suffice. The Cardinal of Lorraine was made coadjutant of the Bishop of Metz at but four years of age. Pope Leo X, who himself was made a cardinal at age thirteen, for a price, made Alphonso of Portugal a cardinal when the boy was only eight years old. Odet of Chatillon was made a cardinal at age eleven by Pope Clement VII. Moreover, I have been informed by my master at the University of Paris, John Major, that James IV King of Scotland bestowed the archbishopric of St. Andrews upon his nine-year-old grandson.

"And these are the more illustrious examples. Need I offer the ubiquitous examples from the ordinary priesthood, such examples would weary in the extreme to recount."

He proceeded in his discourse, laying out carefully the biblical qualifications for the office of presbyter, qualifications that sounded odd to my ears. After an hour, he ceased speaking and a lively discussion ensued, young men telling their tales of benefices purchased by wealth and status. At last one of them directed a question to Calvin.

"Master Calvin, you spoke of cardinals, archbishops, and popes, but what of lesser livings purchased for money or other favors? What of these in your own experience or that of your fellows?"

I studied him closely, for I knew him to be the recipient of no fewer than two benefices himself. His cheeks took on a pastier color than ordinarily they bore, and he stroked his cheek pensively before replying. I felt that what he did as a result of delivering such a sermon and facing this particular question would be most reflective of who he truly was. I did not want to blink as I stared at him, and I found accusation upon accusation mounting up in my bosom against him. For it had been his privileged status that had so rankled me in my youth. Still more it had been the income that he derived from his absentee chaplaincy of La Gesine in the cathedral in Noyon and the hireling priesthood he had long had from his father's birthplace in Pont l'Eveque.

The silence that followed grew so long that it became painfully awkward. Studying him all the while as I was, I felt that there was an inner turmoil of character-defining proportions going on within his bosom. I knew that for him to forfeit his benefices would leave him penniless, destitute of any means of making a living for himself. Such a decision would alter all of his plans, demanding that he take up priestly obligations, which obligations if entered into as he had just herein described them would leave him little time for the scholarly pursuits that he so desired.

The young men began eyeing one another, and throats were clearing, and feet began rustling on the stone floor. When such awkwardness was scarcely to be borne any longer, Calvin at last spoke.

"I am such a one as I have, this evening in my address, described," he began, his voice low and strained. "As God is my judge, I have not heretofore given clear thought to my own income being based on such vile abuses as I have described. But it has been so. I too have received the income, since my twelfth year, of not one but two benefices."

Again he paused, but his voice was firmer and more resolved as he continued. "'Whatsoever is not of faith is sin,' so wrote the apostle. I shall, heretofore, do what I can to correct this foul abuse of privilege and of church revenue of which I have been a participant these dozen years of my life."

He abruptly ended his address, and left the library. I prepared myself for packing his things, for sure I was that we would be undertaking another journey. Next morning we prepared to leave for Noyon. Calvin was in haste.

"Bring only what is absolutely necessary," he said. "We must travel with all speed."

At his words, I began setting aside his Hebrew lexicon, his Greek grammar, his Greek New Testament. Weighty tomes such as these surely would retard our speed.

"Those are absolutely necessary," he said shortly.

"But surely not the letters," I said, hefting one bundle of his correspondence.

"Leave everything else," he said. "But the books and letters, I must have. Leave the rest. We must travel unencumbered."

Presumably he thought food and clothing encumbrances, yet did I dutifully obey him, returning the books, letters, and writing material to his trunk and setting aside spare tunics, breeches, stockings, even the remains of our breakfast.

"At what hour must we board the coach?" I asked in my most servile manner.

"Coach?" he said. "We are walking to Noyon. I can no longer afford to hire a coach. Nor, Jean-Louis, can I afford you."

I looked at his trunk with chagrin. Yes, I prided myself on my strong back, but this might prove to be too much. *Walk one hundred and fifty miles carrying that? Walk all that way for what?* I knew precisely what Calvin planned to do when he arrived in Noyon. He was giving up his benefices. He was about to decline two annual incomes sufficient to provide comfortably for all his needs, food, clothing, housing, travel, books, writing materials— he was about to give it all up. And for what? His scruples about simony?

"But Master Calvin," I ventured to speak. "Unlike those slothful priests whom you described in your discourse last evening, you labor night and day for your livings. If any man deserved to keep his benefices, it is you. Give them up, and they will most surely be given to a slothful man who will squander the money."

"Jean-Louis, you play the role of tempter," said Calvin.

"Not tempter," I replied. "I am the voice of reason. If you give up this money, you will deny yourself the means to do your work."

"What is my work, Jean-Louis?"

I hesitated before replying. "The work of God," I said as matter-of-factly as I could manage.

"Then if it is the work of God," said Calvin, taking up his satchel and slinging it over his shoulder, "God of his bounty is able to provide the means for me to accomplish it."

21

Providence

Judging from the tender way in which Calvin set down his left foot, we were both footsore when we arrived in the village of Artenay in the late afternoon of the first day. I had shifted the trunk from my left to my right shoulder and back again so many times that day I had lost count. My raw shoulders and back felt as if I had carried it not twenty but a hundred miles, and my stomach growled fiercely with hunger. Only one hundred and thirty miles more to tread this way. I was certain that Calvin had not given up on the popish idea of penance, though I had heard him speak against the practice.

We had little conversation on the road that day. I was too irritated with the man for conversation, and too busy juggling his accursed trunk on my back. He seemed too rapt with the beauties of the countryside for conversing, and was busy with his recitations from the Psalms, though I could not be certain of the latter, for he recited entirely in Hebrew, so I could only assume it to be.

"Shall I secure us a lodging?" I asked, lowering the trunk to the cobbles and collapsing on the rim of the fountain in the central square of the town.

"I have no means for such, Jean-Louis," he said firmly.

I knew he had money there in his satchel. I knew precisely how much and where he kept it.

As if he read my thoughts, he said, "What francs I have in my possession are no longer my money. I mean to return them to the bishop as earnest of my resolve to render up my benefices."

"And so how do you propose to eat and sleep?" I asked. "It is many miles yet to Noyon, miles that at this rate shall take us days and days to cover, the covering of which shall require rest and food."

"God will provide, Jean-Louis," he said.

I attempted to conceal my disgust as I rose, leaving him and his trunk at that fountain, to stroll about the village. I had ample means from my royal purse within my tunic to pay for lodging and for food. Calvin, of course, did not know this.

Then an idea began forming in my mind. New energy surged in my veins as I worked it out. I would play an outrageous prank on Calvin. He would not know it. But I would. Out of view from where Calvin rested at the fountain, I stepped into the doorway of a comfortable-looking pension with rooms to let.

After securing rooms and paying out of my own purse for them and for an evening meal, I inquired about coaches traveling north. Upon learning where the public carriage office lay, I went there and paid for two seats and a trunk for travel on to Paris next morning and then on through to Noyon. After giving careful instructions to the conductor, and having him rehearse them back to me, I hurried back to Calvin, eager to share my news.

"God has heard your prayers," I said. "He has provided rooms and food."

I thought this a tremendous jest on Calvin, and inwardly I was prepared to laugh at him. But his reaction somewhat disappointed me.

"Blessed be God for it," he said simply.

After a good meal and much-needed night's rest, I awoke eager for him to discover that we were not in fact proceeding on foot. What fun it would be to render this intelligence to him. After we had breakfasted and gathered our things, Calvin preparing as if to continue on foot, I led him down the street where I knew the carriage office to be. As we approached, I saw that the coach was even then being loaded for the journey north.

As I had carefully arranged with the conductor when I had paid him the evening before, he approached us as we made to pass by.

"There are two more seats available on the coach," he said.

"We are walking, thank you very much," said Calvin.

"But Monseigneur," said the conductor, just as I had instructed him, "these seats have been reserved for you and your companion, and your trunk there."

"Reserved?" said Calvin.

"And paid for," said the conductor, grinning.

"To Noyon?" asked Calvin, wonder in his tone.

"Via Paris, yes," he replied.

So it was that I thwarted Calvin's penance for having received benefices for all his schooling years and beyond. I was proud of my little jest. So he believed God in his providence would provide for him, did he. Little did the man know that it was not God at all. It was I who had done it. As I thus ruminated, smug and condescending in my thoughts toward Calvin, the carriage jolted into motion and we were away.

"'I know, O Lord,'" said Calvin smiling at my side, "'that the way of man is not his own, nor is it given to man to direct his own steps,' so wrote the prophet Jeremiah, who ascribed to God alone not only the might but the choice and determination in all events. And so in this."

He was silent for a moment, and so was I. Pensively, I rubbed my shoulders. Again he spoke.

"Praise be to God in heaven who directs everything and everyone by his incomprehensible wisdom and disposes all things to his own ends."

His words had the effect of taking the edge off my glee. They disquieted me. This was unaccountable to me at the time, but it, nevertheless, made me pensive about what I had been so very smug about orchestrating, as I supposed myself to have done.

Calvin continued, "God's eye and ear are attentive to his children's needs but 'The eye of the Lord is upon the impious to destroy their memory from the earth,' so sang the psalmist. Is it not a marvel, Jean-Louis, that all creatures, above and below, for good motives and for bad, obey God's decree and that he applies each one to any use that pleases him? Is it not a marvel?"

I found it, at that time, not particularly marvelous in the least. It disturbed me greatly to imagine that it was possible that I had, though for evil motives, been the instrument of God's providence, bringing about this happy turn of events for Calvin. I was troubled by these thoughts, and pressed my furrowed brow against the window glass of the carriage and took pains to study the undulations of the vineyards as they flickered by.

When, two days later, we arrived in Noyon, he immediately commissioned me to deliver a letter to the bishop, Charles Hangest. I knew what it contained and so made no effort to open and read its contents. He was resigning his benefices and would be a man devoid of any means of supporting himself. How I was to remain at his side, to observe his movements, to gather evidence, I had no notion.

Why I remained at his side will forever bewilder me. Not only was I remaining at his side, I was now, in a pitiless twist of fate, feeding and housing the man out of my own purse. What is more, I found myself being the unwitting instrument of providence to his needs in a manner that began to seriously erode the contents of that purse. How had it come about that the very man whom I had for so long despised for his status, his attainments, and his means, how had it come about that I was now to pay his expenses out of my own means? If this was, indeed, providence, I was determined to believe that it was a diabolical providence to thus torment me.

The daisies and primroses that had in springtime covered, with such freshness and beauty, the mass graves of my progenitors had now shriveled, fallen off, and were commencing the relentless process of mingling with the decompositions that had fed them. Calvin spent long hours with his brother Antoine and sister Marie, strolling along the banks of the Oise and the pathways through the oak and beech forests nearby the village. I left him to his siblings and to their grief.

For my part, I felt no compelling reason to stay on in Noyon and was chafing to return to Paris. There was a restlessness about Calvin in these months, and so I was not entirely surprised when he announced his intention to return to the city. He insisted that we go on foot. Two days later—weary, backbreaking, footsore days they were—we arrived back in Paris, where he managed to secure a room at College de Fortret.

It was clear from our first hour in the city that things had changed. There was foment and upheaval in the very air. Etienne de la Forge greeted us at Calvin's rooms on that first night of our return to Paris. I recall how earnest and agitated his voice was. I carried Calvin's accursed trunk into his bedroom and undid the clasp. I longed to see the last of that beastly trunk. As I silently arranged his books, bundles of letters, ink pots, and paper, I heeded their conversation.

"One thing is certain, King Francis has ceased vacillating," said de la Forge. "He has declared that he would behead his own children if he found them harboring any who held to the blasphemous heresies of the new learning."

"But his own sister, the Queen of Navarre," said Calvin. "She protects many; the good Augustinian preacher Couraut is under her protection, is he not?"

"True, but it cannot last," said Etienne. "He has stirred up such turmoil in the city against the doctrine of grace."

"But the venerable Lefevre," said Calvin, "he is safely away in Nerac, I have learned."

"Yes, but so determined are the king and his allies at the Sorbonne, there are no truly safe places in all France."

"Meaux?" said Calvin.

"The bishop of Meaux is in grave danger for his support of reformation doctrine," said Etienne, "and the many who have fled to that city will soon find it, I fear, no safe haven for them."

He paused, seeming to notice for the first time Calvin's threadbare scholar's robe. "John," he said, "is it true that you have resigned your benefices?"

"It is so," said Calvin. "How could I preach against the abuses of the church while profiting from them myself?"

"You do not think patronage an evil thing, I trust?" said Etienne. "For I intend to supply you with whatever means you require. You have need of my patronage. Come and stay with me at my house."

All this took place while I busied myself unpacking Calvin's things. Yet had I kept the door ajar and so was able to hear all that transpired between them.

"I must not impose," protested Calvin. "But I am sorely concerned about my trusted attendant, Jean-Louis. His services make me able to accomplish much. Without them, I fear much of my time would be consumed in mundane activities. But do I no longer have the means to retain his excellent services, and yet do I loathe the thought of turning him out. I am not certain what else he is capable of doing for his support."

"Give not another thought to such things, John," said Etienne. "I bind myself as your patron. All my house is at your disposal. Keep Jean-Louis and keep your rooms here at Fortret to store your things and for quiet study, if you like, but do come. I shall pay all your expenses and whatever else you require. I am a respected merchant in the city, and, thus, I can afford you a measure of protection at the House of the Pelican. At the last, good brother, we are in God's hands."

For a fleeting instant, I was moved by Calvin's entreaty on my behalf. So he valued my attendance, did he? But so settled a habit of resentment had I developed over these years that the instant of sensibility to his words rapidly vanished and in its place came high indignation. *Imagine it*, I thought to myself. *He made it sound as if he were accepting the patronage of this wealthy man for my sake.*

"Mundane activities" are they? And you don't know if I'm capable of doing anything else, so you are loathe to turn me out. I was in a huff of outrage by it all, and I may have slammed the lid of his cursed trunk down more loudly than I had intended.

Combine this with the umbrage I had taken at Calvin—or was it at God—for the way in which I had inadvertently been the means of providing for him, indignation still worse because I had sensed more than hints that Calvin knew I had been that means. I felt that he might have been attempting to school me, to create a sort of object lesson in God's providence out of the affair. In any event, combine it all and I was more disposed to my vexation with him than ordinarily I was.

The next day Etienne sent servants to attend us to the House of the Pelican. When we arrived at his palatial residence on Rue St. Martin, we were met with a house fairly bursting with people. Calvin's trunk over my shoulder, I was nearly toppled when an imp of five or six made to scramble beneath my legs as if I were a colossus.

"Sorry, for that," said Etienne to me. "Pierre, you must not run in the front hall. The back garden is for romping, thus."

He then proceeded to introduce us to what seemed like dozens of people, mostly students and scholars, but not exclusively so. There were even families and children, as I have shown. It seems he had converted his merchant's mansion into something of a dormitory for the disenfranchised. And I pitied his silken draperies and satin couches for it.

His lovely wife, Madam de le Forge, was a gracious hostess beyond description, and I came to think of her over time as more of a saint or perhaps even a goddess for her patience, generosity, and unflappable good humor at the unruly state of her home with all of those guests.

It appeared that these were not guests merely for a day or two or even a fortnight. The man and his wife, the very quintessence of hospitality, had happily turned their home, so it appeared, into a perpetual refugee encampment.

Many and frequent were the earnest, sometimes heated conversations at the House of the Pelican. At most of these Calvin's word and instruction were in high demand. From breakfast to bedtime, the young men in the house spent their day reading and discussing Holy Scriptures, comparing them with canon law and with the writings of the early church fathers. But as if Etienne's house was not full enough, others came and went throughout the day and even the night, attending on Calvin's informal lectures and joining in the rousing discussions that inevitably followed. His friend Nicholas Cop was frequently among them.

"God drives the system of the universe," declared one young scholar after breakfast. "But he cannot be credited with directing—or worse yet determining—the actions of individual men. Where then would be the free choice of men?"

"So you insist on drawing a distinction between God's might and his determination," said Calvin.

"Surely God is mighty," agreed the young man, "but it is by his foreknowledge not his predetermination that he drives the system of the universe. How else could all men be invited to come and partake of the grace of God offered in the gospel? Man must be able to regulate his own actions by the plan of his own will if he is to live out the gospel by meaningful sanctification."

"You no doubt draw such conclusions from isolated texts such as John's Gospel chapter one where he declares that those who believe on his name and receive him, that thereby they gain the right to be called children of God."

"Precisely," said the young man, excitedly. "It is our believing in God that gains us entrance into heavenly blessings, is it not?"

"Is it so?" asked Calvin. "Misconstruing God's foreknowledge in this fashion and, thereby, making God a passive observer of human actions is a frivolous evasion of meaning. We are not at liberty to take one statement of Holy Scripture out of its context with the whole. When we do we exchange the Word of God for our ignorant babble, we must beware.

"Allow me to illustrate. Only moments before in John's Gospel he declared that Christ, the light that shines in the darkness, is not comprehended by the darkness. Men's keenness of mind is mere blindness as far as the knowledge of God is concerned. For when the Spirit here calls men 'darkness,' he at once denies them the ability of spiritual understanding. Therefore, he declares that those believers who embrace Christ are 'born not of blood, nor of the will of the flesh, nor of the will of man, but of God.' This means that flesh is not capable of such lofty wisdom as to conceive God and what is God's, unless it be illumined by the Spirit of God. Men only recognize God and believe in him by a special revelation of the Father."

"But by this you make man into an unwilling driven beast," said the student. "Surely the church fathers entertained no such notions."

Several chimed in with agreement, and, dull as I am, it did seem to me that the young man's words made perfect sense and Calvin's words, perfect nonsense. I secretly exulted that Calvin had, at last, been called up short.

"In this you make common cause with Rome," said Calvin. "The church today denies the sole sufficiency of faith when they attempt to blend faith with the merits of works. They indeed allow that man is justified by faith, but not by faith alone. When you make man take hold of salvation by his own free willing choice, you make free will a work, the meritorious means by which the sinner saves himself. Such is not justification by faith alone."

"Yet must the sinner make his choice," said another student.

"Indeed, he must," said Calvin. "But from where does the power to thus will and choose come? John in his Gospel so declared by sure and clear inspired testimony that it is a wonder anyone can have doubts about this. He declared that salvation is laid hold of not by the will of man but by the will of God. Not so the church today, but so the early church believed and taught. Bernard put it this way: 'Draw me, however unwilling, to make me willing; draw me, slow-footed, to make me run.'

"Not only is grace offered by the Lord, but it is this very grace which forms both choice and will in the heart, and the good works that must follow are the fruit and effect of grace, and this grace has no other will obeying it except the will that grace alone has made."

"So man is dragged about like so much cattle," said another.

"No, indeed," said Calvin. "You fail to distinguish necessity from compulsion. Man in sin sins voluntarily and, sinner that he is by nature, he sins of necessity. Grace imparted in the human heart by God's will alone in no way means that man is compelled along against his will without any motion of the heart, as if by compulsion, an outside force acting upon him. Rather the grace of God so affects and alters the will of man that he believes and obeys from the heart. Hence, Augustine declared that, 'Grace alone brings about every good work in us.'"

"But is this grace then," said Etienne, "given to all men?"

"Surely it cannot be," said Nicholas Cop, "or we would see all men walking with God. And that we do not see."

"No, indeed; saving grace is not so given to all," said Calvin. "Augustine in a letter to Boniface wrote—it went like this, I believe: 'We know that God's grace is not given to all men. To those to whom it is given it is given neither according to the merits of works, nor according to the merits of the will, but by free grace.'"

"But why, Calvin, do you quote the church fathers?" asked Cop. "Are not the Scriptures alone sufficient?"

"Indeed they are, and I have everywhere asserted them to be so," said Calvin. "But lest simple minds declare that we innovate a new cult, I herein direct our attention to the wisdom of the church fathers who are ever in agreement with the teaching of the doctrine of grace and not with the papal madness of today."

"But what of those to whom God has withheld his grace?" asked the young scholar. "Why has he done so? And is it not unjust for God so to do?"

"Our flesh cannot hear of the wisdom of God," said Calvin, "without being instantly disturbed by numberless questions, and without attempting in a manner to call God to account. I refer you to the apostle Paul in his Epistle to the Romans about chapter nine, wherein he records the very objection you have posed to his teaching of this his doctrine. His reply? 'O man, who are you who replies against God?' He alters not his teaching, but recollects the prophet's metaphor of the right of the potter to form from the same lump of clay a vessel to honor and one to dishonor. Hence, to those to whom God does not give his saving grace we know that it is because of God's righteous judgment that it is not given. Yet even in those he has ordained to ruin, he has done so that the riches of his glory might be made known in them."

"Wherein does a man discover if he is one on whom God has stooped to give grace or if he is not?" asked the student.

Calvin proceeded to speak of the witness of the Spirit of God in the heart, of true repentance and the mortification of sin, and of other such matters. Finally, looking earnestly at the young man, he concluded, "If it is freedom that you seek, my son, then you must humble yourself and lay aside your flawed notions of human freedom. For as Augustine has it, 'The human will does not obtain grace by freedom, but obtains freedom by grace.' Thus, it is by grace alone, through Christ's imputed righteousness alone, that you shall find freedom."

With dizzying discussions such as this were Calvin's days taken up at the House of the Pelican. So much for bashfulness and liking to be in the shade of things; Calvin had little peace at Etienne's house. He slept little, ate poorly, though I attempted to correct this, but he was happy, or as happy as a man of his sober disposition is capable of demonstrating.

I noticed that after discussions such as the one I have just recorded, Calvin sought retirement in his upstairs room, and asked me to move the writing desk into the better light streaming in the bow window that looked out over the Rue St. Martin. Feverishly would he write after these discussions, and I ventured to ask him of what he was writing.

"I am disturbed at the confusion of belief among many young scholars in our day," he replied, looking up only for an instant from the pages on which he wrote. "I mean to set down, if God wills, a thesis of the pure doctrines of the Christian religion, taught in Holy Scripture, for their use. Hence, I write."

On occasion he would retire for a day or two to his rooms at College de Fortret, therein to read and write letters, and to continue his work on the pure doctrines of the Christian religion, as he termed it. Even here young men sought him out. Were there no other learned men in Paris, I wondered? Surely these earnest young fellows had heard of Roussel, Nicholas Cop, the Augustinian Couraut, and there were many others. But unaccountably to me, Calvin developed a following like no other. I suppose he could be described, young as he was, as the pastor of a network of secret churches, and I found myself accompanying him through dark alleyways from one clandestine place to the next. An unobtrusive house called Pre-aux-Clercs seemed to be the very first door opened to the secret church. But the devotees gathered in crypts, in wine cellars, in garrets, even on boats floating down the Seine—anywhere would they gather, and often at great risk, if only they could hear the Bible read and expounded.

I soon discovered that it was not merely a movement developing among young scholars, a theoretical investigation of obtuse points of theology. Men, women, and children, whole families from all walks of life, from cobblers to lawyers; surgeons to friars; from the royal lieutenant, Fosset, to the stonemason, Poille; from cloaked court officials using false names, to the cloth merchant, Jean du Bourg—tradesman and peasant outnumber the rest, and all were flocking to hear the Bible read in French and to hear preaching from its pages. And, to my astonishment, more and more it was this Calvin they wanted to hear.

There was a great deal that mystified me in those days. Seldom in my life have I been as conflicted as I then was in Paris. I did not understand my own reluctance in all this, but my inner torments had the effect of robbing me of the pleasure and diversion I had, heretofore, gained from the haunts of the metropolis. I felt certain that I must act or forever betray my commission, and that if I did not denounce another, I would, by my neglect, betray my own self. In the midst of my confusions of mind, one thing I was certain I could never be: a *devotee* of the doctrine of grace that Calvin preached.

I recall sitting on my bedside rocking back and forth, with the concerted objective of conjuring up all the animosity that I had ever harbored in my bosom for Calvin and for all of his kind. Thus did I resolve to legitimize my calling by betrayal. My impetus presented itself irresistibly one day as I listened to one of the men who frequently came to the House of the Pelican, Pointent, surgeon of Savoy.

"The king has arrested more printers," he said bitterly. "Many more printers. Indeed, he has prohibited the printing of any books, pamphlets, treatises—anything requiring ink and paper! One printer was condemned to burn merely for reprinting some pamphlets by Martin Luther, and a bookseller met his end at the stake merely for selling the same. If such continues, all France shall soon be a nation state of base illiterates."

I marked this down in the ledger of my mind.

"And the barbarous methods of torture that he has crafted from the diabolical recesses of his hellish imagination," he continued, now pacing about the sitting room, "are destroying, for public amusement, many good men and brethren in this city."

"I have not seen it with my own eyes, nor do I care to," said Nicholas Cop. "But the method is grotesque beyond description. And I tremble for those who must endure it."

"We are those," said Pointent, looking about the room. "Already six of our brethren have been burned to death here in Paris by the king's inhuman method, one to which most pagans have not stooped through the centuries."

"It is, indeed, horrible to imagine," said Roussel.

"I am a surgeon," continued Pointent. "I know of human suffering. King Francis has devised the most horrific suffering for followers of the pure doctrines. He orders that they be lashed to a ladder that is rigged to be moved up and down as a mason employs a davit to raise and lower his bricks and mortar. Then the condemned one is suspended ever lower over a blazing fire until he is scorched but not yet killed, then the man is tormented by being lifted off the flames. Repeatedly does he order his henchmen to lower the man into the fire and lift him off, all so that his agony might be prolonged."

"We must pray," said Cop.

Calvin had thus far remained silent through all this, but I watched him closely. His face had grown a shade paler and his jaw worked as if he were clenching his teeth. At last he spoke.

"By faith," he said, "others were tortured, not accepting deliverance, that they might obtain a better resurrection. Still others had trial of mockings and scourgings, yes, and of chains and imprisonment. They were stoned, they were sawn in two, were tempted, were slain with the sword. They wandered about in sheepskins and goatskins, being destitute, afflicted, tormented—of whom the world was not worthy."

"May God grant us such stalwart faith," said Etienne.

"But what is to be done?" asked Cop.

"I know what I shall do," said Pointent. "As I have denounced the adulterous priests, I do now denounce Francis for the evil he does against true and faithful followers of Christ. May God judge him for the evil he is doing."

His words burst into my imagination like a flash. How simple it then seemed. By his words I leapt at the conclusion: this was not about religion. This was treason against the crown, against the royal person of the King of France. How simple it would all be. Immediately I began planning how I would do it, how I would make my way to St. Germaine l'Auxerrois, how I would honorably fulfill my commission—and replenish my purse.

22

Martyr Burning

ONE WEEK LATER, in the year 1533, again the crowds jostled each other at the Place de la Gréve. Encircled by rows of half-timbered houses, some sagging with age and drooping into the street, the public square before the Hotel de Ville was choked with people, I among them. The mob seemed all elbows as each man clambered for a closer view of the day's entertainment.

"What abyss of madness," murmured Calvin nearby where I stood, "grips a world that does this to good men?" Nicholas Cop nodded in agreement as did Roussel and others, but no one else seemed able to find suitable words. I stood among them as was my public way, but inwardly I had stood with the king and these his executioners. I alone knew it, and I reassured myself of the virtue of what I had done. Yet had I not been quite prepared for how it would affect me. I had witnessed other burnings, but none in which I had had such a particular hand as this.

I watched as with ceremony, the inquisitors paraded the condemned man before the mob that had gathered for the spectacle.

He must have had a hard time of it with those who had cross-examined him. Purpled by bruising, the flesh about his right eye was swollen, and his right cheek and mouth sagged. Over his soiled tunic and tattered britches had been draped the cursed sanbenito, its loose folds crudely ornamented with devils howling in flames.

I tried not to meet the eye of the man, yet could I not help but observe that from his one good eye shone an unrelenting fortitude, a courage I could not then explain nor understand. And there was something more. Battered by torture as his features were, he seemed unafraid, at peace with God and even with his persecutors.

I studied Calvin's face. He was motionless but his eyes revealed a wrenching mixture of indignation and pity, and I was inwardly pleased to see something else in his features, something akin to horror.

"May God grant you grace, good brother, Pointent," whispered a stooped man at Calvin's elbow. The speaker wore the leather apron of a cobbler, and as he spoke, he shifted his weight from a crutch under his left arm to his good leg. "How can such as he be condemned to die for heresy?"

I strained to look about the crowd. Clustered about Calvin, Roussel, Cop, and Etienne were many familiar faces I had seen at secret gatherings around the city in these weeks. There was Canaye, the lawyer, who had become friends with Calvin. His face was red with anger.

"Since when is a fornicating anti-Christ a fit judge of heresy?" said the lawyer.

In this tight-knit circle, others nodded and grunted their assent to the lawyer's words.

"The Word of God," murmured Calvin, his piercing eyes fixed unblinking on the condemned man, "is infinitely above the word of any pope. Yet with a word do minions of the pope condemn our dear brother—condemn him to death for merely speaking the Word of God." Then he added, his voice strained, "but such a death."

I put down in the ledger of my mind his words.

"I feared for Pointent," said the crippled cobbler. "Too boldly he decried the shameful diseases of the clergy, contracted by their adulterous ways."

"Boldness for the truth, Milon," said Calvin, "is ever commendable."

"And so is prudence," said Milon the cobbler.

"When they hobbled to him for medicine," said the lawyer, "he frankly called their pain a just punishment for their fornicating ways."

"But his confession of the pure doctrine of Christ has brought him to this," said the cobbler. And then he drew close in on Calvin's left ear and added, "the pure doctrine you have taught us."

Calvin reacted as if recoiling from an inquisitor's blow to the face.

"It is no offense to proclaim truth," said Etienne in his friend's other ear. "John, there is nothing you can do to stop this," he added, clenching Calvin's arm more tightly.

Then I noticed a change in the look in Pointent's one good eye. "He makes ready to speak," I said.

"Father," he said, his voice raspy but firm, "you know whom you have chosen." As we strained to hear the rest, his voice grew stronger. "Deliver your children with a mighty hand."

"We'll have none of your babble," said the hangman, who, with a flourish, produced a gleaming knife. "Failing to recant with your tongue your blasphemies against the Holy Church," he declared, "I will, therefore, remove your offending tongue."

I cannot now bear to record what followed, but some in the crowd, so intoxicated by violence and brutality, cheered at the spectacle; I may have been among them. Yet did it seem that many were still capable of gasping in horror at the gruesome sight. Calvin at my side was among the latter.

"No! No!" he cried, and it was a louder, more anguished and prolonged cry than the rest. We were all pressed hard against one another, and so I felt his rigid body next to mine, and then with a frantic lunge he began to tear his way toward the scaffold and Pointent. I could only assume he intended to intervene.

"I will not allow you, John Calvin," said Etienne, gripping his cloak firmly, "to throw your life away and deprive your flock of their shepherd."

Straining at Etienne's grip, Calvin's slender face was lined with compassion and empathy, unlike I have seen in any other man. The look in his face and his eyes, as I recollect it to this day, has long haunted me, tormented me; far from comforting me, his expression, stamped indelibly on my memory, has profoundly deepened the misery of my own life.

"He is not alone," said Etienne. "God is with him."

"And soon he shall be," said Moulin, "with God."

There was to be no lowering and raising of the man over the fire this time. Roughly, Pointent was lashed to the stake. Then the hangman ignited the bundles of wood arranged at the feet of the condemned man. Flames leapt upward, igniting first the skirts of the sanbenito, real flames overcoming the mocking, crudely drawn fires of hell. Growing hotter and swirling fiercely, flames engulfed the condemned man.

While his form quavered in the heat waves, barely visible through the flames, to the astonishment of the onlookers, the dying man lifted his right arm heavenward. Apparently the ropes restraining his arm had burned through. He held it aloft, much longer than seemed possible under the circumstances. At last his arm fell to his side. Overcome by smoke and the consuming force of the fire, his head lolled forward, his hair now ablaze, and Pointent, good surgeon of Savoy, expired.

"How can I stand aloof?" cried Calvin. "How can I observe without feeling the agony of a man dying for his embrace of the pure doctrines of Holy Scripture?" He wiped his brow with a thin hand. "Truths I have taught him to believe?"

That evening in the crypt of the Church Saint-Merri, Etienne, Cop, Roussel, Milon the crippled cobbler, Canaye the lawyer, and many others gathered to mourn Pointent's death. There were women and some children present, and there were sobs and tears coming from many. I looked out in the dim light of that musty crypt and saw the wide vacant eye of anguish and incredulous horror throughout this congregation of Calvin's.

Though, in those days in Paris, every gathering of the faithful brought with it great risks, nevertheless, in the billowing wake of martyrdom, these had gathered to mourn their brother. And they were in great need of comfort and consolation from their young minister.

Pale and stooped, Calvin stepped to the lectern and opened his Bible. "Do not fear what you are about to suffer," he read, an expectant hush coming over the place. "Be faithful unto death," he paused and looked about the sober faces as he concluded his text, "and I shall give you a crown of life."

I do not remember a great deal of that sermon, for my mind was in torment. I did not think I could continue in this my double life. How could I? Their grieving looks were fixed intently on Calvin as he spoke, but in their eyes my harrowed imagination saw accusation and condemnation. My handlers at St. Germaine berated me for not delivering the bigger fish, as they termed it. Pointent was an outrage to the priests and doctors of the Sorbonne, but he was merely an irritation to the king. Francis wanted the leaders, and he wanted them now. I was charged to denounce leaders or become food for fishes in the Seine, so they had put it.

Though tormented with these thoughts, I caught some of Calvin's words.

"It is not lawful for us to have vengeful rage at our persecutors. 'Vengeance is mine,' God declared through the testimony of Moses. As Christ committed his cause to his heavenly Father, and forgave his persecutors, so we are called to do good to those who injure us, to pray for those who speak evil against us.

"Doubtless, the feelings of our flesh are far from being in unison with the judgment of God. We want to leap in and take our vengeance on the evildoers who slew our dear brother Pointent this day. But in this we intrude on what belongs to God, and fain would take up his office upon ourselves.

"Let us not dread the insults and reproaches of men, which will one day procure for us the highest glory, as Pointent this day enjoys, and everlastingly so. Let us, therefore, direct all our hope and expectation to Christ who suffered cruel death for our salvation and, thereby, has secured for us the crown of life."

After Calvin prayed, and the congregation dispersed in small bands, Etienne came to Calvin's side. Commending him on his message, he then said, "John, for the sake of these timid sheep, you must not render up your life as you nearly did today at Place de la Gréve."

"The beleaguered church needs you, John," agreed Cop.

"You must use more prudence," said Roussel. "The eyes and ears of the king are everywhere."

I feared that he looked my way as he said this, though I was certain I had been sufficiently discreet to be undetected for my crimes.

"You are their pastor," said Etienne. "God has uniquely gifted you and made you pastor to all of us."

"You are the Luther to all Paris," said Cop.

"To all France," agreed Roussel.

At these words, I knew that there was but one thing for me to do—unless I wanted to be food for fishes in the Seine.

23

Cop Speaks Out

AFTER THE BURNING of Pointent, so fleeting was my petit remorse, I discovered that fulfilling my commission came with more ease, and I entered into a time of near frenzy in my royal calling, as I preferred to call it. My purse grew fat from my covert life of those days, and I took a keen pleasure, not only in counting my francs, but in scrupulously counting lives. In the next seven months, no fewer than twenty-four men, heretics all, so I had convinced myself, were burned alive in Paris. And horrible burnings they were, that is for the one being burned. For the bloodlust of the watchers it had become even more entertaining. Yet unaccountably to my dull mind did the followers of the new learning increase, and I was ever frustrated and mystified by the fact.

Stranger still, though I grew hardened and resolved in my denunciations of others, yet was there a barrier over which I could leap with but the greatest wranglings of mind. Why? I am in a torment to fully explain. On the one hand, I believe that I had come to take a sort of professional pleasure in playing my two-faced role. To denounce Calvin would end everything for which I had lived these past years. All would be over. The charade would be exposed. Part of me would reason that I did not have sufficient evidence to denounce one so influential as Calvin. But I knew that all of my mental vacillations on that score were mere nonsense.

Was there something else constraining me? There were moments when I was in a fevered state of mind and body over this. Was it that I had formed some perverse attachment to him? Was it because he was my countryman, from my place of birth? Was it because I had served him these years, cut his bread and cheese, poured his wine, carried his weighty trunk, however reluctantly, and however ill my motives for doing so? Because I had come to know his inner counsel, had I developed some impossible attachment that constrained my will to do what I had lived to do to him?

Meanwhile, as I halted between two opinions, stagnating in my commission, weeks passed that became months. Then came the autumn of 1533 and new developments in Paris, developments that gave new impetus to my resolves. It occurred like this.

"Great news!" cried Etienne, securing the front door of his house one afternoon. He strode into the dining room, smiling widely. "Cop has been made rector of the university!" Then turning accusingly on Cop, he chided him. "Why did you leave me to find this out on the street? Why did you not tell us sooner?"

Cop set down his cup of chocolate and said, "I did not know it was of such great importance to you."

"Did not know it?" said Etienne, feigning anger. "The rector is one of the most influential positions in the university, and, hence, in Paris, and you did not think it of so great importance!"

"This is, indeed, wonderful news, Cop," said Calvin.

"It may prove most beneficial," said Roussel. "What good will you not be able to effect with such an appointment for the work of Christ in Paris?"

"And you will deliver up your All Saints' address in but a few weeks' time," said Etienne. "On what will you speak? Surely not some discourse on the efficacy of offering up prayers to saints."

"Or how about something original," said Roussel. "You could wax eloquent about buying an indulgence from the treasury of merit, thereby acquiring with money for oneself some of the surplus virtue of St. Denis."

"All will have heard such nonsense many times before," said Cop.

I noticed that at this interchange Calvin began stroking his cheek in thought. Later that evening, Calvin invited Cop to attend us at his rooms at College de Fortret. Late into the night they spoke. Late into the night did I listen. Late into the night did I mark down in the ledger of my mind what I heard.

Two weeks later, within the grand stone edifice of the Church of the Mathurins on the Rue Saint-Jacques, all the doctors and monks of the university gathered for the rectorial address. The place was festooned with pomp and ceremony, with many clerics strutting about in their vestments, and many royal court officials preening in their silk and ermine finery. For hundreds of years, as was the custom, the term of study commenced with an address from the rector, thereby reaffirming the elevated role of learning, and especially of learning under the tutelage of the grand doctors of the University of Paris. In what many considered to be an era of new birth in learning, the metropolis of letters in Paris was thought to be the finest university in the world.

By its dizzying array of colors and by the racket made by the vast array of people crowded into the university church, I recall it appearing to me then as more of an exotic bird sanctuary, rather than—as purported—a God sanctuary.

Nevertheless, was it a grand event, held in a grand edifice. I learned that the Church of the Mathurins was built on the site of one of Emperor Julian's ancient Roman baths, a pagan site by all accounts, and I marveled that here stood a church over the place where such ancient philanderings were part of the liturgical rituals of that world. It was a lovely church with a grand spire and vaulted ceiling and pointed arches rising to the heavens. But I was particularly intrigued by a unique architectural feature. It had been equipped with a splendid spiral staircase, the ancient builder having employed a double stair, wherein one set of steps carried a person upward, and the other set of steps conveyed one downward. All the while, those who climb up do not see those who climb down on the other set of stairs. It was truly remarkable. But I digress.

The Church of the Mathurins is the rector's church and the chancellor's church, if mere men can be said to own churches. Within these elaborately carved stone walls, for centuries, the entire faculty of the university had convened. And so gathered that day the four medieval orders of monks, the Dominicans, Franciscans, Augustinians, and Carmelites, and gathered were the doctors of all the colleges of the university, a frightful host of learned men, masters of grammar, philosophy, theology, and arts, and all eager to be known as such.

There were scarlet-clad cardinals present, as well as wealthy and influential patrons of colleges of grand and illustrious name: of Beauvais, of Navarre, of Boncourt, of Cligny, of Harcourt, of Prémonstré, of Bourgogne, of Saint Benoit, of Cambrai, of Arras, of Bayeux, and a host of others. Where there was still a square inch of flag-stoned floor space available, there were students, fresh faced and eager for knowledge—all crowded into the nave and corridors of that ancient church to hear the rector deliver the All Saints' Day address.

At Calvin's side, I watched as all grew silent and Rector Nicholas Cop ascended the pulpit. "Let us praise the Sciences," he began. His voice rising and falling with eloquence, he elaborated on each one of the disciplines. I felt as I listened, however, that this was a mere prelude, that he was giving the doctors what they had come expecting to hear, but that for Cop, this was not what he had come to deliver. And Calvin at my side sat rigid, his bright eyes fixed on his friend. What followed I was alerted to by a deep in-drawing of breath from Calvin at my side. By his manner I felt that he considered what was about to follow a sort of gauntlet taken up, the weighty consequences of which could not be altered.

"Let us praise all these for the sake of their usefulness. Yet what do all of them mean next to this honored philosophy which all philosophers have sought but none has found." He paused. Though the stone corridors of the ancient building were crammed with human life, for an instant of expectancy there was a suspension of all movement, of all sound. It was as if the Gorgon Medusa had done her stony work on the masses, as if the very stones of the church themselves held their breath.

"God's grace which alone redeems from sins," continued Cop.

A pent-up rustling of breath and garments passed through the church, like the trembling of leaves when the swirling air gathers momentum before spewing out a mighty tempest.

"Let us plead to Christ who has great mercy and who is the only Mediator with God, that his Spirit may enlighten our hearts that all our being and striving might praise him, feel him, and bow before him in awe, so that the Divine Redeemer may fill our hearts and immerse them in his grace."

The rustling grew more agitated at the rector's words, but his voice grew stronger in proportion, and he opened a book on his lectern and proceeded. "Hear and heed the words of Jesus to his followers." And he read the following: "Blessed are the poor in spirit, for theirs is the kingdom of heaven. Blessed are those who mourn, for they shall be comforted. Blessed are the meek, for they shall inherit the earth. Blessed are those who hunger and thirst for righteousness, for they shall be filled. Blessed are the merciful, for they shall obtain mercy. Blessed are the pure in heart, for they shall see God. Blessed are the peacemakers, for they shall be called sons of God. Blessed are those who are persecuted for righteousness' sake, for theirs is the kingdom of heaven. Blessed are you when they revile and persecute you, and say all kinds of evil against you falsely for my sake. Rejoice and be exceedingly glad, for great is your reward in heaven, for so they persecuted the prophets who were before you."

The rector proceeded to deliver an exposition of this text, wherein he declared that true Christians are made known not by outward pomp and ceremony, not by the sacraments, not by indulgences, not by good works, not by prayer to saints, but by the grace of God in Christ alone. "God's free grace he makes known only to the poor in spirit, to those who hunger and thirst for righteousness, a righteousness found in Christ alone."

When he had finished, there were pockets of applause from throughout the church, but there were still more dark looks and rumblings of rage at his words. I felt certain that Cop would need no denunciation after such an address delivered so publicly. My services were not needed to expose one who had so shamelessly exposed himself.

But I knew what no one else knew in that place. It was Nicholas Cop's voice that had delivered the address that November day, but it was not he who had formed the original ideas and words. John Calvin had done it, and he had done so in defiance of all these learned and illustrious men. I convinced myself then and there that he had done it all out of cowardice. Why had not he risen and declared himself a heretic that day? Why had he set up his friend to be the public example while Calvin hid safely in the shadows? Even then, in such a state of mind as I then was in, I knew this was not a fair rendering of the events or of Calvin's character in them. In fact, it was precisely in keeping with the man that he was willing to secretly craft the entire substance of the speech and let another deliver it publicly. This was his way. And it angered me to know that he wanted no credit for his part in it all, not out of fear, but out of genuine humility. Such was the man. I could not deny it, yet did I despise him for it.

In the hours that followed Cop's speech, all Paris was astir. I kept my ear to the ground, as they say, so as not to miss any opportunity presented by these events. I learned that the university was divided: the philosophers and medical doctors defending their favorite, Cop, while the theologians and legal men railed against him. In their deliberations the defenders of Cop would cry, "Here freedom and the gospel; there popery, blind tradition, and subjugation!" Such was their cry. The defenders of the church rejoined with, "Death to the heretic!"

The council of the university petitioned parliament, which was hastily convened to hear the case. Meanwhile, Cop was resolved to face the crown and defend what he had preached.

"Nicholas, I fear for your safety," said Calvin.

Before the address they had agreed to gather back in Calvin's rooms at College de Fortret.

"I have been summoned by parliament," he said, his jaw set with resolve, "and I mean to answer that summons and defend the truth."

"Come what may?" said Calvin.

"It is an opportunity to declare the truth before the king," said Cop, "to declare Christ alone before all France. How can I decline?"

I was equally resolved. I knew that, public as this was, I was constrained to make my usual way to my contact at St. Germaine l'Auxerrois next to the Palace Louvre. If I did not deliver over the information that I knew in such a public case, I would, by my silence, be denouncing myself. I would be declared Huguenot and thrown in the river—or worse.

Cop soon left to go to his own rooms. Meanwhile, Calvin calmly opened his books, and recommended his writing as if all was peace and calm. I sat brooding, plotting a strategy as he worked. Suddenly there was a brisk rap at the door. I opened and saw an agitated Gerard Roussel and Etienne de la Forge.

"My friend, John Calvin," said Roussel, breathing hard, "the Queen of Navarre, the king's own sister—she summons you to her court."

"Within the walls of her brother the king's palace," said Etienne. "Is this wise?"

"To court?" said Calvin, his quill poised over the page. "Why me?"

"Somehow she knows of your part in Nicholas's speech today," said Roussel. "But have no fear. She wants to congratulate you."

"When?"

"This instant," said the royal chaplain. "There is no time to lose."

"What has become of Nicholas?" said Calvin. "Is he safe?"

"An anonymous parliamentarian, apparently sympathetic with the teaching of Holy Scripture," said Etienne, "slipped Cop a note after his address. It warned him to flee Paris immediately."

"But you know how Nicholas can be," said Roussel. "He is determined to make his stand before parliament and the king."

"And he would have done so," said Etienne. "But as God willed it, just when being escorted by royal heralds into the palace, a mob of reform-minded students—friends, all—led by good Canaye the lawyer, formed a human shield, diverting Cop from entering."

"They whisked him into a side street," said Roussel. "There they stripped him of his rectorial garb, disguised him as a tailor, and put him in a private coach bound for Basel, Switzerland, his home, and safety. May God go with him."

"And he leaves his new post as rector to another," said Calvin.

"But he lives, praise be to God," said Etienne, "lives to continue his part in the work of reformation. And so must you, John."

"Come with me, John, to the queen's court," said Roussel. "You must meet her Majesty. She supports all you do."

"And then what?" asked Calvin.

"For now you are safe," said Roussel. "No one knows of your part in Cop's speech. He alone is the object of their rage."

"And if I am found out?" said Calvin calmly.

"Then you must flee, otherwise you will be in jail today and at the stake tomorrow. There can no longer be any doubt about these things. Yet are you safe, for none of our enemies knows of your part in the rectorial address. We must now go. Gather your cloak for it is cold."

"Is this wise, Roussel?" said Etienne. "I am inclined to think that Calvin will be soon known for his role. John, leave at once, before it is too late!"

"You would have him snub the queen's protection?" said Roussel.

There was more, but Roussel prevailed in his entreaties. My mind awhirl, I helped Calvin with his woolen cloak and prepared myself to go with him.

"I shall attend him," said Roussel, taking Calvin by the arm. "You must stay here."

I stared blankly at the royal chaplain.

"Guard his things, and be alert to his enemies," continued Roussel. I heard his words in a tone one might use with a child when one feigns to make him feel useful.

As the door closed behind them, I felt a surge of resentment in my bosom. I knew why I had been left behind. Roussel did not think one such as me fit to be in a queen's presence. And Calvin had made no remonstrance on my behalf. But I was now free to fulfill my office, and, what is more, sufficiently embittered to do so. I looked about his rooms. There were many of his letters that I knew contained damning evangelical encouragements, letters with names and addresses of his correspondents, including letters he had received from his brother Antoine and sister Marie, damning evidence of "conversion," as they termed it. There was his manuscript on pure Christian doctrine lying there on the desk before the window, and, best of all, there were multiple drafts of Cop's speech in a pile on his trunk. Here was evidence and to spare. And I intended to hurl the net as widely as I could and use every shred of it.

24

Flight!

THE DIE WAS CAST. How simple it had been. It is a wonder to me how the words and deeds of but a moment can forever shape the destiny of one's life. So was that November day in 1533 to my destiny. I had done the deed. I had with so much ease fulfilled my duty. And o'er leaped it. Not satisfied with merely denouncing Calvin, I cast about, finally accusing Etienne and his wife, even supplying the street, Rue Saint-Martin, and naming the House of the Pelican. Moreover, I offered what I knew of Cop's whereabouts, and threw in whomever else I could think of in my denouncing frenzy.

The plan was that I would return to Calvin's rooms at College de Fortret and await the royal bailiffs who would arrive to arrest him. I wished it could be otherwise. I did not relish the idea of having to face him as my dark duplicity became known to him. On the other hand, there would be something infinitely satisfying about seeing his reaction to it all, reveling in his astonishment and in his fear at what awaited him for his heresy. There had been suspicions, I was told, but I alone had delivered up the hard evidence that would see Calvin burn, so they assured me. They also assured me that the one who had so done would be well compensated when Calvin was safely in the king's grasp.

Oddly, as I climbed the winding stairway to Calvin's rooms, with every tread I felt as if I, not he, were climbing the scaffold to my death. At his door, I inserted the key, turned it slowly, and entered the room. It was pitchy dark, and I struck a light to see by. There, in flickering silence, I waited, the tiniest scurrying of a mouse in the corridor giving me a start. It was while I waited that my mind began to torture me. What had I done? Dislike him as I so intensely did, even one so hardened in iniquity as I could not help having a certain veneration for him. Surely I, as even his enemies, felt awe at his genius, and for that reason I may have felt as I did, that by delivering him over I had just taken a hammer to a priceless vase from the Orient. But it was something other than his genius that so disturbed me. I had denounced a man who was profoundly unlike the common herd of men, and I knew it. Was it his lack of posturing and pretense, his disarming genuineness, his devotion to duty and to his calling, his diligence to know and practice what he believed to be truth? I did not understand my own mind, yet was I deeply troubled in those hours of waiting.

Then I heard, faintly at first, the scraping of footsteps on the final flight of stairs, then growing nearer in the outer hallway. Not the tread of many but of few. It had to be Calvin with Roussel and Etienne accompanying him. Heretofore, I had been sitting, idly brooding, my eyes mesmerized by the flickering candlelight. At the sounds, I snatched up the nearest book. As fate would have it, or so I then accounted it, the book happened to be Calvin's French

Gospels, gifted him by his cousin, Olivetan. Hastily I opened it, and, where my eyes fell, I began silently reading therein.

"Truly, I say to you, one of you will betray me . . ." I scanned down the page, unable to believe what I was reading. "For the Son of Man goes as it is written of him, but woe to that man by whom the Son of Man is betrayed. It would have been better for that man if he had not been born." My stomach churned at the words, and sweat broke profusely from my forehead. Surely it was not possible that I should alight upon this passage by mere chance, simply by opening the sacred book. Perhaps Calvin knew of my duplicity all along and had set it there, marked to fall open at this page, but I knew that was impossible. As by some inner compulsion, I read on. "Judas came out, one of the twelve, and with him a crowd with swords and clubs . . ." I snapped the book closed. I may have cried out, yet was I unable to read another word.

Just as I closed the Gospels, Roussel, Etienne, and Calvin entered the door. My eyes groped about the room for another occupation, yet was I unable to move, and remained where I sat, the Gospels in my hand. Though I had for so long taken pride in my ability to conceal myself and my inner feelings from outsiders, yet was I in a sort of paralysis, so unable was I then to master my feelings and so my manner.

They spoke in low conspiratorial whispers and at first seemed not to take note of me. When they did, it was Calvin who first addressed me.

"Are you ill?" he asked.

In the few seconds that had elapsed, I had somewhat recovered myself and shook my head for reply.

"I see you have been reading the Gospels," he continued, speaking to me as if aside from the others, Roussel's and Etienne's voices making a sort of background to his words to me. "Perhaps it is reading the Word of God that has made you appear so low and despondent," he said. "His words have often that effect on men in these days."

Suddenly, it all came upon me like a flood. The king's bailiffs would arrive at any moment. There was no time to spare. I had to expose my design to him. But how?

While his friends seemed to be arguing over what to do next, he continued. "Everyone has within him, Jean-Louis, the soul of a king. Hence, nothing is more contrary to the disposition of man than subjection."

I made to interrupt him, but he persisted, lifting a hand to silence me.

"But all those who try to elevate themselves, will have God as their enemy, and he will lay them low. Yet this gracious God looks kindly and favorably to the humble."

Again I attempted to halt him and speak. Again he persisted.

"It is as if God has two hands, one which, like a hammer, beats down and breaks in pieces those who raise themselves up, and the other which raises up the humble who willingly bow themselves down. Let this be to your soul, Jean-Louis, as a celestial thunderbolt. Heed his Word, my friend, and be free."

"I shall," I blurted. "But you must flee. There is no time. You must flee on the instant."

"Of what are you speaking? The queen," said Calvin, "she has only just promised her protection to me."

Etienne and Roussel had heard my words and were now silent.

"I cannot explain to you now," I said. "But if you do not flee this instant, you will in moments be arrested and you will most certainly be accused, convicted, and burned. I know of what I speak. You must flee."

For what seemed like an eternity, Calvin stared fixedly back at me in silence before replying. I felt as if he, with his piercing gaze, were reading my innermost thoughts.

"If we waste another instant," I said, diverting my eyes from his, "all will be lost."

"Then let us pack my things," said Calvin, looking about the room at his books and manuscript, "and be away."

He made to open his trunk and began selecting books.

"It is no use," I said. "We must flee with all speed. You must leave your trunk and bring only the barest essentials. All is lost if you do not."

Then I turned to Etienne and Roussel. "You must be away on the instant. They will be here soon. They may even this moment be mounting the stairway. Do not exit by that way. There is a back way, a room up another stair, the lock of which answers to this same key," I said, handing them the key to Calvin's rooms. "Lock us here within, then make haste, and hide yourselves there."

"But locked within, how, then, will John flee?" One of them spoke. I do not recollect which. "And what becomes of you?"

What does become of me? I am, as I write, still asking that same question of myself. I ran to the window, unclasped the latch, and opened it. The courtyard looked farther below than ever before it had looked to me.

"What is that?" It was Etienne's voice.

My blood seemed to halt in my veins.

"The tread of feet on the stair," said Roussel. "Many feet."

"They are coming," said Etienne. "Our friend is right. We must all away."

231

"Help me tie these together," I said, yanking the sheets from Calvin's bed. "And these," I added, wrenching the draperies from their fastenings at the window. "The knots must be true."

Meanwhile, Calvin calmly selected several books and placed them in his satchel. I felt that he was not selecting them for their lack of weight and bulk as much as I would have done, under the circumstances. In another satchel he placed the manuscript he had been working on these last weeks.

The sound of footfalls grew louder. "You must make your way, with all speed, far from Paris," said Roussel. "Make your way southwest to Angouleme and the court of Navarre. There the venerable Jacques Lefevre resides under the protection of Marguerite's jurisdiction. He lives not far off in the village of Nerac. There is some measure of safety in this region of France, at least there is at the present."

By this time I had secured as best I could our makeshift rope out the window. Not trusting Calvin to climb down that treacherous descent with added burden, I gathered up both satchels, one on each shoulder, crisscrossing their straps over my chest. I consoled myself that two satchels were light by comparison and that I would never heft that trunk again.

I ordered Calvin to stand facing me at the window, and created a seat out of the end of my rope, knotting it securely at his waist.

"Hold tightly here," I said, "with both hands. Walk, as it were, against the wall with your feet, and I shall bear your weight. When you get to the bottom, untie and I shall follow."

The footfalls had become a rumbling in my ears that tormented me as I bore his weight, and still more as he began his descent, a torturously slow descent it seemed. I knew I would soon be grateful for the blackness of night, but though I longed to see his descent, I was forced to be satisfied with merely feeling it around my waist and on the muscles of my arms and hands as I lowered him.

"You, Monseigneurs," I said through gritted teeth, "must away on the instant. Hide yourselves and flee, flee with all your loved ones. Now go."

The trampling of footfalls in the outer hallway was now deafening. Surely they would be upon us in an instant of time. Few sensations in life have given me as much relief as when I, at last, felt Calvin's weight gone and the rope grow slack. Instantly I clambered out the window and, though the muscles of my back and arms ached, rapidly I lowered myself down to meet him. As my feet alighted on the paving stones of the courtyard, I heard, through the open window, thundering blows and then the bursting of the door, and the shouting of men. I only hoped that Etienne had made good his escape.

Grasping Calvin by the sleeve, I nearly carried him across the courtyard, deeper into the still-deeper shadows of the cloister on the other side. As we paused for breath, I whispered close in his ear, "With all speed, follow me. I know the city. I will get you out of Paris. This I swear to you."

I glanced over my shoulder into the darkness back up in the direction of the open window. Suddenly there emitted from the opening a bursting forth of fire. At the same instant, the cracking retort of a harquebus shattered the stillness and echoed off the stone wall of the courtyard. I had heretofore never been shot at, and I feel safe in assuming that neither had Calvin. Nevertheless, I learned on the instant that, when being shot at, no schooling was necessary. The whining of lead pursuing hotly at our heels served to propel us forward by some mysterious energy, born of fear, an energy that I am convinced must discover itself within the heart of any man when so pursued. We ran for our lives, I leading Calvin into the dark labyrinth of winding streets and back alleyways of which I had become so fond and so familiar in my years in Paris.

25

To Angouleme

ALL THIS HAD HAPPENED on the instant, and it was only in the hours that followed that I began to muse at what I had done and why I had done it. I had no clear answers then nor do I now. Here again, in an instant of time I had done things that could have changed the course of my life. But would they?

I knew we dared not stop in Paris, and so we staggered on until exhaustion nearly made us collapse. Thinking it one of the least likely places where we might be thought to go, I took Calvin to the house of Molin the crippled cobbler, one of the faithful men in Calvin's network of secret gatherings. I've never seen a man overcome his deficiencies with such aplomb. Nor did I imagine that a man such as he, tradesman, and crippled at that, would have such vast connections within the city, nor that he could manage to make such use of those connections in the dead of night. Within an hour he had made arrangements for us to make rendezvous at Pont Mirabeau with a Seine barge bound for Rouen and the sea.

"The barge'll be slower than a coach," said Molin, but with a wink, he added, "but the king's henchmen'll be expecting you to flee with all speed by coach, now won't they? So they'll not be searching every barge minding its own business, meandering down the Seine, now will they?" He followed the last with a short laugh, clomping his crutch on the floor for emphasis.

At Pont Mirabeau, after waiting in the cold, damp shadows under the bridge for a quarter of an hour, a silent bargeman steered his craft to the bulwark of the river, alighted, secured his vessel, and without so much as a word, he, with Molin's assistance, trussed Calvin and me into two empty wine barrels. I believe this took no more time for them to accomplish than it has taken for me to write of it.

Between the rhythm of the river against the hull of the barge and the gentle sloshing of wine in the barrels surrounding ours, for my part, I was soon fast asleep, and I can only assume that Calvin, weary as he had to be from our mad flight, slept as well.

Abruptly I awakened when the motion of our sailing halted and I heard voices. Next I felt myself and my barrel being lifted from the barge and set down on some other surface. I heard sounds that assured me Calvin's barrel was being likewise situated. Then came the sound of low voices, but I could only understand a word here and there; Bonnieres-sur-Seine, I heard clearly and can only assume that that was the village where we were being transported. Next I clearly made out the clicking of the tongue so familiar to cart men urging forward their cart horses, and sure enough we jerked forward. The motion of a barge on a river, I was quickly forced to conclude, is far more conducive to comfort and to sleep than is the jolting and lurching of a farm cart on poorly maintained roadways meandering through the French countryside.

As the miles passed, a powerful hunger began to overtake me, and I began groping about, first in Calvin's satchels, hoping beyond hope that in my haste I had not neglected to add some food, though I felt that if I had food in my barrel and Calvin did not in his, that I would not enjoy that food as well as I might have otherwise. Such thoughts were to no purpose, for in my haste I had not thought to grab up anything to eat. But Molin, bless him, had thought of everything. At my feet I discovered a package containing a hard sausage, a block of cheese, a baguette, hard and a bit stale, but nevertheless, under the circumstances, nourishing. Washing the lot down with a small bottle of cabernet sauvignon the good man had thought to include, I blessed that poor crippled cobbler, and I determined that in the unlikely event I were ever made a cardinal I would nominate him for sainthood. I hoped that Calvin had discovered his repast and was enjoying it as much as I had mine.

The hours passed and the irrepressible demands of nature came powerfully upon me, all the more uncomfortably so as the cart on which we were being transported seemed to be passing over a particularly foul stretch of roadway, and the driver seemed to have as his objective to steer his crude equipage into every pothole this side of Paris.

When I felt I could bear my confinement not an instant longer, the fellow halted the cart, and I heard and felt, with relief, the man prying off the lid of my barrel. I drew in great gulps of crisp, country air, and surveyed the small wooded area where we had halted. There were no houses, barns, or buildings of any kind within sight, so there we made free to unbend our stiff limbs, to relieve ourselves, to rest, and to revive ourselves in the nearby stream, and to learn of our fate.

The fellow spoke a manner of French so foreign to my ears as to be altogether another language. Oddly, highly educated as Calvin was and master of many languages, he seemed to have an uncanny ability to comprehend the poor illiterate fellow. Calvin related the cart man's words to me in summary.

Apparently he was to deliver us, with all the speed of which he and his cart and old horse were capable, to friends in Le Mans to the south and west. From there we were to be transported to a proper coach that would convey us, with due speed, to Angouleme. Ours was a journey of over two hundred miles and, though our coach traveled some at night, we took nearly a week to draw near the city. For me it was an exhausting week of sitting in a coach. For Calvin's part, he employed himself in writing on his manuscript, lumpy writing it must have been, inscribed on such roads.

It was a clear November morning, a hovering cloud of moisture lying low over the plain on which we made our final approach to Marguerite's city of Angouleme. Long, low clouds of vapor clung to the fields of grain bordering the roadway, but rising grandly out of those mists, high on a promontory, stood the crenellated towers of the chateau. I could only assume this was the royal home and court of the counts of Angouleme, home to Marguerite of Navarre, that is, when she was not attending the court of her brother Francis in Paris.

There were other prominent towers and structures that formed a mystic skyline rising above the ring of fog, but none so spectacular as those of the cathedral. It came into my mind that it was a stubborn structure, sparse of windows and small ones at that with rounded arches above. To the west stood twin towers, their bulky gables generally directing the eye heavenward, and these were overbalanced to the northeast by a massively high square tower, and to the south by a stout Roman-looking dome.

After crossing a bridge over the River Charente, seemingly encircling the promontory of the town, our carriage labored uphill, hooves and carriage wheels clattering loudly along the narrow cobbled streets. At a turning, I looked back down the street. It was closely bordered by weathered stone houses, whose red clay roof tiles stair-stepped their twisting way back toward the river and the plain. Flooded by recollections, I was forced to think of my home village in Noyon, and I wondered whether Calvin thought of the same.

Winding under a house spanning the narrow street, we turned a corner and then burst into an open square, the façade of the cathedral blocking our way. Our carriage driver reined in his team, dismounted, and opened the door for us.

"Welcome to Angouleme," he said, bowing. "One must always be cautious, but for the present, you are safe here."

I gathered up our meager things: Calvin's two satchels, and another of warm clothes we had been given along the way, and we dismounted the carriage. A biting wind had arisen, and the air was brisk. Bracing myself against the dampness and cold, I was immediately smitten with the intricacies of the wide blocky façade of the cathedral that lay before us. The ancient builders had decorated it with no fewer than forty-one rounded arches—I counted them twice—the ones higher up on the west wall ornamented with a sort of toothy looking pattern. Many of these arches formed niches in which long-dead stonecutters had carved the images of long-dead saints, so I at first assumed them to be. Though as I studied them more closely, I observed that a number of them were depicted in grotesque twistings and writhings as if in torment, and I concluded that these were not intended to be saints—quite the contrary.

We strode toward the great west door, eager to take shelter against the wind and cold. As we entered, the sounds of singing met our ears. Singing was a normal phenomenon in great churches, but immediately there was something that sounded odd about that singing. At first I could not detect what it was, but Calvin did, on the instant. Then, to my astonishment, he joined in, lustily and with full vigor. His eyes grew more intense and his voice, though not loud or deep, grew stronger as he sang. Then it struck me like a blow to the face. It was without precedent. The entire congregation in St. Pierre, Angouleme, not just the monks, and now Calvin with them, were singing from the Psalms—and in French.

La terre au Seigneur appartient
Tout ce qu'en sa rondeur contient
Et ceux qui habitent en elle;
Sur mer fondements lui donna,
L'enrichit et l'environna
De mainte rivière très belle.

Then I began observing another voice joining in that singing. It was no fine angelic voice, to be sure, indeed, more of a peasant growling sort of voice. Yet, almost as if against my will, I found myself, haltingly at first, attempting to intone the words of Psalm 24 with Calvin and the rest.

When the last echoes of the Psalm singing fell silently from the barrel vaulting of that massive church, the congregants began filing out of the nave, wooden shoes clopping on the flagstone floor as they parted. I was astonished at what occurred next. One after another—high and low, noble and peasant, tradesman and merchant, plowman and milkmaid—planted a kiss on each of Calvin's pale cheeks and grasped his hand, some with tears in their eyes, and thanked him for coming to them. It was as if they all knew him, had been expecting his arrival, as if he was a man of stature and celebrity. I felt the high winds of that old resentment beginning, once again, to surge up in my bosom.

One fellow, by the fine tailoring of his cloak and by his bearing, a noble-born man, clearly, stayed at Calvin's elbow until the last of them had passed out the west door and into the November cold.

"My name is Louis du Tillet," he said, "choir director at St. Pierre, and I am at your service. As you can see, we in Angouleme have been eagerly awaiting your arrival."

"It is not fitting," was all Calvin could at first manage to say. "I am astonished."

"You need not be so," said du Tillet. "It is, indeed, I who am astonished at this happy providence. You see, it is my pleasure to be honored with the joyful duty of affording you room and board in my own home. You and your servant are to live with me and my family for as long as you like. All that is mine is at your disposal."

"Du Tillet," said Calvin, musing. "You are brother to the Bishop of Meaux?"

"Indeed," replied du Tillet.

"And is it you," said Calvin, "who has taught them to sing the Psalms in French?"

"With the help of Clement Marot, the poet," said du Tillet. "He it is who has, by his skill, begun to give the Psalms back to the people, for all the church to sing."

241

"And you have, by your skill," said Calvin, "taught them to sing the praises of God in a manner worthy of the object of those praises. It is wonderful to behold."

Calvin and du Tillet talked as we followed him to his nearby home where he escorted us into an oaken paneled dining room, a fire spitting and roaring in a massive stone fireplace, warming and cheering the room. We dined on onion soup, clotted with cheese, on thick slabs of roasted pork, on rosemary legumes, on sautéed mushrooms, and on barley bread, hot from the oven and dripping with sweet butter and honey. When I could hold no more, I leaned back on the velvet chair in which I had been sitting, and, like a contented sow, emitted little grunts of pleasure. I could not help myself. I had not eaten that well for a very long time, perhaps ever. Du Tillet invited us to sit more comfortably before the fire while a servant opened a bottle of Bordeaux and poured out three glasses.

After we had dined and drank, du Tillet escorted us on a tour of our rooms and the rest of his house. At the end of a long hallway, he placed a large iron key in the lock of a door. The thick door of eight carved panels swung open.

"Here, Master Calvin," he said, "is a room you will find most inviting. It is entirely at your disposal."

Rarely in the years I attended on Calvin did I see him so near being what some might describe as giddy.

"Books, books, books—an entire library filled with books!" He was stammering in his excitement. "And such a library! Are all these yours?"

"Indeed, I have for many years collected what I could of the finest books the new learning affords. Under the protection of good Queen Marguerite, I have been at liberty to do so."

With enthusiasm, he began orienting Calvin to his collection. "Here in this corner you will find the complete works of Augustine and the early church fathers, and here Aquinas and the scholastics, and here the Holy Scriptures in Latin, here in Greek, and here the Old Testament in Hebrew, and of course I have acquired many volumes of pagan antiquity."

"Wonderful," is all Calvin managed to say.

"All is yours while you reside with us in Angouleme."

Calvin walked slowly around the room, his eyes passing over the row-upon-row of leather tomes lining the high walls from floor to ceiling. Then he paused, tenderly lifting a volume off its shelf. Carrying it to a wide table, partly encircled by a high leaded bow window, Calvin opened the volume and slowly sat down before it.

"I cannot think of a more conducive environment in which to continue my work," he said at last.

"Is there anything else you require?" asked du Tillet.

Calvin looked about before answering. "Quill and ink," he said, "and paper. I am fearfully low on paper."

"You have come to the right place, for many reasons," said du Tillet, with a laugh. "Angouleme is famous for the making of paper. You shall never want for paper in fair Angouleme."

"Jean-Louis, my satchel, the one with my manuscript within," said Calvin.

As I set them before him, Calvin profusely expressed his gratitude to his host. Then taking up his papers, he fell silent, reading what he had last written.

"I will leave you to your work," said du Tillet, softly.

I do not think Calvin heard him.

26

Caves and Wine

Happy months did Calvin and I pass as guests of the choirmaster du Tillet: happy for Calvin because of the books, the library, and the ample paper, and happy for the peace and quiet so conducive to his studies and writing; happy for me because of the food.

Happy, I say, however, I was far from truly happy. Troubled was I about what I had done. More than troubled, I was afraid. Instead of assisting in his arrest, I had, by aiding Calvin's escape, defied my commission, and in so doing, defied the king. I knew little of royalty and court ways. But I knew that one did not defy kings with impunity. And so, peaceful though they were in other respects, I was often fearful in those months. Looking back on it, my fear served to make me more cautious than I otherwise would have been. Angouleme was such a place of liberty and tranquility—kings did not ordinarily raise siege works against their sisters' castles—that careless presumption would have been the easiest posture to assume. My private fears kept me from such, and so I often looked over my shoulder.

It was that caution that made me see him. The light had always been dim in St. Germaine l'Auxerrois, but one morning while haggling over the price of a small basket of mushrooms in the market before the cathedral, I caught a glimpse of a man I recognized, one I feared I had seen before in Paris. I was sure he had not yet seen me, but there was something odd about the way he went about his marketing. He gave little heed to the wares, but seemed to be studying faces, looking intently for someone.

I ducked behind the *de Nimes* flap of a vender's awning, and studied him more closely. He had a familiar smirk to his facial expression, one I felt I had heard more than seen, if it can be said that facial qualities can be heard. And his eyes, narrow and piercing, were ever roving over the villagers.

Moments later, breathless, I unclasped the library door in haste, and broke in on Calvin's studying, something I rarely ever did.

"Jean-Louis, you look as if you've seen a specter," he said.

"I fear we have been, or soon shall be," I said, "discovered."

"Discovered?" he said.

"It was only a matter of time," this from du Tillet, who must have seen me enter the house in haste and followed me to the library.

"Queen Marguerite's gracious protection," said Calvin, "thrives best among honorable men."

"Are you certain of what you saw?" asked du Tillet.

I hesitated before answering. Had my fears made me imagine it? I wondered, but then I recalled his eyes. He was searching hard for someone, that much was clear.

"How badly is Master Calvin wanted by the king?" I asked.

"Word is," said du Tillet, his brow furrowed with worry. "The king has come to believe that there are but a few key men who perpetrate reformation in his realm. These he is determined to root out and destroy. It is said that you, John Calvin, are one of the foremost he seeks to destroy."

"This man, I have seen him before, in Paris," I said carefully. "I believe he works as a royal agent. If Master Calvin is as sought after by the king as you say, this man, it is almost certain, comes to find him."

"We must away with all speed," said du Tillet.

The next hour was spent in a paroxysm of activity as our host prepared us for flight. Calvin he fitted out as a vinedresser, complete with hoe, and me, he clothed in the tradesmen's garb of a tanner. It was the first time I had worn a leather apron for a very long time. Du Tillet was determined to attend us, but he seemed to have a difficult time coming up with a disguise that suited him. Whatever he told us he was, he still looked to my eye like the comfortably off choir director of Angouleme, and I wondered whether he would be the best man with whom to attempt to travel incognito. He tried to better his charade with giving himself a new name for the occasion, Hautmont. I feared it would afford little aid to his disguise. Determined to go with us, he brought along one of his servants as well.

I was anxious to put many miles between us and the man I had seen and feared in the marketplace of Angouleme. Yet did du Tillet at the end of but one long day of flight suggest a halt. I was desperate to clatter on through the night, but our escort insisted that we halt in Poitou, there to make a call on the venerable Jacques Lefevre d'Etaples in the town of Nerac.

I gazed with curiosity as our cart clattered into narrow cobbled streets lined with half-timbered old houses that wound their way uphill on both sides of a river, the River Blaise, I would learn. An intricate staircase ascended from the left bank of the river to a splendid castle, its circular turrets and stout crenellated walls guarding over the town.

"We draw near his village," explained du Tillet. "It is a town divided into two distinct portions. This bridge is named Pont Vieux and carries us across the river from Petit-Nerac to the more exalted district of Grand-Nerac."

The village smelled of hops and the mealy aromas of brewing, and I was struck by another smell, one that reminded me of the corks used to seal up bottles of wine. From these odors, I drew conclusions about the industry of the place.

I wondered why the venerable Lefevre had chosen this unassuming place for his final days. As if reading my thoughts, Calvin spoke.

"Nerac is within the jurisdiction of Her Majesty, the saintly Marguerite, Queen of Navarre. How odd it is that she should be so ardent a Christian and supporter of reformation, and her brother, the king, the declared enemy of such." He was quiet for a moment, then added, "Perhaps never was a sister so unlike a brother."

Moments later our coach came to a stand before a low stone villa. It was a sturdy house, its flinty walls looking as if they were constructed in Roman days, with windows added when pointed arches prevailed.

We alighted the cart and were invited into the dining room by a servant. There sat an old man, older than any I had ever seen before. His white hair flowed down to his shoulders, and he sat close before a crackling fire, a woolen blanket over his legs, though it was nearly springtime.

I stood aloof in the shadows as Calvin and the old man conversed, my stomach rumbling for something to eat. They seemed absorbed in discussion of a theological question beyond my comprehension, as most of them were, so I fidgeted, longing for meat.

When at last we were called to table, the old man yet remained more interested in talk than in food.

"Such is the sweetness of this divine food. It makes the mind insatiable: the more we taste of it, the more we long for it."

I at first thought he was referring to the lamb roast we were at that moment devouring, but I soon learned he was referring to Holy Scripture, of which he seemed never able to stop speaking.

When the meal had been cleared away and we had retired once again to his sitting room before the fire, he and Calvin spoke long and in earnest about the state of the church.

"If you are a member of Christ's church, you are a member of his body," the old man was saying.

"So is it not necessary to be a member of the Church of Rome?" asked Calvin.

"Religion has but one foundation, one object, one Head," replied Lefevre, his voice escalating with feeling. "Jesus Christ, blessed forevermore. It is the cross of Christ alone that opens the gates of heaven and shuts the gates of hell."

"So you agree that the pope holds not the keys?" asked Calvin.

The old man was silent before replying. "You must be cautious, my son," he said at last. "Be moderate or else you might find yourself tearing down the house of God that you intend to purge of popish evils."

"But what if the building is too rotten to be patched up?" asked Calvin. "What if it must be torn down to its Cornerstone and, thereupon, rebuilt?"

"Take heed," said Lefevre, "that you may not be killed by the cracking walls."

And then, the old man's eyes welling up with tears, he leaned forward in his chair, looked intently at Calvin, and said, "You are chosen as the mighty instrument of the Lord. Through you God will erect his kingdom in our land."

I mused on the old man's words in the weeks and months of near-constant movement that followed. Never sure we were not followed, we stayed but mere days at most in one place before hastily loading our things in a cart and making for our next destination. These months of vast-ranging travel introduced me to many important men and places. In every place we halted, Calvin was sought out by reform-minded people, hungry for his counsel and instruction in holy things, and he was frequently called on to preach. I knew that he was growing restless for the scholar's life, for the library of Angouleme, or some place like it, but for my part I felt less fear when we were on the move, and I found it an exciting several months.

One evening as we passed through low hillsides perfumed with lavender, daylight fading, the setting sun glowing warmly on the fields, we neared the city of Poitiers. Yet a mile or so from the town, abruptly was our cart halted by several young men brandishing pitchforks purpose-grown from the branches of trees.

"It is not safe for John Calvin," one of them spoke, "to enter this city."

They were coarse-looking creatures, and I wasn't at first certain whether they blocked our way as friends to warn us for our good, or whether they were there to threaten us for our hurt.

"But we have been instructed to divert your way," continued their spokesman, "to the nearby grotto of St. Benoit."

"And for what purpose?" asked Calvin.

"Many will gather in the caves this evening," the man said. "We have been expecting you."

I wondered how effective was our disguise if we could arrive near a village none of us had ever entered before in our lives and everyone in the place somehow knew that Calvin was to appear and, no doubt, to preach that evening in some nearby cave. If the common peasant wielding a pitchfork knew so much, why not the king's agents wielding the sword of state? It perplexed me a great deal that we were able without arrest to range so widely in our travels. I cannot, by natural means, explain it.

That evening, with torches burning, Calvin stepped before a peasant band of illiterates, who reeked of the hayfields, of laboring sweat, and of chickens. Standing before a rough stone for a pulpit, opening his Gospels, he read therein to the people. I studied their faces as they listened. For many it must have been the first time they had ever heard and understood the words they were hearing in their own language. Hence, there was wonder glowing in the cheeks of a fair maiden, there were tears of joy in the eyes of an old man, there was hunger and attention on the faces of fathers and mothers and ruddy-cheeked youths. When he completed his sermon, I observed him—nay, I was drawn into assisting him—as he offered the bread of the Lord's Supper to these poor folks. Scowling, I rendered up our last loaf into Calvin's waiting hands, wondering what we would eat that night. He proceeded to break it.

"From the physical things set forth in the sacrament we are led by analogy to spiritual things. This bread is given as a symbol of Christ's body, and as bread nourishes, sustains, and keeps the body, so Christ's body is the only food to invigorate and enliven our soul."

He paused, then continued. "Christ said, 'This is my body which is given for you.' All those here who genuinely hope in Christ alone for their eternal salvation, freely take and eat."

When our last loaf had been mangled by the coarse hands of the attending peasants, and not a crumb remained, Calvin continued.

"When they had eaten, our Lord took up the cup and said, 'This is the blood of the covenant shed for many. Drink all of it.'"

Beckoning me to him, he whispered in my ear for me to bring to him a bottle of wine and a cup. When I had fetched these from our cart and handed these to him, I expected Calvin to do what every priest in Christendom always did: while the peasant masses looked on in thirst, the priest quaffed the wine to the dregs. So it had, in my experience, always been. But not so John Calvin. He did the remarkable, the unthinkable.

Pouring wine into the cup, he held it in both hands and said, "When Christ sets wine before us as a symbol of his blood, we must reflect on the benefits which wine imparts to the body, and so realize that the same are spiritually imparted to us by Christ's blood. These benefits are to nourish, refresh, and gladden our hearts. So Christ, by the mystery of his secret union with the devout, does with his blood for our souls. All you who trust alone in Christ's blood and imputed righteousness for your salvation, take and drink."

He extended the cup of wine to the one nearest him. The poor soul stared blankly back at Calvin. Never before in the Roman Mass had the priest so extended the cup to him. Never before had the elements in both kinds been offered to the common man. Not one of them made a move to receive the cup. Wine was for the priests, but here, for the first time in centuries, Calvin was extending the cup of wine to the peasants.

"Take and drink," he said again. This time he took hold of the man's hand and placed the cup in it. "Now drink," he said kindly.

As the wine was being passed through the cave, du Tillet led them in singing lines from the first Psalm—in French. The grotto of St. Benoit reechoed first with his skilled voice and, as best they knew how, the humbler strains of the peasant farmer and his family joining in.

> Heureux celui qui fuit des vicieux,
> Et le commerce et l'example odieux;
> Qui des pecheurs hait la trompeuse voie,
> Et des moqueurs la criminelle joie...

Leaving the precincts of Poitiers, we recommenced our travels southward and east, away from Paris, away from the king, away from the horrible burnings, away from the scene of all my crimes. Yet did Calvin often speak of Paris, and I felt deep within me that he longed to return to the capital. A disquieting coldness gripped my heart as I sensed this in him.

Yet did we continue traversing the wide plains, the fertile valleys, the rugged ridges of the country. Several weeks later we passed through the farms surrounding the town of Lyon. Here again, before entering the city, we were met by a band of young men led by a zealous youth named Martial Alba, who was attended by others who identified themselves as Louis de Marsac, Mathieu Dimonet, and Denis Peloquin of Blois. They urgently warned Calvin not to enter the city. Apparently Francis had garrisoned a special detachment of soldiers in Lyon charged with arresting all those sympathetic with the reformation cause, a class of people, we were told, not small in number and increasing. And the Inquisitor, as he was known, a man whose name was Nicholas Oritz, breathed out fire against all those who refused to bow to the Roman yoke in that city.

"There is a dispatch for you," continued the young man who had identified himself as Martial Alba. "It has made its way in secret to us," he continued, "from Paris."

"And its contents are known to us," added Louis de Marsac.

Calvin thanked them and broke the seal on the letter, I wondering as he did so, how these young men knew of its contents. Slowly Calvin ran his eyes over the letter.

"You will return, Master Calvin, to the capital," said Martial, "only at great peril to yourself."

His inflection suggested that he was not warning Calvin, but merely stating an irrefutable fact.

"Return to Paris?" cried du Tillet, bending to read over Calvin's shoulder. "What does it say?"

"I have been challenged to a debate," said Calvin, simply, "with the Spanish libertine, Michael Servetus."

"But in Paris?" said du Tillet. "The king, the doctors of the Sorbonne—you are the most wanted man in Paris. To return—you have been denounced. It would be certain death. I cannot advise it."

"It may, indeed, be a trap." Though I seldom initiated conversation with Calvin, or offered my opinion, I felt compelled to

state what appeared eminently obvious to my mind. I knew of
what I spoke.

"There is great peril for the faithful throughout this benighted
land," said Calvin. "Yet ought not the confession of God's sacred
truth be more precious to us than our lives?"

"Yes, but, John," said du Tillet, "Paris will burn you, and the
nascent church, bereft of your gifts, will founder on the shoals
of error."

"It is precisely the correcting of error that compels me to
go," said Calvin. "I have heard of this erring Spaniard. With his
freethinking interpretations, he does much to discredit the cause
of pure reformation. And I know that, through such a public
debate, I shall endanger my life, yet shall I do whatever stands in
my power to heal Servetus."

So it was that we turned our steps toward Paris. In the
days that followed, as we drew ever closer to the capital, dread
grew in my bosom. I felt that my plight was more despairing than Calvin's. He seemed unruffled by the prospects that
lay before us in the city. I mused that he knew that if he was
arrested and burned it would be martyrdom, death for the
gospel. I think he believed it would be an honor to so die for
"the everlasting kingdom of Jesus Christ," as he often termed
it. But I found no such consolations for my tormented self.
If I were denounced, arrested, and burned, it would be for
playing false with my commission, for bungling my obligation,
for failing to complete what I had commenced. My duplicity
had no honor in it, nor was I calmed by sublime reflections of
divine loyalties, and holy resolutions. No, I felt I was caught in
a no-man's land, devoid of allegiance, absent of all honorable
outcome. And in it all I felt desperately alone. How could I

speak to Calvin, to anyone, of these things? What awaited me was hellish. I saw myself denounced and burned for a heretic, yet how horrible to be so, when far from guilty of the martyr's crimes, and so bereft of the consolations of the martyr. So did my stomach churn and my mind grow more troubled as the spires and domes of Paris came ominously into view on the horizon.

27

Royal Feasting

PALPABLE DREAD ENSHROUDED ME, and had the effect of sickening my bowels as we approached the gate of the city near the Bois de Vincennes. I felt short of breath, and so constricted became the muscles of my throat that I had difficulty swallowing. I wondered whether I might cheat the king's henchmen, there and then, by simply dying of fright. I was so certain that agents of the king and the university would be arrayed against us, with axe and sword, lining the thoroughfares of the city, awaiting our entrance, that I became almost giddy with relief as we somehow managed to pass through the gate of the city and into her central streets, all without detection.

But my relief soon gave way to fresh waves of anxiety, as anxious friends of Calvin hastily escorted us to the house on Rue Saint Antoine chosen for the debate with Servetus. My appetite left me, and I had a difficult time sitting still as we awaited the arrival of the Spaniard.

"Will he risk coming?" asked du Tillet.

"I do not know," said Roussel, who had himself just arrived. "Servetus, for his denying of the Trinity, is wanted by the Catholic authorities of the university, perhaps even more so than John Calvin."

"Is it wise to give them so easy a target," said du Tillet, "as we here give them so conveniently."

"If I were an agent," said the cloth merchant, Jean du Bourg, "I would lead the king's bailiffs here to this house on this night, for here might I be rewarded for the catching of not one, but two prize fish."

"A most unappetizing thought," said Canaye the lawyer. "I do trust we are well surrounded by those who watch with all care for such eventualities?"

"We have taken all precautions of which we are capable," said Fosset, the royal lieutenant. "I have arranged certain diversions that will have already begun to occur at the Place de St. Sulpice. The bailiffs of the king will be in great demand there, I assure you, and so will have little interest in what transpires in this place this night. You have my word on these things."

"Where is my good friend Etienne?" asked Calvin. "I long to see him, but he does not come."

An awkward silence hung over the room at Calvin's words, silence at last broken by Jean du Bourg.

"These are dark and trying times in Paris," he began.

"What has become of him?" urged Calvin.

"Etienne has been denounced," said Roussel.

"And so have you been," said Canaye the lawyer. "Roussel is in equal danger, yet does he refuse to flee."

"Etienne was arrested some time ago," said Roussel, ignoring the lawyer. "It happened at the time you fled Paris. He has now been in prison for many months."

"And his wife?" asked Calvin.

"She too lies in prison," said du Bourg. "The House of the Pelican has been turned inside out. Many others have been arrested, and I fear more shall be so, through the evidence discovered therein."

After a moment Calvin asked, "What will happen next to them?"

"The king has determined," said Roussel, "to make a public show of his virulence to stamp out the reformation in all his realm. I wish it were not so, but Etienne, unless God intervenes, shall go to his reward tomorrow, he and five others."

"Is there any way for me to go to him?" asked Calvin.

"Absolutely none whatsoever," said du Tillet.

"Only if you would so carelessly throw away your own life," said Fosset, the royal lieutenant. "It is reported by reliable sources that Etienne, though he grieves for his dear wife, finds strength in God and encourages those about him to do the same."

"God has promised victory in the end," said Calvin. "Yet is it a great mystery how our gracious Lord puts such honor upon his people, whom he has employed to maintain his truth, and how he leads them, as it were, by the hand to martyrdom." He paused. His voice was strained with emotion as he concluded. "We must submit ourselves to the will of this kind Father and sovereign Lord."

It is not possible for me to fully explain my reaction to what I heard that night. I had attempted to reassure myself in these last months that kind and generous Etienne would be safe, that my former denunciation of him and of his saintly wife would be thwarted by the efforts of Molin the cobbler and his capable network of the faithful who risked all to aid men like

Calvin in their flight from persecution and burning. Where were such men when Etienne needed them? Surely Etienne and his wife would be safe, so I had vainly attempted to reassure myself. But clearly it was not so. And there was no single individual more responsible for this evil than I. Why had he not heeded my warning that night as we fled out the window? Had I not told him to flee Paris at once, he and all his loved ones? Yet did I know that it was all my doing. I alone must bear the guilt, weighty beyond measure. To my unsupportable, unforgivable crimes I had now to bear the martyrdoms of these good people.

I recall very little of the remainder of that evening. And I fear that the vast ugliness of my guilt might have that night begun to unhinge my rational powers. Surely what transpired the next day completed the iron castings, the bars and bands, the forged chains and hooks that were to lock me forever in my irrevocable guilt. I do recollect learning, after hours of waiting, that Michael Servetus would not be coming to debate with Calvin. Perhaps he feared the king's latest onslaught against all dissenters more than appearing to lack the courage to have his teaching dismantled by Calvin. In any event, he simply did not show up for the fight.

My sleep that night was tormented by nightmares of fire and burning. I kept seeing Etienne's wife writhing in the flames, her lovely hair ablaze, and her skin charring, and in my dreams she pointed an accusing finger at me, denouncing me before God in heaven as the guilty one. I dreaded the coming of the dawn, and considered feigning sickness to avoid attending Calvin at Etienne's martyrdom. It would have required little feigning, so tormented in mind and now in body was I.

What transpired in Paris, January 21, 1535, I shall never forget, nor, I fear, shall God ever forgive me for my part in the events of that day.

Riding a great warhorse and wearing the velvet finery of his royal office, Francis I, King of France, led a royal procession through the streets of the city. He held aloft a flaming torch, and his queen, Claudia, glittering with jewels, rode at his side. Behind them strutted their three sons, shimmering in their royal finery, and looking with hauteur at the fawning masses lining the streets. Following the royal family came the priests in all their glittering vestments, bearing coveted relics, most notably the crown of thorns worn by Christ on the cross, and Moses' stone tablets on which the very finger of God penned the Decalogue—so the church had declared them to be.

There were many other worthies in the train of the king and queen, including high-ranking nobles and revered doctors of the Sorbonne, all of them bearing torches and candles during their grand march through the city. It was impossible to follow the entire procession, so vast were the crowds that lined the streets to view the royal pomp and dignity. Royal heralds informed the masses that the parade was scheduled to halt in each of the four principal quarters of the city, at which stops the king and his entourage would be seated before an elaborately decorated and loaded dining table. While feasting on roasted pheasant, wild boar, snails, and truffles, and while quaffing the finest wines, the royal family would then be entertained by watching the burning of heretics; eight in all were scheduled to burn that evil day.

Learning at which of the four locations Etienne was to suffer, Calvin and a band of the faithful with him, made their way to be near their friend in his final hour, to pray for him and for one another, to grieve and to encourage one another. I longed to disappear forever in the crowded streets. It would have been a simple matter. Yet did I feel that if I did so, there would be no hope for me. Little hope did I expect by staying with Calvin, but I could not see my way clearly. Where else was I to go? I suppose that there was something, oddly, of penance in my attending them that day. By observing the grim results of my betrayal, I must have crudely imagined that I might, thereby, in some twisted fashion, make expiation for my crimes. It was a muddle to me then, as it remains so to me now.

Perhaps it was merely the effects of sleep deprivation—I had slept little and ill the previous night—or perhaps it was the effect of the smoky atmosphere from the burning, but either way, the tears streamed down my cheeks as I observed the barbaric scene unfolding before me. I had looked on with hardness, even pleasure in the past, but not so that day. I felt that something of my own soul was being consumed in those flames, and that I deserved it and he did not. So I wept, far from shamelessly, but uncontrollably did I weep before the royal inferno that snuffed out the life of Etienne de la Forge.

As the fire burned low, Francis wiped boar fat from his chin on a lacy napkin and rose to his feet. Signaling his three sons to do the same, he paraded them before the crowd.

"I reserve the same punishment," he called out, "for these my own sons, and all who are of my royal household, should any of them by chance be so infected with these most execrable heresies!"

As the royal procession moved on to another quarter of the city and other burnings, Calvin, du Tillet and his servant, and I were whisked from the scene.

"There is no time to lose," said Roussel. "While all Paris is distracted with this madness, you must be gone from this place. Flee now and do not return."

"And so must you," said Calvin.

But Roussel would not be persuaded.

"Flee to the German lands where you can study and write—and where you must pray for our beleaguered land. Now go! With all speed, go!"

Horses were provided for us, and though I had never ridden before in my life, I clung with both hands to the animal's mane and did my best to stay bestride the beast that was to be my salvation from that place. Du Tillet's servant proved to be the best horseman among us, du Tillet himself next in skill, and Calvin and I last, and decidedly in that order. Nevertheless, necessity is a grand teacher, and I developed sufficient skill in a short time to be able to ride. The day after our initial flight from Paris was the second most pain-ridden day of my life, every muscle, every bone in my body crying out for deliverance from the jolting of the beast. I believe that I found a measure of temporary distraction from the torments of my conscience in that physical pain.

28

The Institutes

As the days of our flight passed, I grew, if not skillful, at least more proficient in the riding of a horse. We made our way due east, traversing through such places as Epernay, Verdun, and Metz. Passing into German lands, Calvin seeming loathe to take his leave of France. When we finally arrived in the grand city of Strasbourg, as with other places through which we had passed, many flocked to greet Calvin. Notably, one called Martin Bucer warmly welcomed Calvin, urging him to remain in Strasbourg, there to preach and minister.

"There is much good for you to do in this place," said the kindly Bucer. "Preach in the public square, in the grand cathedral itself—you need not fear the sword or fire here in Strasbourg. God has granted great freedom for his cause in this place. And there is good food and leisure—here you may relax from your work; here you may recreate yourself. Do remain among us."

"The demands of God's beleaguered church," said Calvin, "do not allow for thoughts of food and leisure."

"I know of your dedication to the work of God," said Martin Bucer. "It is unrivaled. But human nature has that weakness by which it cannot always concentrate on grave and serious matters. There must also be provision made for certain relaxations from work and useful studies and a certain recreation of the strength both of the spirit and of the body in play and games. Such you may enjoy here in Strasbourg."

I knew Calvin better than almost anyone, and I knew that, well-intentioned as Bucer's urgings were, they would not be received with favor by Calvin. What is more, in Strasbourg Calvin was accosted on every side by enthusiastic reformers who wanted him to preach, to teach, to debate, and to take pastoral duties among them. These were all things Calvin was reluctant so to do, and I knew this. Hence, I knew that our stay in Strasbourg would not be a long one.

"Tell no one of where we plan to go," I heard him telling du Tillet one evening. "I shall assume the name Lucanius, and thereby shall I be enabled to find a quiet place for study and writing. Bucer and the rest are well-meaning and faithful men, but there is too much activity in this place. We must be away."

I had had my suspicions of du Tillet's servant. There had been nothing of substance, but the man was reserved and surly—as I often had been. Perhaps this was the manner of the servant. In any event what transpired next was nearly to our ruin. We took our leave of kindly Martin Bucer, and Calvin asked him to tell no one of our departure until a full day had elapsed. He arranged for us to board at his home and place of birth in the small village of Selestat, a comfortable day's journey on horseback south of Strasbourg.

It was there that du Tillet's servant showed his evil side. I know it is hypocritical in the extreme for one such as I to record the petty guilt of one such as he, but, nevertheless, did the man do us a great wrong.

It fell out after this fashion. I awoke with a start early next morning. It must have been a sound in the narrow hallway of the Bucer family house. Rising from my bed, I moved with stealth, unlatching my door and straining to see in the predawn darkness. I could make out the barest outline of a man's shape as a light from a lantern in the narrow street shone faintly through a window, partly revealing him to my sight. I followed, but not knowing his intentions, I followed far too slowly.

He had apparently already made his horse ready, for within an instant I heard a racket of hooves on the cobbles in the street. They clattered, echoing against the narrow timbered houses that enclosed the street. Boldly did I attempt to saddle my steed and give pursuit, but by the time I managed to secure the bridle in its place, the man was gone. Certain it was du Tillet's servant, I rode best and as fast as I could in the direction he had traveled, but if it was du Tillet's servant, I knew his riding, and I knew mine. It was a vain pursuit.

Fearing the worst, I at last reined my steed in and returned. "What has he taken?" I inquired as I came back into the house. All were awake by now.

"I have been robbed!" cried du Tillet. "That worthless servant has robbed me of my purse! They are all the same. That scoundrel servant! He has run off with every piece of gold, every piece of silver. We are destitute!"

As we breakfasted, du Tillet fumed in his agitation, cursing his servant, bemoaning how expenses would now be covered, and generally lamenting as if disaster had fallen from the heavens.

I remained quiet, though I frequently fingered the hidden stash within my pouch, concealed deep within my tunic. For some time now I had spent nothing from it. I was loathe to handle it, as if the pouch and its contents were a poison, transmitted merely by touch or by look. I cannot explain my feelings fully on the matter, but looking back, I suppose it had become a sort of blood money to me. There was so much I had not been able to arrange in my thinking; perhaps I never would fully be able to do so.

After we had finished our little meal, du Tillet said, "How can such a one as he, after all of his privileges, most especially hearing the gospel these number of months, how can such as he act so wickedly? It is unthinkable."

Calvin said nothing but opened his Greek New Testament. After reading silently for a moment, he closed the book and said, though I believe he was actually reciting from his instantaneous translation:

"'For if we sin willfully after we have received the knowledge of the truth,'" he paused, looking at each of us, but I felt that he lingered longer when looking into my eyes, "'there no longer remains a sacrifice for sins, but a certain fearful expectation of judgment, and fiery indignation which will devour the adversaries,' this from the Epistle to the Hebrews."

Again he paused, the weight of which pausing seemed to bear down on my soul as if to crush me under its insupportable burden.

"To whom God has granted much," said Calvin, "he will demand far more on the judgment day. Your servant, Master du Tillet, for spurning the grace of God, the many opportunities for repentance, for sinning against the light of the Word of God which he has repeatedly heard, for these your servant, should he persist in his stony-hearted rebellion, must expect fearful judgment and fiery indignation from the Almighty."

Again he looked at me, his piercing eyes, as I felt them, penetrating into my very soul, and continued. "Let us, each one, examine our hearts, and put off the hardness therein. Let us resist the devil, mortify sin, humble ourselves before the grace of God, confess and forsake our sinning. And then let us put on the righteousness of Jesus Christ, mercifully imputed to our unworthy hearts."

I felt his words were for me, and for me alone. I shuddered, and I believe it was such a shuddering as even I could not conceal by my art. If Calvin could say such things about the petty stealing of du Tillet's servant, what would he have to say to one such as I, I alone who was responsible for the great evil of condemning the innocent, of betraying the faithful, of exchanging for money— again I fingered the pouch within my tunic—if he knew that I had for these few glittering coins denounced his friend Etienne and many others, would he so cheerfully extend to me this gospel of grace? Could there be such a grace capable of covering such crimes as I alone had committed? I believed there was not. How could there be?

His words pounded like hammer blows on an anvil in my head: *If we sin willfully after we have received the knowledge of the truth, there no longer remains a sacrifice for sins, but a certain fearful expectation of judgment, and fiery indignation which will devour the adversaries.*

In the days that followed, I liberally spent the remains of my purse on our needs, though I made every attempt to conceal my liberality in doing so. It was a small matter for me to make my way to the market alone and secure food, even lodging and fodder for our horses, now reduced to but three. All of which generosity I credited to others.

"How is it, Jean-Louis," said Calvin, one day as we neared the city of Freiburg. "How is it that we, destitute as we are, are so well provisioned?"

Recalling his words to me long ago when he was determined to render up his benefices, I turned to him and replied, "You do the work of God," I said. "Therefore, God provides for you."

"So he does," he said, eyeing me closely, but smiling as he did so. "And so he does for you, Jean-Louis, and so he does for you."

He meant words such as these as encouragements, no doubt, but they cut like knives. *God, provide for me? Provide hell and judgment of the fieriest and most fearful. Surely that alone was all I could expect God to provide for me.* If Calvin knew my inner counsel, if he knew all that was in my heart, if he knew the rivers of blood that were on these my foul hands, so he too would have expected for me. I was certain of this.

"We near the city where it is reported," said du Tillet, "that the great humanist scholar, Erasmus, now dwells. So it is reported."

"So I too have heard," said Calvin.

"He was a son of the College de Montaigu as were you," observed du Tillet.

"Indeed," said Calvin, "though many years before my time. I owe him a great debt for his New Testament in Greek, but I lament that he has retreated from his earlier criticism of the church and from his grand efforts to make the Bible accessible to all men."

"He loves the Holy Church," said du Tillet, slowly, eyeing Calvin as he proceeded. "And so values the unity of Christ's body, the church. Ought not this unity to be the supreme goal of every Christian?"

"An important goal, no doubt," said Calvin. "But not the supreme one. Truth alone, found in the Word of God alone, is supreme. If the church silences the Word of God and forbids her members to hear and heed the Word of God alone, then unity with such an institution, call it what you may, is unity with the anti-Word, the anti-Christ. Do you not see this, good du Tillet?"

I observed du Tillet to frown deeply at these words, and he fell into a brooding silence.

Several moments passed, and then Calvin began speaking. "I would have the weakest woman read the Gospels and the Epistles of St. Paul," he said. But I had come to detect in his tone when he was speaking from his own mind and when he was reciting. It was a small thing, and I believe few detected it such as I had come to do. In any case, I knew that these words were not Calvin's and that he was reciting them from someone else.

"Do you not agree, good du Tillet?"

"If we desire to have a religion," said du Tillet, "suited to weak women, yes, I agree."

"It is your scholar Erasmus who said those words," said Calvin.

"Surely not!" said du Tillet.

"O indeed, did he speak thus, long ago. He said more. I shall render it as best I can. 'I would have those words translated into all languages, so that not only Scots and Irishmen, but Turks and Saracens might read them. I long for the ploughboy to sing them to himself as he follows the plow, the weaver to hum them to the tune of his shuttle, the traveler to beguile with them the dullness of his journey.' So declared Erasmus, but only for a time. For the sake of unity, he remains within the blinding superstitious unity of the church. It is a great loss."

I observed du Tillet shifting uncomfortably in his saddle at Calvin's words. Only later would I understand why they so discomfited him.

Two days later we neared the city of Basel, in the realms of the freedom-loving cantons of the Swiss. In hopes of finding quiet solitude in that place, Calvin continued to answer to the name Lucanius. I secured, with the last of my coins, a modest stone cottage on the outskirts of the city in a district called St. Albins. Our hostess and landlady, the intrepid Mistress Klein, served as a formidable gatekeeper of that little house in St. Albins, and its tenant. Almost immediately Calvin set to work at his writing again. Feverishly did he labor. He sent me to seek out his good friend and co-conspirator from Paris, the former rector, Nicholas Cop. Basel was his home, where his father practiced medicine, where he now lived and preached without fear of persecution. It was little trouble discovering him, and when I declared my errand to him, he threw his arms about me with delight.

"But Master Calvin," I said, when he had done it, "expressly instructed me to ask you for silence as to his whereabouts. He labors without rest on his manuscript."

"I shall say nothing to anyone," said Cop, "but I must go to him, welcome him to Basel and to freedom."

Cop often visited. I think, though Calvin loved him, perhaps more often than Calvin desired. And he brought but a few others into the secret of Calvin's presence in the city. One Simon Grinee, Wolfgang Capito, the reformer Pierre Viret who would become the closest of friends with Calvin, and the Augustinian Couraut, onetime royal chaplain who had fled Paris for his life and had walked on foot all the way to Switzerland and freedom.

Basel was a free city, free from Roman superstition, from the Mass, from indulgences, and from prayers to saints, and free from all popish errors. Here Calvin thrived among an entire city of Christians whose faith was in Christ alone, who walked by faith alone, who lived by the Word of God alone. Here he studied to master Hebrew, but always he labored on with his manuscript.

"Why do you do it?" asked Cop one evening. "You labor unceasingly at your books as if a novice. I know not another man on this continent with such vast knowledge, yet you labor on for more, always reading, always writing. Why do you do it?"

"I count myself one of the number of those," replied Calvin, simply, "who write as they learn and learn as they write."

"So is it new knowledge that you learn?" asked du Tillet.

"No, indeed," said Calvin. I knew this was a sore point with him. "The enemies of truth call it 'new' and of 'recent birth,' and hence 'doubtful and uncertain' knowledge. They label us 'schismatics' who disturb the unity of the church with new things. But it is not so. All who call the doctrine of grace 'new' do great wrong to God, whose sacred Word does not deserve to be accused of novelty. What we preach and what I herein write is new to them insofar as Christ himself and his gospel are new. For all who believe that 'Jesus Christ died for our sins and rose again for our justification,' they will find nothing new in what I write."

"And what is the summation of what you are writing?" asked Viret.

"God has filled my mind with zeal," replied Calvin, "to spread his kingdom and to benefit his church by expounding the pure doctrines of godliness, so that, without stumbling, his church might believe and do what God desires. Hence, I intend it to be a work that will direct men to true wisdom. And all wisdom if it is to be called true, full wisdom, consists in the knowledge of God, and in the knowledge of ourselves. Man will never arrive at a clear knowledge of himself unless he holds up his weakness against the glory of God. Therefore, I intend to point men to a right understanding of the Word of God, to give them a pure theology based solely on the Holy Scriptures. I intend to dispel popish error and to show that the Bible reveals God as sovereign in his authority over all things in the world, in the individual, and in the church, that it is ours humbly to submit to his divine authority and joyfully to obey his revealed will."

"What will you call it?" asked Nicholas Cop.

"Since I mean it to be the summation of Christian piety and of whatever is essential to know of the doctrine of salvation, I mean to title it," said Calvin, the *Institutes of the Christian Religion.*"

"We must secure a printer, posthaste," said Cop. "And I know the man. Basel is a great city of printers, but none better and none more devoted to proclaiming the doctrine of grace than Thomas Plater."

"There is the matter of funds," said Calvin. "I have no money for food, much less for printing books."

"God shall provide," said Cop, "so, John, I have often heard you declare."

"To whom will you direct the dedicatory?" asked Viret.

Calvin, his eyes sad and gazing as if far away, was silent for several moments. I knew he must be inwardly mourning over the loss of so many of his secret congregation in Paris, of those he counted his friends, of none so dear as Etienne de la Forge. I could not bear to look upon such mourning, and turned away from him. What would he think of me if he knew of my great guilt in the death of his loved ones?

At last he spoke. "I shall dedicate it to Francis I, King of France. I intend to do my very best to appeal for the cessation of the cruelties and brutalities that he perpetrates against the faithful in his realm, and to vindicate from unjust affront my brethren whose death was precious in the sight of the Lord. I only hope that he shall one day soon read it and halt his pernicious violence against his own people and our dear brethren."

"May I?" asked Viret, reaching for the pages Calvin held.

"To his most Christian Majesty of France," read Viret. "Francis, to his prince and lord, John Calvin wishes peace and salvation in Christ. When I began this book I thought of nothing less, Sire, than to write things that would come before your Majesty. . . ."

We all sat transfixed at Calvin's words as Viret read them out.

"'I determined this writing should at the same time exhibit before you a confession of faith. May you learn from it what is the nature of this doctrine which drives the anger of the madmen to destroy your kingdom with fire and sword. . . . It is an outrage to pronounce blood-sentence against a teaching with which one is unfamiliar; fraud and betrayal to brand it without reason as revolutionary and hostile to the state. . . . It is up to you, Sire, not to turn away your heart and ears where such great matters are at stake: to maintain the honor of God on earth, to preserve the honor of truth, and to continue the kingdom of Christ among us. . . . Our God is not a God of anger but of peace. . . . Should it please your Majesty to read this confession, without ill will or wrath, then I hope we would regain your favor. Should this not happen because you leave the power in the hands of those who rage against us with dungeon, whip, torture, fire, and sword, so that we shall continue like sheep to be led to the slaughter, then shall we possess our souls in patience, waiting for the mighty hand of God, which, when the time is fulfilled, will appear armed to deliver us from our tribulation and to punish the proud and spiteful. The King of kings establish your throne in righteousness! Basel, 1 August, 1535.'"

"This is a mighty message," said Cop when Viret had finished reading.

When Calvin had put the final touches on his manuscript, with Cop's assistance, in 1536, Thomas Plater of Basel printed and bound many copies of the *Institutes of the Christian Religion*. It was astonishing to see the result. Within weeks copies of Calvin's book were freely sold throughout Switzerland and Germany, and by stealth and smuggling were copies made available in France and even across the sea in England and Scotland. It was soon known that Lucanius of Basel was really John Calvin, and so his quietude in Basel came to an end. Admiring visitors came to see him, to learn from his teaching, and he received letters in mounds, including admiring ones from his brother Antoine and sister Marie. I know of what I write, for it was my duty to carry all these letters from the city to our cottage in St. Albins, a backbreaking proposition it became.

One such letter came from the court of Ferrara in northern Italy, from the duchess of that small realm, Renee, sister to King Francis's wife, Queen Claudia. In her letter, Renee stated simply that she had been reading the Bible and that she had many questions. Moreover, her letter proceeded as a formal appeal for Calvin to come to her court and teach her and all her household with her. One does not lightly refuse a duchess, especially one with such close family connections to the court of France. Calvin was again restless, eager once again to find a place of solitude for scholarly pursuits. I was as always without rest, and so travel, activity, going to new places, seeing new things, even if on horseback, served as a welcome diversion to me. Hence, we saddled our horses and set out to be guests of honor in the court of a duchess.

29

A Violent World

IT WAS THE FIRST TIME that I had laid eyes on the splendors of the mighty mountains they call the Alps. I wondered as I gazed heavenward whether those who live and work in such mountainous regions do not have the advantage over the rest of us who dwell in valleys and plains. The towering splendor of these craggy edifices, shimmering with glaciers, had the effect of making me feel more keenly my own smallness, so overshadowed was I by their majestic heights. They were to my imagination grand cathedrals in the rough, designed and fabricated for my humiliation.

A different kind of splendor displayed itself to me when we at last arrived in the court of Renee of Ferrara.

"Constancy is rare among princes," observed Calvin as we reined in before the splendid ramparts of the royal castle of Ferrara.

I had not heretofore, nor since, dined with a duchess. She, of Ferrara, was a consummate hostess, and served the finest foods and wines. Court musicians played a concert of enchanting interwoven melodies on the *flute a bec* and on viols. And the duchess appeared to be an appreciator of the latest in Italian paintings. The wall of the great hall where we dined was decorated with painted depictions of grand buildings from Venice, and of contemplative men in Rome wearing flowing robes; there were portraits of people of status and wealth, and idyllic pastoral scenes from Florence that made the world look perfect, peaceful, almost heaven-like. In wonder, I gazed at these, musing on the skill of the artists, and longing to be transported into the world of those paintings.

"I have something, John Calvin, I want to show you," said the duchess when the platters and goblets had been cleared from the table.

As if on cue, a servant brought a large, very old-looking book to Renee, who extended it to Calvin.

Calvin received it with a nod of his head and opened it. He frowned and squinted at its words, I making free to look over his shoulder. It was no language with which I was familiar, and Calvin at first seemed equally baffled by its characters.

"Wycliffe," he said at last. "I have long wished to see this very book. Though I cannot read from it, nor, I am told, but few Englishmen can do so today. Can you read and understand it?"

"No, I cannot," said Renee. "But since my childhood I have been blessed with a governess, Madame de Soubise, who came to Ferrara from Wycliffe's England, bearing this Bible. She it was who taught me from its pages in my youth. And I am ever blessed by God for her doing so."

"So you have had no copy of the Bible in French?" asked Calvin.

"O, I do now," she replied. "At least I have a portion of it. When I lived in the court of Navarre, the venerable Jacques Lefevre d'Etaples gave me one from his own hands."

"And your husband?" said Calvin. "What thinks he of all your Bibles and the reading thereof?"

I must confess, she was a lovely woman to gaze upon. And I had myself dared to wonder why such as she did not have a doting husband at her side, or, if not married, why she did not have a line of suitors from here to Rome seeking her hand in marriage.

The duchess hesitated before replying, her face appearing sad, or was it a hint of fear that I detected?

"I was in my childhood first betrothed to Charles V, Holy Roman Emperor. When that was annulled, my father arranged an engagement to Henry VIII, King of England, but priorities of state alter, and so altered my marital expectations. It has been arranged that I should now be wed to the duke of Ferrara. So I live as his duchess here in Ferrara."

She paused, toying with a goblet, a pensive frown on her lips. "He is ever loyal to the church and to the pope," she said at last. "Hence, he ardently disapproves of my reading Holy Scripture. Alas, he disapproves of my entertaining guests such as John Calvin and the many others I have attempted to protect within these halls from the atrocities of my brother-in-law, King of France."

She blushed slightly and looked earnestly at Calvin as if for his approval. "I have taken the liberty of calling you Charles d'Espeville to my husband. I hope you do not object. If he knew who you really were, I fear it would not go well."

"I do not object," said Calvin. "I am sorry for your unhappiness. These are trying times for such as you." Then, signaling me with a nod of his head, he continued, "I have brought you a humble gift." I handed the copy of his *Institutes* to the duchess, bowing as I thought it appropriate. "It is my little book on the biblical doctrine of salvation," he explained. "In it I attempt to offer a confession of faith, a summation of the pure teachings of our true Christian faith. Perhaps it will be of assistance to you in your trials."

"I have heard of your little book, as you term it," she said, opening the *Institutes*. "I am most grateful and shall commence reading it this very night. But you must pray for me. Pray for Italy. There has, heretofore, been no Wycliffe for Italy, but I have made myself patron to the renowned scholar, Antonio Bruccioli."

"I have heard of the man," said Calvin.

"After several years of diligent labor," continued the duchess, "he completed an Italian translation of the Holy Scriptures in 1532. Even now faithful preachers risk their lives proclaiming the gospel from its pages. But there is great persecution. The pope, my brother-in-law, King of France....." Her voice trailed off. "My own husband. He it was who burned the preacher, our brother, Fanino Fanini, and dumped his ashes in the Po River. Others have died. More lie in prisons."

She told how for many months she had given protection to the court poet, Clement Marot, employing him as her secretary.

"He who translates and versifies the Psalter into French?" said Calvin with interest. "Is he here at present?"

"No. He has returned to the court of France," she said.

"To the court of France!" exclaimed du Tillet. "In doing so, does he return to the church of Rome?"

"I do not believe it possible of him," said the duchess. "My brother-in-law, King of France, has declared a peace, of sorts, and so Marot has returned."

"May God protect him from such a peace," said Calvin.

They spoke more of these things, and then the duchess implored Calvin to preach to her court. He proceeded to deliver a homily on Hebrews chapter ten. "Hold fast the confession of your hope, without wavering, for he who promised is faithful."

He concluded with this charge to the duchess and her court: "I implore you not to swerve from the straight path in order to comply with the world. Call upon God and trust his sufficiency to help you in this your sad infirmity. Ever meditate on his noble promises by which he will lift you up in hope of the glory of heaven."

I mused with some degree of anxiety on all the duchess had told of cruel death and imprisonment going on in her realm, and I wondered at her inviting Calvin to come. For my part, I longed to be away, and hoped we might make our way far from France and her dominions, some place safe, peaceful, with good food. I cared not whether I ever set foot in France again. I reflected on how ironic it was that I, by my vacillations and inconstancies, was now a fugitive from the very things I had perpetrated in Paris.

So it was that I detected something in Calvin's manner that led me to worry that he had it in his mind to return to France, perhaps to Paris. He spoke outwardly only of making his way back to Strasbourg, and I wondered whether Martin Bucer warning him to make some small time for recreation in the midst of the rigors of his studies had not hit its mark. I felt certain that if Calvin kept working, kept writing, kept preaching and teaching as he was that he could not long survive in this world. He was ever pale and sickly, and I knew that his digestion was not what it ought to be. He often grimaced while eating, and still more often in the hours after taking food.

To make our way north required us either to brave the precipices of the Alps or to pass through France. I wondered how difficult scaling the ice and rock of those forbiddingly steep mountains might be. Surely it would be better to take our risks there than with the savagery of the King of France, whatever promises of peace and safety such as he had extended. Calvin did not agree.

"Word afoot is," said Calvin, "Francis I declares a cessation of persecution, at least for a time."

"As a ploy to lure you into his net," said du Tillet.

"I cannot help but agree," I felt compelled to add.

"But my brother and sister," said Calvin, "the only surviving members of my family, they yet remain in France, and I fear for their safety."

I could not help thinking of the final days of my own family, and I felt it was right that he should want to assist his own, but at what risk?

"Paris holds no good for you," said du Tillet. "It would be best if never you set foot on the Champs-Elysees again."

I had encountered Calvin when he had made his mind up to do something. I knew that, whatever the risk, we were bound for France, Paris in all likelihood.

So we traveled mostly by night, blindly making our way through dark forests and sparsely populated villages, I always with a keen ear for the thundering hooves of the henchmen of the king, and with a heavy heart.

I shall not belabor the journey, for to do so forces recollections too painful of my own terrors at once again walking the streets of the place where I had committed such great crimes, and where I knew that I would most surely be destroyed, by either side, if ever I was exposed for my foul duplicity in it all. It is sufficient to record that Calvin, with tenderest joy and familial affection, enfolded his brother and sister into our little fugitive band, and then, with all speed, we made for Strasbourg and freedom.

If one were to examine a map of France, it would be simply impossible to reconcile the course of our journey. Calvin was a far better theologian and preacher than he was ever to be at efficient route finding. All this was, of course, because he had entirely different objectives than did I, and I believe du Tillet often agreed with my remonstrances. Calvin made his decisions about what city we would next make for, based on the urgings of faithful Christians who had last welcomed him into their homes, or barns, or wine cellars, or caves. So ours was a zigzagging tour, a crisscrossing of hostile territory, with Calvin frequently and ill-advisedly pausing to commit more of the very crime, preaching, for which the territory was so dangerous to us and, thus, rendering France all the more so with every passing day. Hence we were forced often to travel at night. In my memory, our travels in those weeks were to me a labyrinth of anxiety.

Then one early morning as we neared the environs of the city of Chalons-en-Champagne we became increasing aware that there was something odd in the air. In the waning night sky, I observed a glow on the horizon, orange and white, with patches where the glowing seemed to grow hotter, brighter, then recede, and then once again increase in brightness.

All the while, as we drew nearer, dumbly observing these things, there came a low rumbling, with deeper cataracts of sound, sound that could be felt more than heard, and deep within the core of our bodies did we feel it. As dawn began to break on the eastern horizon, the glowing became more difficult to observe, yet did we feel the low rumblings for a time.

"We had best discover a place for rest," said du Tillet. "I fear our way may be blocked by some mischief."

Yet did we find ourselves plodding ever nearer the odd glowing and rumbling before us. It was as if our footsteps were drawn against our wills. For my part, I felt a rush of excitement and longed to gain a vantage point and observe what lay in our path. We mounted a long wooded ridge that followed the eastern banks of a river, and as the morning dawned fully, we saw in the valley before us two vast armies arrayed against one another. Arrayed, I say, but at this hour it seemed that only one army was advancing.

It was a chaos of color, of smoke and fire, tents, cargo wagons, men at arms, men of horse, plumes, heraldic banners snapping in the breeze. And in a smoky wafting from all was the acrid stench of burning saltpeter, the explosive aromas of artillery, and the firearm they call the harquebus.

"It appears that the army to the south has suffered a crushing defeat," said Calvin, his face drawn and sober. He placed his arm about the slender shoulder of his sister Marie. "And the conqueror—if my eyes do not deceive me, flying the royal standard of the King of France—advances to the plunder."

"There lies the Swiss phalanx," said Calvin's brother, Antoine, excitement in his voice. "As one, they make a stand—in defense of the Hapsburg Charles V and his Holy Roman Empire, I am certain—with pikes leveled, to repel the cavalry charge of the French."

Fascinated, I watched and heard, for now we were close enough to hear the shouts and cries of battle. I breathed it in like some intoxicating aroma. From our vantage point I was easily deceived into feeling a sense of invincibility, as if those were not genuine men, engaged in genuine battle, a real-to-life death struggle, as if none of it mattered to me. I felt an overwhelming urge to shout and cheer for the Swiss as they made their desperate stand. Over and again did they level their pikes and repel the thundering cavalry of the French, men and horses impaled on their pikes and falling in death. The more of the French cavalry that fell the more their corpses formed an inadvertent defensive mound, behind which the Swiss could more easily defend their corner of the field.

"The Swiss fight not for the empire," observed du Tillet, who seemed to have assumed the detached manner of the tactical theorist as he watched. "Mercenaries, all, I should think, the premier export of the Swiss cantons, so it has long been. While the Spanish and German forces of the empire scatter for their lives, those sturdy Swiss will hold that corner of the field against the French in defense of their honor and their lives. You may count on it. A raw fashion in which to make one's living, but the disciplined Swiss have long bred stout warriors, to be sure."

"What is that?" I cried. I pointed to where a regiment of men appeared to be drawing, with cart horses, wheeled carriages nearer to the intrepid Swiss pike square.

"Cannon," said du Tillet, shortly. "Artillery at close range—'twill be a bad business, I fear, for the Swiss."

Meanwhile, as Calvin watched, his face grew more pale, and I am certain I observed, if not actual tears on his cheeks, nevertheless, the welling up of them within his eyelids. His sister buried her face in the folds of her brother's cloak, and he stroked her hair, speaking soothingly to her as he did so.

"May God have mercy on them," he whispered.

By this time the imperial cannons had been positioned in a broad arc, their mouths agape in the direction of the Swiss pikemen. An order must have been given for the cavalry to withdraw, for what remained of the men of horse suddenly reined about and ceased their attack.

"The poor doomed souls," said Calvin, his voice low. "They imagine themselves victorious. It is too much. We must get Marie clear of this."

I felt the gut-thundering report as the imperial cannonades put fire to their ordnance. For the first time, I began to feel that real men were fighting and that real men were dying in that valley.

"It is as if God plays at ninepins," said du Tillet, awe in his tone.

An apt description, for the cannonball entered that Swiss pike square like a ball rolled on a village green, mowing a path through the men as if they had been made of wooden game pins. Another rumbling, and another cannonball did its deadly work. By the time the last cannon roared, the Swiss who remained alive had fallen back in despair, their disciplined ranks shattered, their brothers and friends mangled on all sides. Mayhem followed. The Swiss had acted, whether intentionally or of necessity, as a rear guard, the last stand of men holding off the rage of the triumphant forces of Francis I and the French. When they fell, the French soldiers poured in like a wave of the sea when a dike has failed.

"I cannot bear to see any more," said Calvin. Marie was sobbing by this time.

I had heard of the ruin and devastation soldiers could effect as they overran the countryside in their fury. We were frightfully close to it all, and I was certain that those crazed soldiers would not hear when we attempted to explain that we had no part in this fight, were merely passersby, spectators, not participants. I felt certain none would stay his sword to hear such explanations, and I suddenly felt a rising panic in my bosom to be away.

"We must get clear of this," said du Tillet, pulling our map from within his tunic.

I looked over his shoulder as he studied the map.

"We must not go to Lyon, deeper into France," he said, then paused, biting his lower lip.

"Why do we not make our way here?" I said, pointing to the southwest end of a blue crescent that appeared on the map. "Geneva. Why not make our way there with all speed?"

Calvin looked on and said, "And from there we can continue north to Strasbourg. It seems a good plan."

So it was that we turned our backs on the slaughter of that battlefield and, for our lives, made our way toward Geneva.

30

Fiery Farel

EAGER TO PUT as much distance as we could between ourselves and that bloody battle rout, we arrived at the source of the Rhone River, Lac Leman, and the bustling commercial city of Geneva. The sun was painting the Jura Mountains a brilliant purple, and the breathtaking scene was duplicated by reflection on the deep waters of the lake.

"So this is Switzerland?" said Marie, her eyes wide with wonder and her mouth slack as she gazed at the unfolding beauty.

"It is," said du Tillet. "Switzerland it is, though the city of Geneva is almost entirely encircled by French lands, and if the king had his way, he would absorb it. We shall have more time for exploring later. We must find accommodations."

Winding our way steeply up the cobbles of the town, as we made to enter the guesthouse we had been directed to, suddenly a woman accosted us.

"Welcome to Geneva," she said, seeming to appraise us. She was an alluring feast for the eyes, I am forced to confess, and I was immediately flooded with arousing memories of Paris and my night revels. By her loosened manner of carrying herself, her stance, her flirtatious eyes, her silken voice, I knew her for a woman of ill repute, so those of her employment were generally termed.

She came near. I shall not say that she walked near, or strode near. It was more of a hovering or a floating, and I felt my pulse quicken. But she passed me by and made her way to Calvin, displaying herself before him as if she were a fine mare and this were market day.

"You look like someone who works too hard," she said in a soothing tone, making with her hands as if she wanted to caress his cheek. "Come with me, and I will give you pleasure."

I studied his face. Would he be moved, as I am forced to confess I was, by her seductions? Calvin was a man, with the anatomy of a man, the desires of a man, and she was—or had been—a lovely specimen of a woman, and was here offering her body to him for his sensual delights. I watched all this with the keenest of interest.

It would not accurately describe what transpired next for me to merely say that he resisted her advances because, for what she proffered to him, he had no such natural longings within his bosom. Such would misrepresent entirely what I observed that first night in Geneva. Calvin was, indeed, a man. And I could see in the flush that instantly inflamed his cheeks, and his sharp intake of breath, that he was not sensually unmoved by her.

But I saw that day that not only was Calvin a man, subject to the temptations of men, he was, in the profoundest sense, a man of God. I felt certain that had he been alone, without attendants, without brother or sister, had he known no other living soul in Geneva that night, had he and she been the only inhabitants of the planet, he would not have followed that pathetic young woman to her bed. He was a man of God, and as such he lived before the face of God. I observed this many times over the years that were to come. He was a man, true enough, but a man of integrity, a disciplined, self-controlled man of God. And I began that night hopelessly longing to be, in some small way, like him.

Drawing in breath, he looked heavenward and smiled. Then he recited the following: "All at once he follows her, as an ox goes to the slaughter, or as a stag is caught fast till an arrow pierces its liver; he does not know that it will cost him his life. Let not your heart turn aside to her ways; do not stray into her paths, for many a victim has she laid low, and all her slain are a mighty throng. Her house is the way to Sheol, going down to the chambers of death."

He then, master of himself, gazed into the painted eyes of that prostitute and said, "Leave your sins, dear woman, and live. Repent, and flee for mercy to Christ, for no adulterer shall have a place in the kingdom of heaven. But with Christ there is abundant mercy."

I looked on in awe at Calvin as we entered that guesthouse in the old town, and I felt that the conquest we had witnessed in battle that morning was something far less than what I had just witnessed on the street that evening.

Du Tillet disappeared soon after we settled in our rooms, claiming to be on an errand to fetch us food. When he returned not moments later, the door burst open, and with du Tillet came the oddest-looking fellow I believe I had ever seen. So frightful was he that Marie gave a squeal of alarm as he entered.

The man looked almost the ascetic, his scholar's robe shabby and threadbare, and his beard, untrimmed and draping carelessly down his chest, was a fiery red like that of a wild Celt. His face was speckled with blotches of pigment the color of his beard, and presumably his hair, though I could not be certain of this, for his head and ears were covered with a scholar's skull cap. Remarkable as were the rest of his features, it was his eyes that had a sort of terror about them, though a benevolent terror, if that is possible. They glowed like red-hot embers in a blacksmith's fire.

No sooner had he entered the room than his voice thundered, and I felt pity for the timbers of the little place. In all, the man burst into the room like a storming, breathing whirlwind. I felt certain that I was not the first person to feel the sensation I have described at his entrance.

"John, I have taken the liberty of—" du Tillet began, but it was no use. The man cut him off.

"John Calvin, is it?" cried the man. "I have only just completed reading your book, *Institutes of the Christian Religion*, and, by God's kind providence, here you are in Geneva. I am most honored to make your acquaintance."

"And you are?" said Calvin.

I thought he was behaving in something of a cooler manner than generally he did.

"William Farel is my name," said the big red man, though he did not speak in a fashion that is best described as merely saying anything. He fairly roared when he spoke. "God has guided your steps to Geneva," he continued, "a place where, God be praised, the city council has only recently cast its votes in favor of bringing reformation to this benighted city."

"When?" asked Calvin, his curiosity clearly piqued, but it was impossible not to detect his reserve at such a one as Farel.

"May 21, 1536, the citizens of this republic gathered in St. Pierre and swore on solemn oath that the gospel of Jesus Christ, without popes, Masses, idols, or indulgences, would alone be what guides faith and life in Geneva."

"A turning of events, indeed," said du Tillet. "It is now August and some months have elapsed. Does the work of reformation proceed with encouragement?"

"It is a vast work, in a vast city," replied Farel, "vast, I fear, with corruption, profanity, and sin. There is much work to do, far more than I can manage."

Here the man paused, looking intently at Calvin. "It is for this reason that I have come. I believe that God has called you, John Calvin, to undertake this work of reformation in Geneva with me."

Calvin stared back at the frightful-looking man for a moment before replying. "I am honored that you believe this," said Calvin. "But I am already engaged to travel north to Strasbourg, there to commence further studies. What is more, one such as I would be of little aid to you in this place."

"But surely you will consent to preach on the Sabbath," said Farel.

"We stop in Geneva but one night," said Calvin. "We must resume our travels on the morrow."

Farel's face broke into larger, more fiery red blotches than before, and his flaming eyes flashed in a terrific manner, not easy to describe. When again he spoke it was like a Jeremiah speaking. "You must not leave this place. It is clear to me that God has ordained you for this work. Hence, he has providentially brought you to this place this night. There is much he has for you to do in Geneva, and you are not leaving."

I studied Calvin's pale features. His eyes reminded me of those of a hare I had once caught on the banks of the Verses River in my youth, terrified eyes desperately searching for some means of escape.

Farel continued. "You have seen Geneva. Though the ignorance of Rome has been overthrown, and papal abuses exposed and condemned, there remains much work to be done. The monks and priests labor to regain their control, and libertines who mock religion abound on every corner. It is your gifts, John Calvin, that we need, your knowledge of Holy Scripture, your expositions of the Word of God, your teaching of the Bible to the wayward ignorant in this city, of which there is no shortage."

"Teach?" said Calvin. "Why am I so implored to teach? I who have need of learning? I must have quietude for study, for thinking. I am not fit to take up such duties in such a place. I must deepen my knowledge, learn from men who are far more fit to teach than am I: Bucer, Capito, Luther. I want to increase my learning before presuming to teach."

"But now is the time for doing," said Farel, holding up his hands as if fending off Calvin's words. "To sequester yourself and indulge in your contemplative study—it is to desert the cause of reformation in this city! I have good men like Froment and Viret who assist me, but they—good men that they are—have not your gifts and learning. And I am all bluster and impetuosity. I know it well. I have not your learning, your powers of reasoning. I can wail and threaten, I can entreat and cry down anathema, but I cannot carefully, systematically expound Holy Scripture as can you. I wonder whether any man can. I know all this well, and hence I entreat you. You must remain in Geneva."

I could see that Calvin was preparing for another line of defense, though it appeared to me that there could be no defense against such a man as William Farel.

"What you require for such a task is a man of energy, of vigor, and of strength," said Calvin. "A fighting man. But I am a man of weakness, ill health, and peace—a faint-hearted man. What you require in such a violent place as Geneva, is other than who I am. I will be of no help to you before the city council, before riotous crowds of libertines, before resentful priests and monks who plot to regain the city. I am not your man for these Genevans."

"Tearing wolves they are," cried Farel. "These Genevans, these Genevans! Yes, it is a riotous city. But like Thessoloniki of old, it will only be tamed by the Word of God, skillfully and faithfully expounded, taught and applied to the lives of these wicked, and so needy, people. There is much to do among these Genevans that you are, of all men, most gifted to do. God wills it! Put off your personal comforts and ambitions. Now is the day of battle. Geneva is the place of battle. The outcome is the kingdom of God. You must remain and fight!"

"In the name of God, man," said Calvin, the sweat breaking on his pale forehead now. "Allow me to serve God in a manner that is different from yours. Though you are the most pertinacious man, I cannot do what you demand."

Their voices by this time had risen to a pitch that gave me concern about our status in the guesthouse. Might not such an altercation, such vociferous dialogue, get us ejected from the inn? So I feared it. Yet did they persist, heedless of the racket their voices now made.

"John Calvin," said Farel, now pacing before him, "do you care to heed the will of God in this matter, or your own will?"

"No, it cannot be so," said Calvin, now twisting his fingers in his beard as he spoke.

Farel halted in his pacing, squaring his body before Calvin's. "If you refuse, then I denounce unto you, in the name of God Almighty, that if you depart under the pretext of continuing your studies and refuse to labor with me in this work of the Lord, God will curse your labors, he will damn your sequestration. On your rest and studies shall no blessing fall, only fearful cursing and flaming indignation."

I had been thoroughly convinced myself much earlier in this discourse that we were to be staying on in Geneva. There was always the matter of our purse, or lack thereof, and I began thinking that if Calvin was given a situation in Geneva, our financial troubles might be ended. But it took Farel's final denunciation to halt Calvin in his steps. He gazed up at the fiery Farel, his eyes welling with tears. I wasn't certain whether they were tears of intimidation, resignation, or simply of unmitigated terror at the man. Calvin stroked his pale, concave cheek and passed a hand over his brow. I knew of what he thought. There was to be no peaceful scholar's life, no quiet study, no behind-the-scenes role for John Calvin. By submitting to this violent preacher, Calvin knew what he was rendering up. And I could see in his eyes the tumultuous anguish it was causing him. Winding a fold of his robe in his long fingers, he sat gazing at the wall. Twisting and wrenching with his garment, I knew that he was actually wrestling with this man Farel, and wrestling with his own soul, and, perhaps, wrestling with God himself.

At last he unwound the fold of his robe, smoothed the wrinkled cloth with his hands, rose to his feet, and stood before the red-bearded prophet. Extending his right hand, he said, "Hereby, I denounce my will and obey God."

31

Geneva

WHEN THAT HANDSHAKE was concluded, things began happening in a flurry. Farel immediately secured permanent lodging for Calvin and, for the time being, his sister and brother. I was given a small servant quarters in the house. No sooner had we set our things down in our rooms and Farel commenced planning, excitedly developing a strategy for how best to employ Calvin in Geneva.

I feared for Calvin's health in those first days. Many a candle fizzled and had to be replaced in those early nights of discussion. Weary as I grew, there was something compelling about it all. There was an electricity, as it were, in the air. Surely, Farel's whirlwind persona, his unflinching obstinacy, his flaming passion for the progress of the gospel contributed to that atmosphere. But Calvin caught it, too. Once resolved, he entered into his new calling with unstinting zeal.

I shall always remember what Calvin said that first night, rather, in the early hours of that first morning. When Farel paused for breath in his exuberant strategizing, Calvin spoke.

"The subject to be taught is the Word of God," he said firmly.

"Absolutely, but on what themes will you commence?" asked Farel. "Now it is in my mind that Genevans need to hear—" Calvin cut him off.

"The best way to teach the Word of God," he said, "is by steady and methodical exposition, book after book, *lectio continua*. By continuous exposition, I am guaranteed to teach nothing but the whole counsel of God. By this method I am forced to address even those lesser desirable portions of God's revelation, and thereby neglect nothing. You have bullied me into preaching here in Geneva, and preach, by God's grace, I shall. Preaching is the living voice of God in his church. By it God begins and multiplies his church. It is only by means of his Word, by the faithful preaching of the grace of God alone, that the church is kept from perishing."

"And it is for this that I have so bullied you," said Farel.

The two men continued talking, but more of their time they spent praying, on their knees, praying the Scriptures back and forth, their voices rising and falling with earnest petition. I had heard Calvin explain to Farel, "Two things are united, teaching and praying; God would have him he has set as a teacher in his church to be assiduous in prayer."

Calvin refused to go with Farel to the city council that first week, reminding the man that he had promised to handle city council matters so that Calvin would be free to preach and teach.

"But you must send Jean-Louis," said Farel. "He can be your representative."

I nearly panicked and bolted from the room at the prospect.

"This is not France, my boy," said the big red man, clapping me on the back. "This is free Geneva. A free man has nothing to fear before free men."

I wondered whether I was, in fact, a free man. I felt very much as if I were not so. The city hall in Geneva was a grand edifice, with a massive hall surrounded by arched compartments that overlooked the proceedings below. I came to understand in an instant why Farel had referred to Genevans as tearing wolves. Every man was his own sovereign in that place, and there were shouts of defiance, bold-faced speeches, railing declarations, and all and every man had a voice, though there was at times so much racket no voice of any one man could be distinguished above another.

Until Farel rose to speak. I realized at once why it was that this man had so moved such free-thinking men as these city council members. For one thing he was louder than any of them. His voice thundered above the chaos, and soon all eyes were fixed on the red-bearded giant who stood before them.

"God in his kindness," he roared, "has sent us his servant John Calvin."

"Sounds French," hollered a fellow in the back.

"Yes, is he a Frenchman like yourself?" cried another.

"*Ille Gallus? Ille Gallus?*" More took up the cry.

"John Calvin is a fugitive of France," thundered Farel above them all. "Under sentence of death by the King of France. As are many of you! Whether he is French or not matters not at all. In an age of new learning and prodigious scholarship, however, there is no more gifted teacher than he. With so great a scholar in our midst, Geneva will become the envy of all Europe, and her city council shall be still more highly esteemed."

With his wit and rhetoric, Farel soon had the vote of the council to approve Calvin for employment as a teacher in this rambunctious place. Then they began haggling over how much they were to pay him.

"Scholars require little," said one.

"And he is not even a citizen of Geneva," said another.

"A Sonnentaler now and then for books and a bit of food should suffice," added another.

"Since a preacher serves God," declared one, "let God pay him!"

The council roared with mirth at this jest. At last it was agreed to install Calvin as preacher at the cathedral of St. Pierre and as lecturer in theology, to provide him with housing and a modest stipend, far too modest it sounded to my ears.

Therein commenced my new life in Switzerland. I had come to understand that my role, if role I had in Calvin's life, was to free him from all distractions so that he might study, read, write, preach, and teach. I entered into this role with the diligence and devotion of a penitent. I suppose it had now become for me, in my distorted and so-partial theology, a penitential means of grace to so attend him. Though I felt the disproportion of it all; so great were my crimes, and so hidden, and so little by comparison was my labor to amend them.

Calvin determined to preach through New Testament books at Sunday morning worship, and to preach through Old Testament books on weekday lectures. He commenced his Sabbath day preaching on the Epistles of St. Paul.

I accompanied Calvin that first day whereon he began his teaching in Geneva. It was a brisk September morning, the mists hovering over the broad expanse of Lac Leman, when we made our ascent to the cathedral. It was a sturdy structure, Roman-like, with few of the delicacies of the cathedral in Bourges, or of the unified splendors of Notre Dame in Paris. No flying buttresses, no vast stained-glass windows. Yet for its location alone, high atop the hillside overlooking the rooftops of the city and the stretching expanse of the lake, it had a magnificence that transcended other places of worship I had seen. It seemed that morning as if a gateway into truth and freedom, so I indulged in imagining.

Up the narrow cobbled streets we walked slowly, Farel speaking excitedly, gesturing, expostulating; Calvin quiet, meditative, and sober. I shall never forget my first time passing through the polished panels of the west doors and coming within the twelfth-century simplicity of the place. Stone vaulting, held firmly by grand columns, rose above us, as in many such medieval churches I had been in. I immediately noted, however, that this place of worship was fundamentally altered in one important respect. It was free of nearly all images; there were no clusters of candles burning before statues and shrines to saints; there was no smoky incense hovering about the capitals of the thick columns or curling its way in and through the circular candle lighting suspended high above and giving light to the nave and quire. There were no elaborate mural paintings of apocryphal scenes garishly decorating the walls. There was an unadorned, undistracted splendor about the place that, I confess, over time I grew to prefer, even to love.

A tentative crowd of freedom-loving Genevans had gathered to assess the new preacher; among them I observed many from the city council, presumably to pass judgment on the value of the new preacher. The nave was perhaps a bit more than half filled with worshipers that early autumn morning in 1536, and there was a reverent expectancy in the place.

After the singing of Psalm 100, and after an enthusiastic and booming introduction by Farel, Calvin, his Greek New Testament under his arm, walked to the pulpit. He hesitated for a brief moment at the foot of the carved circular stairway. I wonder whether he had any idea how many times over the next decades he would mount that very pulpit, his voice echoing off those very stones. Slowly, reverently, he mounted the pulpit stairs. When at last he arrived before the lectern, he set his book down, opened it to his text, then gazed out over the upturned faces of those standing before him. I seldom saw Calvin smile broadly or laugh hilariously, but he smiled that morning, in his own way, as he looked out over his new flock.

"We owe to the Scriptures the same reverence which we owe to God," he began. His voice, so unlike Farel's thundering, was, nevertheless, clear and penetrating, and rang with force off the ancient walls of that cathedral. "We owe this because the Word of God has proceeded from God alone. And it must, therefore, have nothing of man mixed with it. When the Word of God is faithfully preached in your hearing, dear people, it is as if God himself comes into the midst of us. May he do so this day.

"Hence, we must all be pupils of the Holy Scriptures, even to the end; even those, I mean, who are appointed to proclaim the Word. If we enter the pulpit, as I have done this day, it is on this condition, that we learn while teaching others. I am not speaking here merely that others may hear me; but I too, for my part, must be a pupil of God, and the word which goes forth from my lips must profit myself; otherwise, woe is me! The most accomplished in the Scriptures are fools, unless they acknowledge that they have need of God for their schoolmaster all the days of their lives."

Then he said, "Hear the Word of Christ," and began reading out his text, his voice clear, measured, and penetrating. "Blessed be the God and Father of our Lord Jesus Christ, who has blessed us with every spiritual blessing in the heavenly places in Christ, just as He chose us in Him before the foundation of the world, that we should be holy and without blame before Him in love, having predestined us to adoption as sons by Jesus Christ to Himself, according to the good pleasure of His will, to the praise of the glory of His grace, by which He made us accepted in the Beloved. In Him we have redemption through His blood, the forgiveness of sins, according to the riches of His grace which He made to abound toward us in all wisdom and prudence, having made known to us the mystery of His will, according to His good pleasure which He purposed in Himself. . . . In Him also we have obtained an inheritance, being predestined according to the purpose of Him who works all things according to the counsel of His will."

I would hear Calvin, verse-by-verse, word-by-word, expound on Paul's Epistle to the Ephesians many times over weeks and months in Geneva, and I was far from alone. More people filled the nave with every sermon he delivered. Many tradesmen and commoners and their families came to hear the Word of God in their own tongue. Others came as libertine critics, there to find grist for mocking him in the taverns over their ale, still others came as pietistic Anabaptists gathered to fault-find his doctrine, while others were miffed city council members there to inspect their investment in the advancing of the intellectual status of their city. But many more came, harried by persecutions from their homelands, as hungry refugees, thirsty for pure doctrine, eager to hear and heed what Calvin taught them from Holy Scripture. I was ever among all of these, and found myself at times troubled by his teaching, though I could not gainsay that he was true to his word, that what he delivered had nothing of man in it. I could not dispute this, though the king in my own bosom writhed and squirmed during many of his sermons.

I suppose it was for Calvin's unrelenting determination to proclaim, verse-by-verse, all of God's Word to God's people and to the citizens of Geneva that he would inevitably make enemies. For so he did.

While Calvin rested one day after teaching in the *auditoire* next to the cathedral, I indulged myself in a pint of beer at one of the public houses in the city. What I there overheard alarmed me for Calvin's sake and for Farel's.

"Fry me up a Farel fish for my supper," cried one fellow, too long at his ale.

"A Farel fish, is it?" said the barmaid, all the men roaring with laughter. "All leathery and fizzled like the man himself, coming up in a tootles."

I at first did not comprehend the charade that one fellow attempted. Much to the delight of his fellows, the man feigned a sober solemnity, making his cheeks sunken, taking great draughts of wine, his eyes downcast. Another stepped before him and asked, "In what passage of Holy Scripture did the Holy Spirit specify just how a fair maiden is to wear her hair?"

"Aye, and if Absalom had lived in this our once-fair city," added another, waggling his face to within an inch of the man's playacting to be Calvin, "would you not have marched him off to have his tresses shorn off?"

"Is it pale-as-death Lazarus?" said another, gasping in terror at the sight, "or just John of Noyon?"

More guffaws and hilarity burst about the public house.

One man took up his fiddle and, sawing away and stomping his feet, made more racket than what could be called music, with lyrics invented to mock the solemnities of the reformers and their message. One went like this:

This somber man from Gaul
Has built a ten-stone wall
Against our fun and games,
Our brothels and our dames.

There was more, pretty barbaric it was, and it forced on me an uncomfortable recollection of the carousing of my early days in Paris.

Though there were many in pleasure-loving Geneva who found much for which to criticize Calvin and Farel, yet were there still more in the city, and pouring into the city, who could not hear the preaching of the Word of God often enough. Hence, Calvin was pressed to commence a Bible conference that came to be called "the congregation" that met in the auditoire next to the cathedral on Fridays. This was eventually to expand beyond what any could have imagined, but I shall tell more of that if time permits.

In those early weeks in untamed Geneva, Calvin feared for the safety of his brother and sister and sought permission from Farel and the council to accompany them to Basel. Farel was at first suspicious.

"Will you turn aside after so soon a beginning?" he asked sternly.

"This is no turning aside," said Calvin with near-equal sternness. "Basel will provide a more suitable place for my sister Marie. Geneva is yet early in her reformation, and I desire to protect my sister and brother from the coarseness of this place. Besides, it is so near to France, and so desired by King Francis that I feel they would be safer the farther they are from here."

Farel gave his leave. I could tell when Calvin revisited the cottage at St. Albin's and secured lodging for Antoine and Marie in the good landlady Klein's house, that he longed to remain with them. But he had made his commitments and would keep them, though at times with great consternation. Once back in Geneva as the weather turned colder, Calvin fell ill with a violent cold, for which I retained the best doctor I could find in Geneva. The man administered endless fomentations and remedies, including twice the more drastic procedure of letting Calvin's blood. Meanwhile, sick or not, Calvin labored at translating his *Institutes* into French, all the while preparing sermons and preaching upwards of five times per week. Little wonder that he was taken with such a violent cold. But, God be praised, he recovered, though I do not know whether any of the physician's remedies had any role in that recovery.

Calvin had been preaching for scarcely six weeks in Geneva when a letter arrived from Viret. He had been visiting friends in Lausanne, and assessing the readiness for the preaching of the pure doctrine of grace in that lakeside city, when encouraging word arrived from the Council of Bern. He had eagerly written to Farel of the news.

"The city council of Lausanne has called for a disputation!" cried Farel one evening. "Viret has arranged everything. We are to go and debate with the Romanists. This is a glorious providence. Let us pray God shall deliver that city from the pernicious error of idolatry."

Lausanne was less than forty miles down the lake from Geneva, and it was thought most efficient to go by boat. Thus, before dawn, October 1, 1536, with expectation in the wind, we set sail on board a sturdy sailing craft bound for Lausanne. Little did I then know of how grateful I would be for the stoutness and the seaworthiness of that sailing craft.

32

Lausanne Debate

AS THE SUN ROSE, dissolving the chilly mist, it sparkled blindingly off the water, as if a giant had scattered precious gemstones on the surface of the lake, and we sailing gently through a sea of mystic diamonds. For the first hour. Suddenly we encountered autumn winds rushing like a fury down the Jura mountains to the north and west of our course. Such winds gave us speed, frightful speed, to be sure, but they also gave us waves that made me think of Jonah, storm-tossed for fleeing the command of the Lord.

My sailing experience had, heretofore, been restricted to small river craft in calm water. This was something otherwise entirely. As the wind howled in the rigging and the sailors took reefs in the main and mizzen sails, I clung in earnest to the gunwales of the heeling vessel for my life. The craft strained and groaned as we crested the foaming waves, then, hesitating for an instant as if to torment me with the prospect, plunged into the gaping troughs of those seas.

Somehow gazing from the steps of St. Pierre in Geneva at what had from that firm vantage point appeared to be flat water on a tranquil inland lake had ill prepared me for the unsettling turbulence of what I then experienced.

Words are inadequate to describe the relief I felt when at last the sailors doused the sails and secured the vessel to the *place du port* in Ouchy, and I was once again standing on fixed and unmoving earth, though for a time the pavement under my feet seemed as if to roll and crest like the waves of Lac Leman.

Good Pastor Viret met us at the pier, and escorted us to our guesthouse and evening repast. After a sumptuous dinner of *coquelet aux morilles, poisson du lac, fondue au fromage Suisse,* and *vin du Rhone,* I fell into my bed and slept. I suspect, though I was not conscious to know this, that Calvin slept considerably less than I, he praying, no doubt, as I observed him doing often, and more and more in Geneva, and perhaps reciting to himself principal passages that he intended to use in debate in the days ahead.

Early the next morning, October 2, 1536, still rubbing sleep from my eyes, I followed as Viret led us from our guesthouse on Rue Cite-Derriere to the site chosen for the debate. The sun rose, brilliantly illuminating the many spires of the grand cathedral of Lausanne. High atop the city, it rose as a magnificent specimen of gothic architecture, one of the finest I had seen, and it dominated with splendor the skyline of that tidy city.

As we neared the cathedral, it was obvious that this was to be no small gathering. Crowds of people converged on the steps, waiting to enter the massive doors. Bells from high atop the west tower rang unceasingly, echoing throughout the narrow streets and rows of medieval houses that surrounded the great church. I wondered whether that ringing sounded ominous and foreboding in the ears of the nervous papists there gathered that day.

We left behind the more festive atmosphere in the plaza before the cathedral as we entered. Within, we were met with a breathtaking masterpiece of the medieval cathedral builder. The vaulted nave into which we entered was flooded with brilliant morning sunlight glittering colorfully through large stained-glass windows on the south side of the cathedral. Far more light illuminated Lausanne's cathedral than in Geneva's, and the effect was astounding. Speckled with elongated shafts of colored light, the vast columns separating the nave from the ambulatory were decorated with intricate paintings in reds and yellows.

The corridors of the ambulatory were crammed with curious onlookers from all walks of life. Not a few peasants, many tradesmen had shut up their shops for the opening of the debate, and there were a number of black-robed students from the university. Midway in the nave opposing chairs had been placed, and these were now filling up with delegates from Bern, all resplendent in official gowns of red and black, with lawyers expert in canon law, and with a staggering army of Roman priests, to my count, no less than one hundred seventy-four of them. On our side, Calvin's side, there sat but three participants who were to defend the reformation cause against so vast an array of papal clerics and doctors of theology.

Farel and Viret arranged stacks of books before themselves, ready at hand for quick reference when needed. The principal Roman delegates, led by the apologist Blancherose, did the same. Meanwhile, Calvin sat himself down calmly in his chair before a table with nothing but a copy of his cousin Olivetan's French Bible, yet incomplete, and so, unbound.

There were formalities aplenty that opening day of the debate, so much so that I began to be bored with it all and gazed at the stone magnificence all about me, speculating on the motivations of its designers and builders. Conspicuously absent at his clerical seat, the cathedral, was the Roman bishop, who, perhaps out of dread at the outcome, had made the decision not to attend. A brief edict from the Holy Roman Emperor, Charles V, forbidding the debate, was indifferently read out, and as indifferently disregarded.

When at last the battle was to be engaged, it was fiery Farel who lobbed the first cannonball, in a manner of speaking. My stomach churned. How was our side, I had come to term it so, how was our side to stand against so vast an opposition?

"Speak straight from the shoulder!" thundered Farel, his voice reverberating off the stone vaulting, echoing here and there. Confident in their numbers, nevertheless, at his voice the Roman doctors came to attention. "We do not here engage in disputation with galleys, fire, and sword, prison and torture awaiting! This is not Rome! It is not France! We have no hangmen for preconceived opinions. We do here debate the truth. Let Holy Scripture alone be the final judicatory. If the truth be on your side, step forth!"

I smiled at his words. There was no one better suited to deliver such a salvo than Farel. It was what he did so well. For the duration of that first day, Farel railed against abuses in the church, copiously citing example after example of priestly philandering, of money-grubbing friars, of papal incompetence, and of the shameful ignorance of the priesthood, especially ignorance of the Holy Scriptures. From there he proceeded to decry idolatry.

"And there is no better illustration thereof," he cried, pointing toward the chancel and the high altar of the cathedral, "than your pagan veneration of the golden Virgin given the central place in what is supposed to be this House of God. From many poor men's purses, throughout the centuries, has Rome defrauded the price to adore this base idol!"

For three days it went, Farel and Viret answering all questions, rebutting all argument, with the topics becoming more substantive, more theological in character. Meanwhile Calvin sat before his empty table, silent, not offering so much as a single word.

"Why do you not speak?" asked Farel over dinner.

"You and Viret need no assistance. You answer with force and power, for thus proceeds the debate. I am well content to hear your replies."

"But you, John Calvin," cried Farel, "you who penned the *Institutes*, you have such vast knowledge of Holy Scripture, why must you have still greater reluctance?"

Calvin merely smiled and dipped a hunk of bread in the pot of simmering cheese before us.

But the next day was different. The foremost apologist for the teachings of Rome, a priest called Mimard, rose and gave an elaborate defense of the transubstantiation of the Mass.

"For was it not Christ himself who declared, 'This is my body'? And was it not Christ himself who declared, 'This is my blood?' *Ergo*, the common elements of bread and wine are, by the unequivocal declaration of the Son of God himself, transubstantiated by the intercession of the priest in the miracle of the Mass into the very body and blood of Jesus Christ. Moreover, so the Holy Church Fathers have always taught, and so the church has always practiced."

Farel's chair legs scraped on the flagstone floor as he made to rise and thunder a reply. I was pretty certain he would declare the opinions of the Church Fathers of no value, for this debate was to be about the teachings of Holy Scripture. I had heard him so speak already.

But Mimard was not finished. "But what the Holy Church Fathers have always taught is of no concern to you innovators, now is it? It is in my mind that reformers like you care nothing for Augustine and the Holy Fathers. Did I say, 'care nothing'? I believe I did. Forgive me. I have misspoken, and in so doing I misrepresented these esteemed doctors who sit before us in this exalted place."

He stepped from behind his table and stood triumphantly before Farel, Viret, and Calvin.

"It is not a matter of caring nothing for the Church Fathers. One must know something in order to care one way or another about the thing under consideration. No, you upstart innovators in religion, you *know* nothing of the Church Fathers. There, I have said it. Nothing at all. You care nothing, because you know nothing!"

Farel had risen from his chair, fists clenched, his mouth open, but before he uttered a word, Calvin silently rose. I observed all of this from close at hand, from under one of the archways between the nave and the ambulatory.

Calvin appeared frail next to the giant Farel, but he stood erect and looked steadily back at the scornful eyes of Mimard. Farel returned to his chair.

"If Christ is sacrificed in each and every Mass," said Calvin, "he must be cruelly slain in a thousand places at every moment. This is not my argument, nor is it an innovation. It is the apostle's argument in Hebrews 9:25–26, in Holy Scripture. But I have forgotten. Mimard prefers the Church Fathers to the apostles. Forgive me. Honor to the Holy Church Fathers. You declare that they have all taught your transubstantiation of the Mass. It is a pity that you are not more carefully and thoroughly read in them. Allow me to elucidate from their writings."

Farel and Viret were frantically pawing through their books, Farel extending an open copy of Chrysostom. Calvin ignored it.

"Mimard is undoubtedly aware of what Gregory of Nazianzus, in his treatise *To Amphilochius*, declared concerning the apostle's own utterances, that they cry out a hundred times that the Supper is without blood."

Calvin proceeded to recite freely from Gregory, "from his thirty-seventh argument, if my memory serves," he declared when he concluded his recitation. Then he proceeded to expound on what Gregory had written.

"I ask the Mass-doctors here present," continued Calvin, looking from Mimard to the one hundred seventy-three other priests, "how they can believe that God is pleased with a way of celebrating the Supper of our Lord in a manner for which there is not one syllable of scriptural support? Ah, but I forget myself. You are the ones who care more, because you know more, for the opinions of the Holy Fathers of the church."

He turned, waving off another tome extended to him, this time by Viret.

"Yet was it Augustine, *Against Faustus*, the twentieth chapter, I believe, who declared that 'the Christian, by the most holy offering and partaking of the body of Christ, does so as a remembrance of a sacrifice already made.' Where is your erroneous innovation of transubstantiation in Augustine? Or in Fulgentius, *De fide*, chapter nineteen, if I am not mistaken—you do remember Fulgentius, the bishop of Ruspe in Africa who died, I believe, in AD 533?—he it was who declared, 'In this sacrifice are thanksgiving for and remembrance of Christ's flesh, which he offered for us, and of his blood, which he shed for us.' Remembrances and thanksgivings, not literal meat and blood."

311

I looked at the blank faces of the priests. It was in my mind that few if any of them had ever heard of a Church Father called Fulgentius, let alone read, what is more, could recall at will, any of his writings. But Calvin was just warming to his argument.

"Or consider Chrysostom's *Homilies on Hebrews* wherein he states—I might add, Augustine agreeing in his rebuttal to the *Letter of Parmenianus*—'it would be the voice of Antichrist to say that a bishop is intercessor between God and man.'"

Never once consulting any of the books proffered him by Farel and Viret, who soon gave up the effort, Calvin cited freely from Tertullian, cross-referencing to Chrysostom, then back to Augustine "in his book against the Manichean heresy, approximately the middle of his argument." And all by memory, without book or manuscript before him. I had, of course, seen Calvin do this kind of thing before, in Orleans, in Bourges, in Paris, but the force and wit of his recitations and expositions of the Church Fathers that day was unrivalled.

The people crammed into that church fell absolutely silent as Calvin spoke. Even those who understood not a word of his Latin, comprehended by his manner, his tone, and by the astonishment of those who did understand his words, that extraordinary things were occurring in that place.

"Judge for yourselves," continued Calvin, sounding much like a lawyer making his closing arguments. "Who are the innovators? Who are the ones who are ignorant, not only of Holy Scripture, but of the Church Fathers? Confess that you have hardly seen the bindings of their works.

"But why do I seek proofs from men? The Scripture alone is sufficient. The Lord's Supper cannot be without a sacrifice, in which, while we proclaim his death and give thanks, we do nothing but offer a sacrifice of praise. Nor do we, his royal priesthood, come before God without an intercessor. The Mediator interceding for us is Christ, by whom we offer ourselves to the Father. He is our pontiff, who has entered the heavenly sanctuary and opens the way for us to enter. He is the altar on which we lay our gifts. Thus, we are bound to our Savior, by grace alone, through his body and blood, by a spiritual communion which binds us through a spiritual bond, the bond of the Holy Spirit—that is the Lord's Supper."

Calvin took one last look at Mimard, wiped his brow, and sat down. At least a full hour had elapsed since he had begun speaking. Now utter silence filled the place. No one wanted to move, to speak, to break the spell of the moment. Farel sat rooted in his chair. Mimard would not meet Calvin's eye, nor the eyes of his companions on his side of the nave.

Then an extraordinary thing occurred. A man rose to his feet, a Franciscan by his habit, and awkwardly he made to speak. I later learned he was one of the foremost preaching friars in the Canton Vaud, known for his eloquence and his staunch defense of the Roman doctrines.

"It seems to me," he began, clearing his throat loudly to continue, "that the sin against the Spirit which the Scriptures speak of is the stubbornness which rebels against manifest truth. In accordance with that which I have heard, I confess to be guilty, because of ignorance I have lived in error and I have spread the wrong teaching. I ask God's pardon for everything I have said and done against his honor." He paused as if to regain composure. Then looking about the faces in the cathedral, he continued. "And I ask the pardon of all of you people for the offense which I gave with my preaching up until now. I defrock myself henceforth to follow Christ and his pure doctrine alone!"

Seven days were scheduled for the debate, and duly endured by the clerics of Rome, but after that fourth day, when Calvin first spoke, it had been over, and not a soul in the place thought otherwise. One of the first events to follow the debate was the tearing down of the idol of the golden Virgin. It was hauled to Bern and there broken up, melted, and minted into gold coins. There was great rejoicing in the city and throughout the Canton Vaud, as the region was called. Houses of prostitution were closed, whores who cared not for their souls were expelled from the city. Within a few months two hundred priests, like the Friar Jean Tandy, as I learned his name, confessed their sins, and professed their faith in Christ alone for salvation. Among these were some of the most ardent defenders of the doctrines of Rome in the canton—including Calvin's nemesis Mimard.

33

Banished!

WHEN WE RETURNED to Geneva, Calvin threw himself into the work with zeal. Not satisfied with merely preaching at least six times a week and his work on the translation of his *Institutes* into French, he labored to prepare a catechism for the instruction of children in the chief articles of pure religion, and he began work on a formal doctrinal statement to be proposed before the City Council—by Farel.

"We confess our faith based alone on Holy Scriptures, without any additions from human wisdom," so his proposed confession began. It would be up to Farel to see it approved by the council.

Meanwhile, unholy factions and unresolved disputes waged between influential families in Geneva, libertines on the council opposed Calvin and his preaching, and Anabaptists leveled accusations of heresy against him. Though rending beasts of various species encircled him, yet did Calvin quietly study the Scriptures and faithfully climb the spiral staircase into the pulpit and deliver the Word of God to that turbulent city.

Winter came on, and the first snowfall covered the Jura mountains like a confectioner's sugar finely dusting a birthday cake. Though I had rejoiced at our victory in Lausanne, and still more as news of the conversion of many priests and monks came to our attention in Geneva over the subsequent months, yet did I continue to believe that such joys, such liberating conversions were for the souls of others and not for mine. I believe there was not a single sermon or lecture that Calvin delivered, either in the cathedral or in the auditoire that stood next to it, that I did not attend. As if by some penitential compulsion, I went. What Calvin preached on the free grace of God and forgiveness, as he so often did, sweet though it sounded in my ears, was for others to imbibe; while all he preached on God's holy judgment and wrath ever filled my bitter cup, and I drank it to the dregs. Deeply troubled was I by those sermons, yet did I, as if at a whipping post, stand and hear them.

In a letter to his old friend Francis Daniel, Calvin rejoiced at the progress of the gospel in Switzerland, but he also lamented the lack of pastors. I read his mail far less in these days, feeling that doing so added to my already great condemnation, but at times he would dictate letters to me and I would actually set quill to paper on his behalf. Such a time was this. "You can hardly believe the small number of ministers compared with the very many churches that need pastors. If the idle bellies with you, who chirp together so sweetly in the shade, were only as well disposed as they are talkative, they would instantly flock hither to take on themselves a share of the labor, to which we must be inadequate, since there are so few of us. How I wish, seeing the extreme necessity of the church, that, however few they may be in number, there were at least some right-hearted men among you who would be induced to lend a helping hand. May the Lord preserve you."

Farel had formed a consistory of spiritually minded leadership in the church, small though it was. These men gathered on Thursday evenings, in the warmer months in the auditoire, but in the colder ones in our rooms.

"*Ille Gallus!*" cried Farel at one meeting of the consistory. "Why do you prefer to be known as Ille Gallus, why so prefer the shade? The council believes that your confession of faith, penned by your hand, is mine. I have remonstrated and told them repeatedly that it is the work of John Calvin. Yet do they render you no credit."

"If we served ourselves or other men, good Farel," said Calvin, "we would be poorly rewarded, indeed. It is of no importance. But now, I implore you, present to the mayor and the council this little catechism."

He handed a sheaf of papers to Farel.

"Couraut has reviewed it and made his additions and comments, as have you. It is needful for the nurture of the spiritually ignorant and for the children of this place."

Farel proceeded to read it out before the small group of pastors. I looked about the table. They were, indeed, few, and Couraut was aged and now totally blind, though keen of ear and mind, and devout of heart. Calvin's lament at how few they were in so vast and unruly a city was well-founded.

"Long for the spiritual milk," read Farel, "as newborn babes, being ready always to give answer to every man that asks you a reason concerning the hope that is in you." So it began.

"We believe that all the elect are united in one church, one communion, one people of God, whose prince and leader is our Lord, Christ. All the elect of God are to be united and bound to

Christ their head, that as members of one body they grow with him and have the same faith, the same hope, the same love, and, therefore, also the same spirit of God, and have been called to the same inheritance of eternal life."

July 20, 1537, Farel presented Calvin's confession and catechism before the City Council of Geneva. It was heatedly debated for hours, railed against by the libertine factions, but hailed as a spiritual triumph by the devout mayor of the city, Ami Porral, and many others.

I shall explain in as few words as possible my understanding of what transpired over the nine tumultuous months that followed that day. As a consequence of confessional church law being adopted by the civil government in Geneva, moral laws were imposed by the magistrates on a citizenry more eager for the moral and spiritual transformation of their society in theory than in practice.

Ironically, it was a city councilman to be reprimanded first under those new laws, and after him a citizen of high regard, Matthieu Manlich, was punished by the council. A jester who frequently performed masquerades on the streets of the city was punished for public indecency by being forced to publicly kneel on the stone floor of St. Pierre for an hour. Another who refused to close the doors of his gambling establishment was placed in the pillory for an hour, his neck draped with a halter of playing cards. An adulterous couple, caught in the very act, were led in shame by a bailiff through the streets of the city for their crime. Others were reprimanded by the council for debauchery, drunkenness, or theft, or for failing to send their children to school.

I worried for the outcome of such reforms. I had never lived in or heard of a place with such mild forms of punishment. I, who had frequently been whipped in my apprenticeship, did not know such a place existed. Yet did I fear anarchy would be close on the heels of such benign justice. In Paris, in Noyon, in every other city I had heard of, punishments were far more severe. When a thief was caught, his hand was promptly chopped off; if he stole again, he would be hanged; when a man became known for seduction, he was castrated; when an adulterous woman was exposed for her harlotries, her nipples were snipped off; when a man cheated at his trade, he could be branded on the face, or his nostrils slit; when one was accused of treason, he was tortured and publicly hanged or burned. No, these Genevan laws were far too mild when compared with all other civil laws and punishments of which I was aware.

Yet did the libertines and the Romanists rail at such imposed morality, as they termed it. The commoner in Geneva, however, the fisherman and his wife and children who faithfully attended worship at St. Pierre, the vinedresser and his family who heard and heeded Calvin's preaching, the ordinary Christian family delighted in the new laws. By them Geneva would become a haven of the family, a haven for women, a haven for religious fugitives, a haven of opportunity for the honest, upright man.

"Do you follow the oppressive strictures of the foreign clergy who rule our city?" one man might ask another on the streets; I often heard thus. The German-Swiss citizens who lived on the Rue des Allemands made a pact to oppose the foreigners. One day in the street, I witnessed a blasphemous caricature of Calvin administering the Lord's Supper. The jongleur who played Calvin narrowed his eyes and attempted to make his cheeks sunken. In this fashion he looked with terror into the crowds, shaking his head dismally at each face, and finally passing over everyone; then the fool feigned eating and drinking the elements alone. Far too many in the crowd broke into hilarity at the dramatic farce.

In February 1538, Mayor Ami Porral was ousted and new council members were elected. The new civil leadership in Geneva stood staunchly against Calvin, Farel, and the reformation of the city. Outspoken libertines, though they were far from the majority, now unleashed their fury on the preachers.

I awoke with a start one cold March night. The rain driven by wind off the lake had beaten against the windows through the night, but what had awakened me was a new sound. I jumped from my bed and listened. A clatter of stones, then shattering glass. Calvin had heard it and joined me in the sitting room. I observed that only one pane had been broken as I flung open the window.

What I saw were the upturned faces of a band of street revelers, their cheeks flushed with wine. One of them emitted a prolonged belching, to the amusement of his fellows. "We hash come," he slurred, "to sh-erenade his Majesty, J-John Calvin. We hear that heesh departing our fair city. Thish ish a departing song."

What followed could hardly qualify as singing. I had heard more tuneful bawling and cowbell clanging from the bovine in the pastures surrounding the city. When the next morning Andre the town fool was led before our rooms with cries of "La parole d'Andre," I could only speculate at the meaning. Instead of the Word of God, these libertines were acting as heralds to the word of the village fool, whose word, they apparently desired to convey, they preferred to Calvin's preaching.

Farel appealed to the City Council to pass a resolution forbidding the singing of songs in mockery of citizens of Geneva. Of course, this excluded Calvin and Farel who were French subjects in exile and not citizens of the republic of Geneva. Nevertheless, did the libertines resent being told how they might sing in their drunken revels. Easter approached and the turmoil mounted in the city.

"These Genevans!" blustered Farel. "These Genevans! They break off every appearance of peace by their lack of self-control. They tear us in pieces, publicly and privately, so as to make us a stench to all."

"We are in God's hands," said Calvin. "These men are not able to afflict us except for God's good purpose and by his permission. Let us, without retaliation, consider what God has for us in this affliction. And let us humble ourselves, lest we strive with God."

"Yet, I fear," said Farel, "that we must make plans in the event of an emergency."

"Flee?" said Calvin. "It may come to that. But it grieves me sorely that my companion and friend Louis du Tillet has fled."

"Fled?" said Farel. "I fear he has done more than that. But what of our immediate concerns? Is it possible that such as we are now in this so-troubled city, is it possible to celebrate the Supper?"

"In the thanksgiving of the Lord's Supper," said Calvin, "are included all the duties of love. When we in the love feast embrace our brethren in these duties, we honor the Lord himself in the feast."

"The duties of love?" said Farel. "There is no embracing among our brethren in such duties. Not in this place at this time. We would be serving damnation to most, not thanksgiving and love. But what of preaching? The council has forbidden you and me to step into our pulpits and preach. What are we to do?"

"God's truth is to be asserted against false accusers," said Calvin, "who evade it by their shifts. Of this today we have abundant experience in our great efforts to rout the enemies of pure and wholesome doctrine. With such crooked and sinuous twisting these slippery snakes glide away unless they are boldly pursued, caught, and crushed."

"So we must preach," said Farel.

"Our summons into these pulpits came not from men," agreed Calvin, "but from God. Therefore, we will preach his Word to his people, let come what may."

That night rocks beat against the shutters, and poundings came upon our door. "Into the Rhone with the foreign traitors!" A gathering throng took up the chant. "Into the Rhone with the foreign traitors!" I confess that I slept little and very ill. And I must confess that, while Calvin spent the night in prayer, on his knees, I spent it shivering in my bedclothes, covering my ears at the terrors without. Then in the early hours of the morning, I heard the unnerving concussion of a harquebus discharged at close range on the street beneath our windows. After a brief pause, another, and then another. I was nearly unhinged by the incessant rumbling of that firearm. Sixty discharges, if I did not miscount in my disordered state of mind.

Then came the morning, Easter morning. I half expected to see a siege work barricading the narrow street that led from our house to St. Pierre. I knew that Calvin had determined to defy the council and preach, but I wondered what the outcome of that day's defiance would be. St. Pierre was crowded with people. To be sure, some had entered the church to worship and celebrate the resurrection of Christ. Yet many, by their scowls and murmurings, had awakened that Easter morning to decry Calvin and his gospel of grace.

Calvin, as was his habit, climbed the steps of the pulpit deliberately and with solemnity. I wondered whether it prefigured him

mounting the steps of a scaffold, for in this act he was defying
the civil authority of Geneva, made up of men who, like hungry
wolves, had been waiting for him to fall into their jaws. I observed
a number of men standing in the nave wearing a dagger or a sword
at the hip, and I fretted at the knowledge of this, and wished I
might give warning.

Ignoring the rabble in the crowd, Calvin read out his text from
Holy Scripture and preached the gospel. No listener hearing his
sermon on John's Gospel chapter fifteen would have known that
in the act of preaching, the man delivering the sermon had defied
the City Council, had been threatened with gunshots through the
night, had been taunted and shamefully abused by enemies on
every hand. In but one place in his message did he make reference
to the crisis.

"Before all of you we testify that it is not a question of leavened
or unleavened bread that prevents us from celebrating with you the
Lord's Supper. Think of the strife, the revolts against the gospel,
the blasphemy that prevails among you. Think of the manifold
defiance against the Word of God and the Lord's Supper."

I felt my pulse quickening as Calvin neared the conclusion of
his sermon. What would happen next? Would he be set upon and
torn apart by the mob that had come to discredit him, to seize
him for his defiance? When Calvin pronounced the benediction
and descended the pulpit, I moved to his side, though there was
little I could do, unarmed as I was. However, no hostile hands
reached out to him; no swords were brandished; none shouted
out, railed, or cursed at him.

That afternoon, though, when Calvin preached in the Franciscan chapel, all the pent-up chaos broke free. My hands ached
for a stout sword that afternoon. Many others gathered around

Calvin with me as if to make a human shield against his foes. No sooner had he begun to preach than his words were drowned out by the shouts and cries of libertines, by the blows of fists on jaws and torsos, by the shying of steel and the clanging of sword fighting, all in a house of God, on a Sabbath day, on Easter Sunday, while the Word of God was being preached by a servant of God. Remarkably, though there were many bruises and blackened eyes, not one man was wounded to the point of shedding blood.

Monday, the council met and heard the testimony of those who rose to accuse Calvin and Farel. All efforts to address the real problem, the libertine hatred of truth and morality, were hastily silenced. "These foreign clergymen have defied the council. They have preached despite the prohibition."

That Monday in 1538, with a stroke of the magisterial quill, Calvin and Farel were officially banished from Geneva. They were to quit the city within three days. One day was too many as far as I was concerned. I could not help resenting the place and all connected to it. I could not help looking darkly in Farel's direction, for he it was who called down damnation on Calvin if he would not remain and serve in the city with him. And it had come to this. I was angry with everything Genevan that day.

April 25, 1538, leading blind Couraut with us, we trudged north. Calvin and Farel were determined to go to Bern and Zurich, there to raise support for their reinstatement in Geneva. To my mind, this was more Farel's plan than Calvin's. After encountering the dizzying twists and turns of Swiss politics, I began to notice a change in Calvin's manner. The Bernese Council sent a delegation with Calvin and Farel back to Geneva. The City Council of Geneva called a special session to hear the appeal. When it came down to a vote, hands raised against reinstatement far exceeded those in favor. "Kill them!" cried libertines on the council, drawing their swords and making after the Bernese delegates.

The die was cast. There was no hope for Calvin and Farel except in flight. Farel halted on the outskirts of Geneva, bent down, and removed first his left shoe and then his right shoe. "I beat the dust of Geneva from off my feet," he said viciously pounding his shoes together. Then we turned, a sorry, dejected little band, and trudged off. When we first set out, I am not certain either Farel or Calvin knew where we were heading.

"Your brother and sister remain in Basel," said Farel. "And there is always Strasbourg. Bucer is forever attempting to woo you to that city. Your preaching would be well received by the Germans. I am certain of it."

Calvin halted and turned to his friend. "Above all I fear to return to the yoke from which I have only just been freed. In Geneva God's call held me bound. Now freed from that calling, I fear I would tempt God were I to assume again a pastoral burden which, as I have discovered, is unbearable to me."

Farel frowned deeply at Calvin's words.

"And where will you go?" asked Calvin.

"I may return to Neuchâtel. It is not so strategic a city as Geneva, nor is it so furious and untamed. But for now, let us make for Basel."

The more miles we traversed the lighter seemed Calvin's step. There was a look of profound relief on his features, and he breathed in the crisp spring air like a man newly released from a foul, stinking dungeon. I knew what he was thinking. At last he was free from the calling of a public life as minister in the church. None could accuse him of talking and not acting. None could gainsay his willingness to labor for the advancement of the kingdom of God. None could point the finger at John Calvin and declare him to care more about his personal comforts and studies. I knew he had longed for death ten times a day while in Geneva; hence, his banishment was a liberation, a joyous unshackling. For Calvin, it was as if the hangman had cut him free from the noose, absolved him of all charges, and set him free.

We made our way along the southeastern shore of the Lake of Neuchâtel, the grassy fields painted with blue and yellow and red wildflowers, newly sprung up and shimmering in the breeze. A great deal of snow had fallen that winter, and the warm sunshine of spring rapidly melted the snowpack in the mountains and caused the River Aare to swell its banks, roaring and foaming with frigid rushing waters.

We came to a place where we were forced to traverse a narrow pathway that ran dangerously close to the swollen river. While I made to assist the good man Couraut, blind as he was, my foot suddenly slipped off the path. Into the deafening tumult of the river I felt myself falling. I cried out. Couraut, reaching blindly toward my cry, attempted to grasp my tunic.

I have never felt water so cold. As it enfolded me in its icy grasp, it seemed instantly to squeeze the breath from my body. If it were any colder, it would of natural necessity been solid ice. Of this I was absolutely certain. There was to be no attempt at swimming, futile as such an attempt would have been for me in waters so cold, nor was there to be any breathing. Crying aloud as I fell, my mouth was suddenly choked with water, and I felt myself sinking beneath the turbulent river.

This was not the Seine, and there was to be no resurfacing, sinking, and resurfacing again. So rapid and so churning was the Aare that it pulled me ever deeper. Then, just when I felt certain that all hope was lost, I felt myself being lifted. Spluttering and gasping for air, my skin taut and blue with cold, I saw the red features of Farel, felt his iron grip on my tunic and the firm ground of the pathway beneath my body. My lungs heaving, I gazed up at the blue expanse above, the sun warming me. *Once again*, I mused at the heavens, *you have saved me.*

Within days we found ourselves in Basel. Word of the expulsion of Calvin and Farel had traveled rapidly. A friendly printer, a man named Oporin, welcomed us into his home and gave us food and lodging.

"For as long as you need it," he said, smiling warmly at us.

But I looked around the place. It was small, modest in décor, and clearly not the home of a man of great means. How was he to provide for all of us? Du Tillet had left some money with us, in my keeping. "Calvin will give it away in an hour, and you both shall be destitute," he had explained to me. But it was an amount that would scarcely feed us for another week.

"Welcome to the Athens of Switzerland!" declared the Hebrew scholar Sebastian Munster. We were greeted and warmly welcomed—Calvin was, that is—by the scholars, theologians, and pastors of this city of printing, learning, and piety.

Pastors Oswald Myconius and Heinrich Bullinger enthusiastically invited Calvin and Farel to preach in the church in Basel, and noble Grynaus and other reformation-minded of the faithful contributed to our needs. But it could not continue. Calvin set to work studying Hebrew and writing, and he made attempts at selling some of his books. But the majority of his time he spent expanding the *Institutes*. I believe it was his confrontation with error and trouble in Geneva that so immediately inflamed him with the desire to instruct more thoroughly the reformed church with this revision.

Frequently he was forced to pause and write letters, for he received, as always, many letters. And no one wrote more often than Bucer.

"It is always the same with Martin Bucer," said Calvin. "He ever urges me to come to Strasbourg. He is almost as pertinacious as Farel, though not as violent in his urgings."

"And you have again refused him?" I asked.

"Indeed," said Calvin. "Farel has returned to Neuchâtel, and urges me to attend him there. The congregation in Lausanne has extended a pastoral call; even the church in Basel urges me to take up pastoral duties. Good Couraut has accepted the pastorate at Orbe. But I am not suited to such a calling. Geneva is proof of that. It is the scholar's life for me, as has always been my desire."

I hesitated to remind him of our finances. "Master Calvin," I began, "there is the little matter of the purse."

"The purse?" said Calvin.

"Yes, it grows ever lighter," I said, trying to ease him into understanding my meaning.

"We do the work of God," he said.

"Yes, and, hence, God shall provide the means thereof," I said. "I know this full well. But might not God be doing so by prompting Martin Bucer to invite you to preach and teach in Strasbourg, there to receive a stipend for your labors?" I could not help remembering the words Bucer had said to Calvin, words of caution about overworking himself. I felt that Strasbourg would be good for Calvin and for his health.

"You too would have me hasten thither," said Calvin, not unkindly. "But I shall not comply with Bucer or with you, my trusted Jean-Louis, unless a greater necessity compels me."

Another letter arrived, this from du Tillet. The gist of his epistle was grievous to Calvin. It was one of the times I observed him to weep. "Your expulsion from Geneva is clear and unequivocal evidence, a divine sign, that God disapproves of your labors with the reformation of the church."

Louis du Tillet went on to explain that he had come to disapprove of Calvin's labors as well, and that he, forthwith, was returning to the Church of Rome. The threats and railings of Genevan libertines grieved Calvin. Such news, however, from a friend cut more deeply than a knife.

I made sure that Bucer's letters and those from others in Strasbourg, especially Capito, Niger, and Hedio, were placed on the top of his pile of letters, to be read first. These I made free to open for him, even to lay them out on his writing desk.

"I see you have been at my mail, again, Jean-Louis," he would gently chide me as he sat down to read his letters.

At last in September 1538, Calvin announced that we would make a visit, "merely a visit, mind you," to Strasbourg. Eagerly I packed our things. He had acquired another trunk, which I uncomplainingly shouldered, and we set out for Alsace and the Rhineland.

34

Strasbourg

"MERELY A VISIT" TO Strasbourg proved to be one of three years' duration. Three gloriously peaceful years they would be, for Calvin, ones sprinkled with joys and pleasures that I believe he had resigned himself never to know.

One must not imagine that Calvin was idle in Strasbourg. Within a short time, he preached four times a week, often in the grand cathedral that rose so loftily above that amiable city near the Rhine. Additionally, he taught young men how to expound the Scriptures, and he frequently engaged in debates. Critics who came to spar with Calvin often were won over by his gentle frankness as much as by his vast knowledge of Scripture and his compelling rhetoric.

The French congregation in Bucer's German church welcomed Calvin, hailed him as a great preacher and the esteemed author of the now well-known *Institutes of the Christian Religion*. The Table of the Lord was celebrated with solemnity, humility, and unity of mind and heart, "a true sacrifice of praise," Calvin once remarked. He was honored, not cursed, by his congregation, and even the councilmen of Strasbourg loved him, supported him, encouraged him, heeded his instruction, and bowed willingly to his discipline. They elected Calvin as delegate for the city of Strasbourg, sending him to appear in defense of the pure doctrine before the Holy Roman Emperor in Regensburg.

Though ever busy with his labors, and though underpaid for his work, Calvin was happy in this place. Even word of the death of his cousin, Pierre Robert Olivetan, grieved though he was at the news, did not mitigate his satisfaction with his new life in Strasbourg. Eagerly he brought Antoine and Marie, his brother and sister, to live with him there, and took in boarders both to help cover his expenses and as a means of providing daily train- ing for young men who might be future pastors in the reformed churches. Visitors crowded around our table, including a friend and colleague of Martin Luther, Philipp Melanchthon, with whom Calvin developed a lasting friendship. Mealtimes in our lodgings were frequently marked by vigorous discussion and debate, yet more often by high devotion, prayer, and the reading of Holy Scripture. These things surrounded me in Strasbourg.

How infinitely different were the people of that city from the hordes of revelers, profaners, and libertines who had littered the streets of Geneva. Here was a people teachable and hungry for the Word of God, and Calvin was very happy. Here Calvin published a treatise on the Lord's Supper, a topic he was certain Satan, the foul fiend, had raised to trouble and divide the reformed church. He published a revision of his *Institutes* and began a series of expositions of Paul's Epistle to the Romans, delivered before his attentive congregation in the cathedral.

"To praise the blessing of the book of Romans for Christian knowledge," he declared, his voice sounding clearly throughout the high nave,"would be a vain undertaking. Our words do not reach the height of this epistle. It must speak for itself. Who enters into it receives the key to all the hidden treasures of Holy Scripture."

For months he expounded word-by-word through Paul's great epistle. One such exposition made a deep impression on my mind. Here, as in Geneva, the cathedral was packed to capacity, and so it always was; it mattered not whether it was a sermon for the Lord's Day or one preached in the middle of the week. As Calvin mounted the pulpit and prepared to deliver his sermon, the sun shone through the massive stained-glass windows, flooding the nave and his attentive congregation with light.

"Jacob have I loved, but Esau have I hated," he read from Olivetan's now-completed French Bible, his earnest voice ringing like a clarion. "What shall we say then? Is there injustice with God? By no means! For he says to Moses, 'I will have mercy on whom I have mercy, and I will have compassion on whom I have compassion.' So then it depends not on human will or exertion, but on God, who has mercy."

After a brief and unadorned reminder of the previous sermon and an explanation of Paul's words, he continued.

"We shall never be clearly persuaded, as we ought to be, that our salvation flows from the wellspring of God's free mercy until we come to know his eternal election, which illuminates God's grace by this contrast: that he does not indiscriminately adopt all into the hope of salvation but gives to some what he denies to others. This Paul will later assert in Romans 11:5–6. Here he denies that this grace which needs so much to be known can be known unless God, utterly disregarding works, chooses those whom he has decreed within himself. Hence, our salvation comes about solely from God's mere generosity—we must be called back to the course of election. Yet do many rail at such a teaching. Those who do, who wish to get rid of all this, are obscuring as maliciously as they can what ought to have been gloriously and vociferously proclaimed, and by so obscuring election they tear humility up by the very roots.

"They who shut the gates that no one may dare seek a taste of this doctrine wrong men no less than God. For neither will anything else suffice to make us humble as we ought to be, nor shall we otherwise sincerely feel how much we are obligated to God. And as Christ teaches in John's Gospel 10:28–29, here is our only ground of firmness and confidence: in order to free us of all fear and render us victorious amid so many dangers, snares, and mortal struggles, he promises that whatever the Father has entrusted into his keeping will be safe."

Ever torn by longing and by my guilt, I listened with a troubled heart. In the tranquility of Strasbourg, I had attempted to forget my past, to rid myself of my crimes by a delusion. Calvin's words cut deeply, distracting my bosom that day, and I fairly writhed in anguish as I listened.

"From this we infer that all those who do not know that they are God's elect will be miserable through constant fear."

I felt certain he delivered this sermon for me alone. I often felt thus. It was I who was miserable through constant fear, certain that my crimes against Calvin, if not against God, so I then perceived them, barred me forever from grace. How could one such as I be elect?

"Let them remember that when they inquire into predestination they are penetrating the sacred precincts of divine wisdom. If anyone with carefree assurance breaks into this place he will not succeed in satisfying his curiosity and he will enter a labyrinth from which he can find no exit. God would have us revere but not understand that through the doctrine of God's merciful election he should also fill us with wonder. He has here set before us, by his Word, the secrets of his will. And it is insane to seek any other knowledge regarding predestination than that which the Word of God discloses to us."

How was I to revere a doctrine by which I was forever shut out from mercy, disenfranchised from divine grace, cut off for eternity, and from all heavenly kindness? While Calvin continued his sermon, I persisted in my self-imposed lament.

"There are others who require that every mention of predestination be buried; indeed, they teach us to avoid any question of it, as we would a reef. Yet Holy Scripture is the school of the Holy Spirit, wherein nothing is omitted that is both necessary and useful to know, and nothing is taught but what is expedient to know. Therefore, we must guard against depriving believers of everything disclosed about predestination in Scripture, lest we seem either wickedly to defraud them of the blessing of their God or to accuse and scoff at the Holy Spirit for having published what is, in our all-wise opinion, more profitable to suppress. Let us, I say, permit the Christian man to open his mind and ears to every utterance of God.

"Profane men, I admit, in the matter of predestination abruptly seize upon something to carp, rail, bark, or scoff at. But if their shamelessness deters us, we shall have to keep secret the chief doctrines of the faith, almost none of which they leave untouched by blasphemy. An obstinate person would be no less insolently puffed up on hearing that within the essence of God there are three Persons. Such men will not refrain from guffaws when they are informed that but little more than five thousand years have passed since the creation of the universe. Nothing, in short, can be brought forth that profane men do not assail with their mockery.

"False apostles, however, could not make Paul ashamed by defaming and accusing his true doctrine. Many say that the teaching of predestination is dangerous for godly minds, because it hinders exhortations, because it shakes faith, because it disturbs and terrifies the heart itself, but this is nonsense!"

I wondered. Such teaching felt to my soul as a terror, for surely it disquieted me. From where I sat amid the grandeur of that gothic edifice, a carved face gawked down at me, cadaverous eyes, bared teeth, mocking, tormenting me. I was that chained ghoul, writhing, gnashing under the judgments of the Almighty. Yet did Calvin, unrelenting, continue.

"Augustine admits that on the basis of these objections he was frequently charged with preaching predestination too freely. It is true, that just as we should not investigate what the Lord has left hidden in secret, yet must we not neglect what he has brought into the open, what he has revealed in his Holy Word for our instruction and for our sanctification.

"For those who are so cautious or fearful that they desire to bury predestination in order not to disturb weak souls, with what color will they cloak their arrogance when they accuse God indirectly of stupid thoughtlessness as if he had not foreseen the peril that they feel they have wisely met by so being silent where the Scripture clearly speaks? Whoever, then, heaps odium upon Paul's doctrine, hence, on the Bible's doctrine of predestination, openly reproaches God, as if he had unadvisedly let slip something hurtful to the church. Yet Paul elsewhere, in his Epistle to the Ephesians, declares that chief among the spiritual blessings the believer has in heavenly places, chief among those is God's loving predestination, whereby alone the believer may be truly grateful for such lavished kindness on his unworthy soul."

Again did his words fall like hammer blows pounding against the iron bars of my soul. And these his words forced me to recollect that previous text, so despairing to my soul. *If we sin willfully after we have received the knowledge of the truth, there no longer remains a sacrifice for sins, but a certain fearful expectation of judgment, and fiery indignation which will devour the adversaries.* Such was I, and no man such as I could be elect—except to damnation. Of this I was certain. Yet did my heart ache with longing for it to be otherwise.

In Strasbourg Calvin encountered something new in his experience. Whereas in Geneva the congregation sang metrical versions of the Psalms only, here, under German Lutheran influence, hymns written by poets on biblical themes, but not strict versifications, were freely sung in worship. Not once did I hear Calvin speak against this practice, and I did observe him joining with his congregation, lustily singing hymns written by Martin Luther and other poets.

One day as I tidied up his writing desk—it could become so surmounted with his books, manuscripts, ink pots, and quills—I discovered something new on which he had been laboring. It immediately captivated my attention for its dissimilarity with the manner in which he wrote other things. The *Institutes* he had laid out in paragraphs, but this page was laid out in short lines, of near equal length. Poetry, I took it to be, and my curiosity got the better of me, as it usually did. So I read it.

> I greet thee, who my sure Redeemer art,
> My only trust and Savior of my heart,
> Who pain dist undergo for my poor sake;
> I pray thee from our hearts all cares to take.

Thou art the King of mercy and of grace,
Reigning omnipotent in every place:
So come, O King, and our whole being sway;
Shine on us with the light of thy pure day.

Thou are the Life, by which alone we live,
And all our substance and our strength receive;
O comfort us in death's approaching hour,
Strong-hearted then to face it by thy power.

Thou hast the true and perfect gentleness,
No harshness hast thou and no bitterness:
Make us to taste the sweet grace found in thee
And ever stay in thy sweet unity.

Our hope is in no other save in thee;
Our faith is built upon thy promise free;
O grant to us such stronger hope and sure
That we may boldly conquer and endure.

I was never absolutely certain that these glorious lines of poetry were original to Calvin or whether he had transcribed them from another in Strasbourg. Nevertheless, were they so perfect a likeness to Calvin's devotion, his adoration, and his dependence on God, expressed in his sermons and other writings, and were these lines so like his fervent praying, on which I had eavesdropped a great deal.

That same evening after I had cleared away the remains of our dinner, Calvin appeared distracted, preoccupied, inattentive to those at table with him.

"Well, well," said Melanchthon, nodding his head knowingly at Calvin. "It seems to me our theologue is thinking."

"He is ever thinking," said Calvin's sister. "He is overtired this evening, that is all."

"I think not," said Melanchthon.

"And of what do you divine that I am thinking?" said Calvin.

"You are thinking," said his friend, "about a future spouse. Make no protest. I know the signs."

"Do you think thus, dear brother?" asked Marie. "O you must marry!"

"Hold, hold," said Calvin, lifting a hand in protest. "I shall not belong to those who are accused of attacking Rome, like the Greeks fought Troy, only to be able to take a wife!"

"Luther has married," said Melanchthon, "and is ever happy with his rib Katie."

"Dear brother, you must," said Antoine.

"Indeed, you must," said Marie. "You are twenty-nine years old. The time is ripe for marriage."

"What qualities must a young woman exhibit," said Melanchthon, "to capture the attention of John Calvin? Expound upon them."

"The graces which might capture me for a woman," said Calvin, "are discipline, gentleness, modesty, good housekeeping, and patience."

"She will have need of the latter," laughed Marie, "if she is to be happily wed to you, brother!"

I was ever disquieted by these discussions, of which there were a growing number in these days. What would become of me if he married? The things which I attended to on his behalf would be cared for by his wife, would they not? I would not be needed. Nevertheless, all his friends and acquaintances in Strasbourg seemed determined to see Calvin married. Farel wrote letters extolling the virtues or beauties of this charming girl or that. Though her dowry would have, with a word, dispelled all future want, Calvin waved off the suggestion of a rich nobleman's daughter, and he dismissed another young lady because upon meeting her he sensed deficiencies in the graces he looked for in a woman.

Meanwhile, Calvin found himself engaged in discussions, as was often the case, with a young Anabaptist man, Jean Stordeur, who had come from Belgium to Strasbourg.

"The magistrate's office," declared Stordeur, "is a carnal office. The sword of the magistrate is to be rejected by true Christians. All civil government lies outside the perfection of Christ."

"It is true that Christ's spiritual kingdom," said Calvin, "and all civil jurisdiction are completely distinct, and must not be unwisely mingled."

"More than distinct!" cried Stordeur. "Paul declares that in the kingdom of God there are no political distinctions."

"By your interpretation of Paul to the Galatians," said Calvin, "the reign of Christ would also end all sexual distinctions. Once the grace of God lays hold of a sinner, he ceases to be male or female any longer?—a nonsensical interpretation, indeed!"

"Look around you," said Stordeur. "Kings, magistrates, city councils—they never can control themselves."

I knew the man's words would force on Calvin a painful recollection of the tearing wolves of the Genevan City Council.

"A system compounded of aristocracy and democracy," continued Calvin, "because of men's faults and failings, far excels all others. It is far safer for a number to exercise government so that they may help one another, teach and admonish one another, and, if one asserts himself unfairly, there may be a number of censors and masters to restrain his willfulness. All these things, however, are needlessly spoken to those for whom the will and Word of the Lord is enough."

Whereupon, Calvin began freely citing from Scripture to the man, copiously referring to passage after passage where civil government, though admonished, is not condemned or absolved.

"When David in Psalm 2:12 urges all kings and rulers to kiss the Son of God, he does not bid them lay aside their authority and retire to private life, but he bids them submit to Christ the power with which they have been invested, that Christ alone may tower over all. Similarly, Isaiah, when he promises that kings shall be foster fathers of the church, and queens its nurses, does not deprive them of their offices and honors. Rather, by a noble title he makes them defenders of God's pious worshipers, and all this in a prophecy that looks forward to the coming of Christ."

These informal discussions took place over some weeks, on the steps of the cathedral after a sermon, on the street corner before the baker's shop, on the crest of a bridge spanning the canal, and eventually over humble meals in our lodgings. Often in these meetings, at Stordeur's side was his wife Idelette, their two children at her sides. I observed her for the intensity of her attentions to Calvin's arguments. I felt at times that she longed to speak, but she never did. She struck me as not only a singularly chaste and attractive woman, but as a woman of intelligence, even one of wit, if I may make so free, herein, to observe these qualities.

Then tragedy struck. Jean Stordeur fell gravely ill, perhaps with plague. Calvin tenderly prayed and offered the consolations of the gospel of grace to the man as he lay dying. I often attended Calvin as he ministered to the ill and dying, and so in this case. I had hastened from the room to fetch another bowl of cool water, and when I returned, with his last strength, the man gripped Calvin's hand, attempting in his weakened extremity to sit up in his bed. Calvin leaned close, and the dying man seemed to be speaking earnestly in his ear.

I do not know what Jean Stordeur said in Calvin's ear in the final moments of his life. Calvin expressed heartfelt condolences to his widow, Idelette, and assured her of her husband's confession of faith in the pure doctrine of Christ in his dying moments, but I always wondered whether the man had said more to Calvin with his last breath.

For days after Stordeur's death, Calvin was at times deeply distracted, sitting idly gazing out the window, a thing he rarely indulged in doing. Calvin proposed that out of his means he would provide food and basic needs for Idelette and her two children, now left destitute: she without a husband, they without a father. I strongly protested at his proposal, citing the meagerness of our own means. Yet did he persist. One day I entered the room, intending to raise the question of our straitened means. Apparently he did not hear my approach, for I overheard him murmuring to himself at the window.

"Discipline, gentleness, modesty, good housekeeping, patience, perhaps, friendliness, and . . ." His voice trailed off.

Within a short time, in August 1540, Calvin made another proposal, this one a proposal of marriage to Idelette. There was to be no protesting on my part; I felt little inclined to such. She humbly and graciously accepted his proposal. She was a winsome woman, and in spite of my worries about my status in Calvin's household, I found myself inwardly happy for him, for her, for the little ones at her sides. After receiving Calvin's letter announcing marital intentions, Farel was elated and insisted on traveling from

Neuchâtel to Strasbourg to solemnize their wedding vows before God and the people of the city.

I have never met another like Calvin's Idelette. In the contented years that lay ahead, I observed many times a woman of the most extraordinary piety, a mother to her—to their—children, who cared more for the holiness of their lives than for any other quality in them. I had seen many wives storm and rail, even strike and hurl, at the real or perceived failings of their menfolk. Never did I see such in Calvin's Idelette. And he adored her. I alone as their servant could tell of the genuine sweetness of their life together; they were never more kind to one another than when they were alone, under their own roof, with none to impress. He often endearingly referred to her as "precious helper," and "excellent companion." I believe that if it came to it, Idelette would have died for her Calvin, and I know that he would have willingly done so for her. A mere servant in their household, I was, of course, not a confidant of their intimacy, but observing from afar, I watched the most enviable, the most profound, the most genuine love deepen and grow between them, of any I could imagine between a man and a woman. Naturally I envied all this. But something had begun to change in me, and even my envy would not have desired to mitigate their happiness in the slightest degree. I observed all this; keenly, wonderingly, longingly did I observe it.

Yes, Strasbourg had given Calvin everything for which he had longed. But would it last?

35

One Hundred Deaths

DISTURBING NEWS was on the wing from Geneva. While Calvin and Strasbourg were at peace, and the Word of God advanced, the city at the mouth of the Rhone River had sunk into near anarchy in those three years. Perhaps inevitably, the ousted Roman bishop of Geneva, Peirre de la Baume, had not been idle after Calvin's banishment. Determined to reclaim the turbulent city for the Roman pontiff—and for himself—la Baume had conspired with his friend, the eloquent scholar and moderate, Cardinal Sadoleto, to craft a letter to the erring city on the lake.

"It is a clever piece of rhetoric," said Martin Bucer. "And it must be answered." He eyed Calvin as he spoke thus.

"What is so clever about it?" asked Calvin.

"Sadoleto addresses, with subtlety and flattery, the mayor, the council, and the citizens," said Bucer. "I have a copy. Read it yourself."

Calvin read portions of it aloud. "Peace be to you, most faithful brothers in Jesus Christ, and with us the Catholic Church, namely your and our mother; love and unity through God, the Father Almighty . . . ."

He scanned down the letter. "What prevarication! He claims that Rome has always believed in justification by faith. What misleading nonsense! The order of faith and works means everything to the doctrine of salvation. With this he will pursue the ignorant and, alas, Geneva is not short of such."

"It must be answered," said Bucer again.

Brilliant though he was, Calvin was often slow at picking up on hints his friends attempted to give him. I knew that it was only a matter of time before Bucer would prevail, and Calvin would take up his quill and answer this letter, and I had suspicions of what might follow. I wonder whether Calvin had known what lay ahead, if he would have ever written that letter.

"Word is that the bishop and his supporters have entered the city and make ready to reclaim Geneva for Rome." This again from Bucer several days later. "Did you notice, John, that he attacks you for ambition and money grubbing."

"Money grubbing!" Rarely did I do so, but it was I who had spoken, thus. "I am the keeper of the purse for this household, and I can assure you that if what Master Calvin was paid in Geneva, for hard labor, is money grubbing, then the pope is a pauper, and I am the emperor!"

"Peace, Jean-Louis," said Calvin. "God shall vindicate his own. Yet, as his servant, shall I write a reply to this pernicious letter."

And he did. Pacing about his study, he dictated portions of it to me, of which portions I am more familiar; hence, I shall render them here.

"Not long ago you wrote the council and the people of Geneva soft words in order not to embitter those whom you needed to accomplish your goals. You attacked violently only those who, as you say, have caused disturbance in this poor city with their craftiness. Be it known to you, Sadoleto, I am one of those whom you slander and, although at present I am not pastor of the church in Geneva, I hold her with fatherly love.

"In order to sow discord among us you accuse us, against better knowledge, of ambition and love of money. Well, were I looking out for myself for those ends I would probably never have cut myself loose from your party. Our only goal is to increase the kingdom of God by our smallness and humility. To assert the contrary is highly unbecoming to the respected gentleman of science, the prudent, cunningly calculating Sadoleto."

I recall not the precise words of his next repost, but he made an impassioned appeal for the centrality of the Word of God, loyalty to which is "the true mark of the church." He appealed against the evil of depriving helpless souls of the Word of God, and accused the pope of severing the visible church from the Word of God.

On he went, defending the pure doctrine of grace over against the false doctrine of justification by faith and works, everywhere taught by the Roman church. He defended the reformed doctrines as the pure doctrines believed and practiced by the early church, alluding to Augustine and others as his proof. Line by line, he rebutted Sadoleto's attack.

"We demand a peace in which the kingdom of the Redeemer reigns—you believe that everything that has been won for Christ is a loss for you. May the Lord grant, Sadoleto, that you and your people will finally come to realize that there is no other bond of our church than Christ the Lord who offers us his communion so that his words and his spirit unite our hearts and thoughts."

Silence followed Calvin's letter. Sadoleto and Rome had decided to withdraw. There was to be no defense against the force of Calvin's rebuttal. But I awaited the next developments. I wondered whether he had misspoken, or perhaps overstated, when he referred to his fatherly attitude toward the church in Geneva.

Geneva was due for another election, and word of a landslide victory for the supporters of Calvin and reformation came north. Such news was received with hesitant rejoicing in Strasbourg, for perhaps they, if not Calvin, could see what I had foreseen in all this. Soon the letters from Geneva poured in, and my back began once again to ache with hefting them to our lodging.

Ami Porral had been reinstalled, now as First Syndic, and he promptly called Pierre Viret back to Geneva to pave the way for his friend. "Triumph, come quickly, brother, come, come, that we may rejoice in God our Redeemer. Do not linger, come to build up and to gladden the church which lies in misery, grief, and sorrow."

Another letter, this from one of the compromising pastors elected to take Calvin's place, one who had exulted in Calvin's banishment. "Do not say 'No.' You would resist the Holy Spirit, not men. Remember the fruits waiting to be harvested in France. The Genevan church is important, and no mortal man is able to direct it with such force, so wisely, and so ably as you."

It was an astonishing appeal, especially coming from such a man.

Calvin flung the letters aside on his desk and buried his face in his hands, Idelette hurrying to his side.

"I would rather submit to death one hundred times," he moaned, "than to this Genevan cross, a cross on which I would be subjected to death a thousand times daily."

Yet did the letters continue to pour in from Geneva.

"We, the mayor and the council of the city of Geneva, to Doctor Calvin, our good brother and our distinguished friend," so it began. Calvin was so moved with distress in these days that he actually broke off into audible sobbing as he read.

"Inasmuch as we know that your desire is none other than to further the growth of the honor of God and extension of his Word, we wish sincerely to commend our request to you, and to beg you. . . ." Here he broke down in sobs, knowing what was to follow. I offered to read further for him. The letter was, as Calvin feared, an official request for Calvin "to betake yourself hither to your old office." The council assured Calvin that the people wanted him in the worst sort of way, and further assured him that he would be kindly and respectfully dealt with by all, and that in Geneva, "you will have no cause to find trouble and grief."

Then Viret sent another urging letter. This time Calvin broke into laughter. "My good friend expresses so much concern about my health, and then urges me to return to Geneva! It is a non sequitur! He might as well have urged me to my grave, as to compel me to return to the torments of that place of torture."

Then it arrived. February 1541, a letter came from Farel. It is of little use to record its contents. Farel thundered and roared relentlessly, giving Calvin distress beyond words. I feared for their friendship after his first reading of the letter. It was yet another violent denouncing of Calvin if he did not return. If he refused, then he cared nothing for his brethren being mercilessly butchered for their faith in France. Geneva was the key to it all, so claimed Farel, and Calvin was the key to Geneva. At last he rendered his reply to the fiery Gascon.

"I yield. I surrender! Had I the choice at my own disposal, nothing would be less agreeable to me than to follow your advice.

But when I remember that I am not my own, I offer up my heart, presented as a sacrifice to the Lord, promptly and sincerely. And for myself, I protest that I have no other desire than that, setting aside all consideration of me, they may look only to what is most for the glory of God and the advantage of the church. Therefore, I submit my will and my affections, subdued and held fast, to the obedience of God."

September 1541, Calvin, with Idelette and his new family, returned to Geneva. The Genevans had slightly exaggerated their promise of no grief and no trouble for him, for there would be many times of grief and trouble. Nevertheless, in the twenty-three years that would follow, there were to be many years of triumph and enduring blessing for all.

On the first Sunday of his return, the nave of St. Pierre was jostling like a sea composed of silk and satin and broadcloth, so many had crowded to see and hear the banished reformer. It was an unusually warm and still September morning, and the press of bodies emitted a hovering cloud of stench. I buried my nose in my sleeve and blinked against the smarting sensation in my eyes. I was not alone.

A hush descended over the cathedral as Calvin deliberately climbed, tread by tread, the stairs of the pulpit. Three years had elapsed. He had been banished, driven from the city in disgrace and humiliation. Now all Geneva had begged him to return. Would he exult in triumph at his return? Would he rail at past wrongs? Only those most blinded by their resentment could think this of him. Would he review the City Council's errors, admonish, rebuke their past arrogance? Would he commence a study of the role of ministers, their high calling, and the obligation of all to hold the ministry in highest esteem? Would he begin an exposition of a new book of the Bible? All waited expectantly as Calvin laid his Bible on the lectern and faced his congregation.

"When last we gathered in this place to hear God's Word, from John's Gospel we saw how we are to abide in Christ's love, that we are to obey Christ's commandment, that his commandment is for us to 'love one another' as he has first loved us.

"Hear now the reading of Christ's words from today's text, John 15:16–17. 'You did not choose me, but I chose you.... These things I command you, so that you will love one another.'"

No railing, no admonishing, no rebuking, Calvin had simply and faithfully returned to the very passage he had left off three years before. With little preamble, he launched into his exposition. "Men commonly imagine some kind of concurrence to take place between the grace of God and the will of man, but here our Lord makes a clear contrast, 'I chose you; I was not chosen by you,' and thereby claims exclusivity for our salvation. It is Christ alone."

With passion and simplicity he continued. "We must not measure the gospel by the reputation of those who preach it, for they will be feeble men. We are to understand, rather, that it is Jesus Christ addressing us. We must receive his Word and acknowledge that he is in control of our lives. We must be willing to be taught in his name; for whenever his Word is preached, though it is uttered by the lips of men, it is spoken with the authority of God."

With piercing clarity, point by point, he made his way carefully through his exposition, drawing to his conclusion. "Now let us fall before the majesty of our great God, acknowledging our faults ...."

Nothing was more important to Calvin in his labors than his preaching, and he gave his best energies to it. But there was so much to do in Geneva. Calvin set about to revise and expand the moral laws governing life in Geneva. It was exhausting labor, and yet did Calvin rarely lie down and sleep the night through. Many nights, I feared when I awoke, he had not slept at all. In a letter he once wrote to a friend he said, "I have not time to look out of my house at the blessed sun, and if things continue thus I shall forget what sort of appearance it has. When I have settled my usual business, I have so many letters to write, so many questions to answer, that many a night is spent without any offering of sleep being brought to me by nature."

In the first of these years, Calvin had Idelette at his side, the excellent companion of his life, but in matters of church and state, he was alone. This time there was no fiery Farel to handle the City Council, and he was sorely short of men able and well-equipped for the ministry in the growing city.

One day during his first year back in Geneva, Idelette rose suddenly from the breakfast table, her chair clattering to the floor. Hastily she left the room, and I distinctly heard retching from the far corner of the house. Concerned, Calvin rose and went to her side. I am not privy to what was said between them when he made to comfort her in her illness, as I then thought it to be. But over the next weeks and months she grew large in a family way, and she and Calvin often smiled at one another confidentially. I observed him stroking her tautened belly as the infant in her womb kicked, and I once saw him lay his ear close in an effort to hear the signs of new life in his wife's womb.

But all was not well. Idelette grew weaker as her time drew near, and I was anxious for her strength, for surely she would have need of it. When at last little Jacques was delivered July 28, 1542, with tears and prayers Calvin cried out to God for the life of his young son. The child was sickly and frail, and ate little or nothing. Within but a few days, amid his parents' grief, always tempered with faith, he departed this life, and they laid his tiny body in the earth.

Yet was there little time for prolonged grief in those days. Calvin was needed at City Council, and I attended him. "Some persons, in their hatred of discipline recoil from the very name, let them understand this: if no society, indeed, no house that has even a small family, can be kept in proper condition without discipline, it is much more necessary in the church, whose condition should be as ordered as possible."

Their assurances notwithstanding, it appeared to me that not a great deal had changed with the magistrates in Geneva. To be sure, Calvin had more supporters than detractors, but I learned in those days that lying or discord in a few is all that is needed to disrupt the whole.

There was the young upstart Sebastian Castellio, master of the school, who wanted to make a name for himself by publishing a creative translation of the Bible in French. Offended by Calvin's suggestions and criticisms of the work, he set about to make Calvin's life miserable.

There was the playing-card maker, Peter Ameaux, whose wife became an outspoken Anabaptist and demanded a divorce. She not only—shrew-like and publicly—repudiated her husband's authority, but that of Calvin and the church, as well as the constitutional laws governing divorce passed by the City Council.

A man called Jacob Gruet posted scandalous pamphlets about the city, even on Calvin's pulpit at St. Pierre, and published treasonous fliers attacking the City Council. Gruet called Christ an evil seducer, wretched visionary, a conceited churl, a drunkard, hypocrite, and traitor who was rightly executed. He declared the apostles rogues and rascals, and the Virgin Mary a harlot. And he persisted in these blasphemies. Calvin had no part in it, but the City Council tried, condemned, and executed the man by beheading.

Another vengeful critic, Jérôme-Hermès Bolsec, onetime Carmelite friar, set himself up as a theologian and scandalously attacked Calvin for preaching the doctrine of predestination. In a public debate—I was there—Calvin so carefully and thoroughly refuted the man's attacks, using the Bible alone, that Bolsec gradually fell awkwardly silent, played idly with a thread on the sleeve of his tunic, and could make no rebuttal. Further investigation of the man by the council found him to be a spy commissioned by the Duke of Savoy to disturb the city. The City Council tried him and found him guilty of sedition and exiled him. Yet did I suspect it would not be the last the world would hear of such a scoundrel.

Hence it was that Calvin gave great attention to the role of discipline in the state, and especially so in the church, whose condition, he believed, should be as ordered as possible. Calvin had desired to celebrate the Lord's Supper once each month, but, to his frustration, the council intervened and would only allow it four times yearly. Furthermore, Calvin's great care not to profane the Supper, by admitting scandalous offenders to the table, led to mounting tensions with libertines in the city.

"The ancient and better church guarded the purity of the Supper," he declared in a sermon from 1 Corinthians 11, "while lawful government flourished. For if anyone had committed a crime that caused offense, he was ordered first to abstain from partaking of the sacred Supper."

I looked about the nave of St. Pierre as Calvin spoke. There were scowls and some shuffling of feet by a few at his words. Calvin continued.

"Nor is it enough if a man, who by setting a bad example through his misdeed has gravely injured the church—it is not enough that he be chastened only with words. He ought for a time to be deprived of the communion of the Supper until he gives assurance of his repentance. For Luke records Paul's sermon in Acts 26:20, wherein the apostle 'preached that they should repent and turn to God and prove their repentance by their deeds.' And in Matthew 3:8 we are told to 'produce fruit in keeping with repentance.' Yet must church discipline be practiced with the gracious object of producing such fruit in the offender. Hence, so that no one may be injured by severity, the punishment must not be harsh, so that by it sinners will find their way back to the Lord."

With libertines on the council, any chastisement was too severe for their liking, and it was perhaps inevitable that Calvin's teaching on church discipline and the Lord's Supper should come to a crisis. And so it did.

Tried and found guilty of sexual promiscuity by the elders, a lawyer and prominent libertine, Philibert Berthelier, was barred by the church from partaking of the Supper. His fellow libertines on the council, however, succeeded in getting the civil magistrate to overrule Calvin and the church elders. They lifted his suspension from the Table. The next day was Sunday, and the Lord's Supper was to be celebrated at St. Pierre.

I overheard Calvin speaking with Idelette the night before. "I would rather be dead a hundred times than to commit such terrible mockery to Christ. I swear rather to die than to have the Lord's Supper defiled."

She expressed her deep concern that it would not come to such drastic means.

I did not sleep well that night. But while I worried, dozed, and fretted, I am certain Calvin spent a good deal of that night in earnest prayer.

St. Pierre was crammed with people next morning, some chatting excitedly and behaving as if they had come to a jousting tournament or a theatrical production. Calvin stepped into the pulpit and delivered a powerful message from the Word of God.

"Let us learn that God does not intend there to be churches as places for people to make merry and laugh in, as if a comedy were being acted here. There must be majesty in his Word, by which we may be moved and affected."

When he had completed his exposition, and had urged his congregation to fall before the majesty of God, he proceeded to the table to administer the solemn feast to the faithful. Suddenly, Berthelier and some of his libertine friends entered the church with swords drawn. Amid gasps of alarm and scurrying feet as the congregation drew back, they proudly strode down the center aisle of the cathedral. Calmly, Calvin stepped in front of the table, barring their way.

Had this been a tavern brawl or a street fight it would have been comic. Stout and hale, Berthelier and his minions, swords in hand, halted before frail, sickly John Calvin, alone and unarmed. Sweat broke from my face and I felt that I should go to him, stand by him. Then I looked again at the malevolence in Berthelier's face, at the cold steel of their swords. These men were in earnest, and if they capitulated, this was public, and all eyes would see their humiliation. I halted.

I have never seen a man so physically slight with such power in his features, his posture, his eyes, and his words, as Calvin that day.

"These hands you may crush," he declared boldly, extending his naked hands to them. "These arms you may lop off; my life you may take; my blood is yours; you may shed it. But you shall never force me to give holy things to the profaned, and so dishonor the table of my God."

There was a suspended silence in the cathedral. No one breathed. All eyes were fixed on Calvin and his opponents. At last, his face twitching with rage, Berthelier sheathed his sword, spun on his heel and walked briskly from the church, his friends at his heels.

There were other critics. The Spaniard libertine, Michael Servetus, who had failed to come to the Paris debate in 1534, began writing letters to Calvin, Calvin making reply to correct his pernicious theological errors. In his own written confession of faith, *The Restitutes*, no doubt intended to be a clever salvo to Calvin's *Institutes*, Servetus blasphemously decried the doctrine of the Trinity, and hence of the deity of Jesus Christ; he railed against justification by faith, and he equally railed against the Roman Catholic Church, terming it the Synagogue of Satan.

Fleeing Catholic condemnation, he arrived in Geneva, immediately defying Calvin and the council, and was soon tried and exiled from the commonwealth. But he persisted. It seems he had a plan to overthrow Calvin and set himself up as head of the Genevan church, perhaps of the entire republic. Calvin and he sparred on theological questions in letters, but Servetus wanted to meet Calvin face to face. In violation of his sentence, he returned to Geneva. Confident of libertine support, he slanderously attacked the church and the council. Again he was arrested, and this time thrown in prison. Libertines came to his aid, assuring him of vindication, and the lawyer Philibert Berthelier gleefully took up Servetus's case, eager to trouble Calvin and his supporters in Geneva. Aided by his new lawyer, Servetus wrote to the council.

"I demand that my false accuser be punished, and that he be imprisoned until the trial be decided either by his or my death."

The gauntlet was hurled at the feet of the magistrates. It was to be Calvin or Servetus, and one of them must die. At last the civil authorities in Geneva decided to do away with the troublemaker who kept returning when they merely exiled him. Amid protests from Calvin, they sentenced Servetus to death by burning, along with a copy of his book *The Restitutes.*

Calvin immediately appealed to the council on Servetus's behalf, urging them to alter the form of execution to a more humane one. But they refused to listen. Calvin went to Servetus's cell and pleaded with him to retract his false beliefs and teachings, to believe on the Son of God and be saved by Christ alone from eternal ruin. Servetus obstinately refused Calvin's words, and the gospel freely offered in them. Again Calvin appealed for a mitigation of the form of execution, but in vain. The Genevan City Council burned Servetus, yet did I fear that his critics would see to it that Calvin would bear the blame for it.

36

Triumph at Last

THROUGH THE WINTER of 1548–49, Idelette had developed a slight cough. At first she insisted it was nothing, and kept up her household duties, caring for the children and caring for Calvin, who was plagued by intense pains in his stomach and abdomen, and by near-constant headaches. But the cough persisted. One day it came on her and she coughed so violently that she nearly collapsed. Calvin helped her to bed. He prayed earnestly with her and for her. He sent letters to friends, begging them to pray for his wife, and he sought out the administrations of the best physicians in the city. But she grew worse. At last she could no longer hold food in her stomach, and she wasted away.

Calvin was ever at her side, and, I believe, she knew the end was near. April 2, 1549, after reading Scripture with his wife and praying with her, Calvin attempted to calm her concerning her children.

"I will not fail you, dear Idelette, my love, in caring for our children." He spoke tenderly and close at her ear.

She smiled faintly. "I have already committed them to God." Her voice was barely audible, so weak was she.

"But that shall not prevent me," said Calvin, "from being his willing instrument."

"I know," she said, her lips pale, almost transparent, "you will not neglect what you know has been committed to God."

There were tears of grief in readiness at his eyes. He stroked her pale forehead, and gently squeezed her hand.

"I want them," she continued, "to live holy lives, like my dear husband lives."

He attempted but could say no more to her.

Three days later, Idelette de Bure, in her final moments on this earth, cried faintly but clearly, "O glorious resurrection! God of Abraham . . . I trust!" And then she died.

Over many years had I, by this time, observed Calvin in every possible situation. I had seen him in the extremity of his own grief at the martyrdom of friends, and as he gently comforted others in their grief. But it was the first time I had been there to observe a man wounded so deeply in his loss and yet so unbroken in his spirit. It puzzled me. How could a man like Calvin, with so much innate tenderness, to whom nothing more difficult could have happened, for whom no trial could have been more weighty to bear, how could he find so much comfort and strength to continue his labors? How could a man who believed so completely in the absolute sovereignty of God who orders all things, how could he bear patiently such an affliction without resentment toward a God who would so order the death of his wife? I did not understand. Yet did I marvel as he, with patient composure, entered the pulpit of St. Pierre the very next Sunday, there to adore in his preaching the same God who had seen fit to take from him his dear Idelette.

Without a word did I serve him in those dark days, and he was ever gracious and considerate of my feeble attempts to render comfort to him in his loss. And still he labored on.

Detractors continued to level their cannons at him. Libertines continued to name their dogs for him, drunkards to mock him in their alehouse songs, yet did he labor on, and more and more did the faithful gather to hear him proclaim the pure doctrine of Christ. One capable young man from Lausanne, Theodore Beza, Calvin invited to participate in the ministry in Geneva. Beza was often at Calvin's side and labored with the zeal of a disciple to his master.

Farel had once predicted that Geneva would become a haven for French refugees, called Huguenots, fleeing the brutal persecutions in their homeland. His prediction was not vain. In ones and twos, in families, in vast waves, the disenfranchised from everywhere came to Geneva, waves that precisely corresponded with the persecutions in France, in Holland, in Hungary, in England, in Scotland. Libertines petitioned the council to make immigration more difficult, to keep out these French Calvinists and their like, who would swear the oath, become citizens, and thereby diminish libertine power in the city. When legal means failed them, a band of troublemakers, led by Berthelier and others, planned a ruthless night assault on French refugees, intending to murder them in their beds. It was thwarted "by the hand of God," as Calvin said. The wickedness of the libertine plot, now exposed to all, proved to be a turning point in Calvin's work in Geneva.

In the years of triumph that lay ahead, young men like Beza flooded Geneva to learn at the feet of John Calvin. Many from France, to be sure, but when a Catholic queen ascended the throne of erstwhile Protestant England, a wave of refugees came to the commonwealth of Geneva. Calvin met the challenge of new immigration with energy and zeal, and with creativity. He helped establish a velvet cloth industry in the city, established hostels for travelers and hospitals for the sick and aged, and he established schools for physicians and for training the youth. But it was his special concern to establish an academy where he might train young men for the ministry and for preaching. Hence, he added to his labors weekly teaching in the auditoire, surrounded by men from many lands who had flocked to Geneva. Over these years the population of the republic doubled as more people were drawn to this bastion of truth, this refuge from oppression, this grand citadel of the Christian world.

John Knox, a fiery man from Scotland, who reminded me of Farel that first day we arrived in Geneva, had fled the persecutions of the monarch they called Bloody Mary. I overheard him one day after listening to Calvin deliver a sermon from Psalm 93. Books in hand, Knox halted in his stride as he exited the auditoire. Gazing out over the city, wonder in his tone, he murmured to himself, "Here exists the most perfect school of Christ which has been since the days of the apostles on earth."

And there were others. Court poet, turned fugitive, Clemont Marot joined Calvin in Geneva and was immediately set to work translating and versifying the complete Psalter for use in singing in worship. Musician and composer Louis Bourgeois was encouraged to use his gift by writing new melodies for Marot's Psalm poetry. I overheard Calvin speaking earnestly with these men about the role of music and poetry in Christian worship.

"Although music serves our enjoyment rather than our need," said Calvin, "it ought not on that account to be judged of no value; still less should it be condemned."

"No, indeed," agreed Bourgeois the composer.

"There is scarcely anything in this world which can more turn or bend hither and thither the ways of men than music," said Calvin.

"Hence, Doctor Calvin, is music most profitable," said Bourgeois.

"Music can be made profitable to men," said Calvin, "if only it be free from that foolish delight by which it seduces men from better employments and occupies them in vanity."

"Thus, when rightly employed," said Bourgeois, "music is a great aid to men in the worship of God?"

"Indeed, it may be so," said Calvin. "when it is remembered that music in the Word of God is always about the worship of God. 'Make a joyful noise to the Lord, all the earth; break forth into joyous song and sing praise!' So the Psalmist sang. Indeed, music has a secret and almost incredible power to move hearts."

"But what of poetry?" said Marot.

"When melody goes with poetry," said Calvin, "every bad word penetrates more deeply into the heart. Just as a funnel conveys the wine into the depths of the decanter, so venom and corruption are distilled into the very bottom of the heart by melody."

"But when melody is matched with worthy poetry, with sacred poetry," said Marot, "what then?"

"Danger may still lurk. We must beware lest our ears be more intent on the music than our minds on the spiritual meaning of the words. You must remember this, Louis, as you form your music. Songs composed merely to tickle and delight the ear are unbecoming to the majesty of the church and cannot but be most displeasing to God. Augustine approved of music but added strong caution. 'When it happens that I am more moved by the song than the thing which is sung, I confess that I sin in a manner deserving punishment.' We must beware of these dangers, dear brothers, in our use of music in worship."

Forthwith, these two men began producing Psalm versifications set to spirited music that critics mocked as "Geneva jigs." Yet was it glorious to hear the voices of God's people joyfully raised Sabbath by Sabbath in St. Pierre in Geneva. When young men completed their theological training at the Academy, many of them returned to their homelands, I am told, there to translate Marot's poetry and to lead their new congregations in sung worship with Bourgeois' melodies.

There was great joy in those years of triumph, but not unmixed with sadness. News filtered back to Geneva that grieved Calvin greatly. Many of those zealous young men who had fled persecution to Geneva, whom Calvin had trained to preach the pure doctrine of Christ from the Holy Scriptures in the Academy, whom he had come to love as a father, returned to their villages and boldly proclaimed the gospel of grace. With tears of deep sadness did Calvin receive the news of their arrest and cruel martyrdom.

A young man named Peter Chapot—I recall him as a bold and cheerful youth—for smuggling French Bibles from Geneva into France, was arrested, condemned, and burned. Word was that so loudly and so long did he testify to the grace of God in his burning that, thereafter, the hangman resorted to cutting out the tongues of the martyrs before lighting the fire. There were men Calvin never heard from after they left Geneva, but he did hear of thirteen unnamed men martyred for proclaiming the doctrine of Christ in Paris, and of other nameless men who died in the flames. Another, Stephen Polliot, was arrested with a bag of French Scriptures and Gospel books in his satchel. Without a trial, the king's hangmen promptly cut out his tongue and burned him for his crime. In 1553, the shoemaker Nicholas Nayle, for distributing copies of Calvin's *Institutes* and French Gospels, was arrested and burned soon after. In 1554, Dionysius Vayre, for smuggling Bibles and other prohibited books into France, was seized in Normandy. Sentenced to die by burning, he was "thrice lifted up, and let down again into the fire," so Calvin was informed in a letter. Another, this the bookseller Bartholomew Hector, was arrested in 1556 and burned. All of these were denounced by agents of the King of France or of the doctors of the University of Paris.

When word of these, and many others, came to Calvin, he mourned them as if they were his natural-born sons. "O Stephen, Peter, Nicholas, my sons," he would lament them. "O that the King of France had read and heeded my preface."

On one of these occasions, Beza was at hand attending Calvin and made the remark, "It belongs in truth to the church of God to receive blows, but the church is an anvil that has worn out many hammers."

Hearing the names of these martyrs left me numb. I heard them with horror, and wondered who was guilty of the crime of denouncing them, and how much he was paid for his services. Their names gave me a still deeper unrest, one I did not entirely understand at that time, though now I do. Their names sounded in my ears as a portentous litany, an eerie requiem that pressed down on my conscience, like a great marble slab on a grave.

While I nursed my secret woes, Calvin, driven by his tender concern for his persecuted brethren in his native France, labored on. His output was staggering. I would awaken in the morning astonished at the mounds of paper covered with his handwriting, wondering whether troops of elves or fairies had done it all. When did the man sleep? Massive volumes of letters, precise and detailed commentaries on nearly every book of Holy Scripture. And, in 1559, he completed his final revision and enlargement of the *Institutes*; the book had grown to many times its original proportions, and thousands of smuggled copies of it circulated throughout Europe.

On Christmas Day of the same year, Calvin was, without requesting it, offered much-coveted citizenship in Geneva. I shall never forget his reply; it was so like the man. "Do not think it unkind, noble Sirs, that I myself have not long ago asked to become a citizen. My only reason was to avoid any false pretense."

That afternoon, as I attended him from the City Hall, tragedy struck. I thought at first that he had merely stumbled on the cobblestones. But it was not so. Calvin doubled over, clutching at his chest, and fell to hacking and coughing most uncontrollably. I did what I could, supporting his weight, patting his back in my helplessness. But it was no use. His body stiffened and the coughing turned to retching, and a horrible vomiting of his life blood followed.

At last, with the aid of his brother Antoine, who had seen his brother's distress from his bookshop window, I succeeded in getting him to his house.

"An artery has burst!" declared the physician who attended him. But I was not certain this was correct. What was certain, and became increasingly more so in the months and short years that lay ahead, was that Calvin was very ill, that he was in fact dying.

His last years, infirm as he was, he continued his tireless labors, at times needing to be carried to preach in St. Pierre. Yet did he never grow slack in his duties, though he lamented his weakness and even wondered whether the city ought to reduce or eliminate his pay. I strongly suggested that this would not be a good idea. He had so little. Even the furniture in his house, the very walnut-tree bed he slept in, he had on loan from the city. He was forever giving his means away, and even refused a substantial gift offered to him by the council, embarrassed that he was incapable of laboring for it as he longed to do. His friends and fellow pastors, Theodore Beza, Raymond Chauvet, Michael Cop, Louis Enoch, Nicholas Coladon, Jacques Desbordes, and Henry Seringer, urged him to rest, to cease his labors for his health's sake.

"Am I still working?" said Calvin. "Bear with me that God will find me watching and busy at his work until my last sigh."

February 6, 1564, would be the last time that Calvin would make the trek, for trek it had become, up the spiraling staircase to his beloved pulpit in St. Pierre. In his condition, that climb was no less labor than that of an alpinist ascending the lofty precipice of Mont Blanc. There with quavering voice, he delivered his last public sermon. There were many tears, for we all seemed to know by his manner, his condition, and his words, that this was to be the last time we would hear John Calvin preach the Holy Scriptures to our ears.

As springtime came and the snows on the high slopes of the Jura mountains towering above the commonwealth melted into rushing torrents, Calvin was clearly nearing that last sigh. As he diminished into his final hours, and I knew he would be forever gone from me, the greater became the vain turmoil in my bosom. He summoned me on April 25, urging me to bring quill and paper to him.

"I am too weak, good Jean-Louis," he said. He had for some time referred to me as "good Jean-Louis," and it augmented my distress, for I alone knew how false and evil I had been. For all these many years, a hypocrite, was I not so?

"Take down for me," he said, wheezing as he spoke, "my last will and testament."

So I sat before him that April morning, the brilliant Swiss sun radiating through the leaded panes of his bedroom window, giving me light as I wrote down his words. He broke off frequently as coughing overcame him, racking his fragile body. I shall herein recollect the merest parts thereof.

"In the name of God, I John Calvin, servant of the Word of God in the church in Geneva, thank God that he has shown not only mercy toward me, his poor creature, and has suffered me in all sins and weaknesses, but what is much more, that he made me a partaker of his grace to serve him through my work. I confess to live and die in this faith which he has given me, inasmuch as I have no other hope or refuge than his predestination upon which my entire salvation is grounded. I embrace the grace which he has offered me in our Lord Jesus Christ and accept the merits of his suffering and dying, through which all my sins are buried, and I humbly beg him to wash me and cleanse me with the blood of our great Redeemer . . . ."

There was more, and then he prayed, passionate and earnest was his conversation with the Almighty.

April 27, 1564, Calvin called members of the City Council to his side. Extending an emaciated hand in blessing, his body a living cadaver, he blessed and exhorted them. I render here only a portion thereof. "You older ones be not jealous of the gifts which the younger generation has received, but be glad and praise the Lord who has given them.

"And you younger men, be humble and seek not to achieve greater things than you can do; for youth is seldom void of ambition and tends to despise the opinions of others."

The next day, a Friday it was, he called the ministers to his bedside. Beza knelt at his side as Calvin blessed and exhorted them. He reviewed the years of struggle in Geneva, and commended them for their faithfulness to him and to the Lord. He asked forgiveness for any wrong he had done any. "I have not falsified a single passage of the Scriptures, nor given it a wrong interpretation, to the best of my knowledge." He urged them to avoid subtle and doubtful interpretations and to aim at simplicity, as he had done in his preaching. And then he added. "I pray you, make no change, no innovation. People often ask for novelty. Not that I desire for my own sake out of ambition that what I have established should remain, and that people shall retain it without wishing for something better, but because all changes are dangerous and sometimes hurtful."

He said more and then he shook each of their hands in turn, and all were silent as they, stricken with emotion, attempted to compose themselves.

His voice faint, at last he prayed with them all. "Almighty God, grant us the grace humbly to resign ourselves to you, not to falsify our service for you by our own imaginations, and in obedience to your will to persevere, as it has been revealed to us through your only-begotten Son."

For another month he lingered, sleeping often, eating little, growing ever more slight and faint. For hours at a time, I remained at his side, wretched and of all men most unworthy to be near him. I attempted to pray as I had observed Calvin to pray, but my hidden evil stopped my mouth. At odd times, when I thought he might be gone, Calvin began reciting from Holy Scripture, often from Psalm 39.

"O Lord, make me to know my end and what is the measure of my days; let me know how fleeting I am!"

At other times he recited, with more energy than seemed natural in his dying condition, from Psalm 93, a Psalm I had come to believe to be his favorite, if it were possible to say this.

"The Lord reigns; he is robed in majesty. . . . Your decrees are very trustworthy; holiness befits your house, O Lord, forevermore."

I was tormented by it all, yet did I feel obligated to remain at his side to observe the horrific realities of death, as if performing a penance in so doing. Yet did I look on in wonder and envy from afar at such intrepid faith, at such dying grace. Then early one morning, late in May 1564, he stirred, and opened his eyes. We were alone. Suddenly, I knew what I must do. I knew I must confess, tell him everything, who I am—who I was—yet did I kneel in fear at his bedside.

"Master Calvin," I began, my throat so dry I could barely speak. "I must confess to you."

"Confess to Christ, my son," said Calvin. "He alone is the mediator between God and sinful man."

"But must not a man who has deeply wronged another," I said, "must he not confess his wrong to the man?"

Emaciated as he was—he had to be at death's door—he gazed deep into my eyes, and nodded. "Speak," he whispered.

I told him everything, every detail, all that I had done against him, how I had hated him, how I had denounced his friends, how I had denounced him. It was as if a vast water course had built up behind an earthen dam, churning and foaming at the frail rampart, and then when the pressure was greatest, it suddenly broke through all resistance. So it was with me, and I wept, uncontrollably at times, forced to break off my speaking. I feared that the magnitude of my evil might so disturb his breast that he would immediately expire, and I un-absolved of my evil against him.

"Am I forever damned?" I said, at last. "There can be no hope for such as I, can there?" I feared his answer, yet did I hope.

He said nothing for several moments and I feared he might have slipped from this life, but I saw his eyes fill with tears as he gazed at the ceiling. I wondered whether he was seeing Etienne or his wife, dying in flames at the stake in Paris, by my doing, and I feared what he would tell me.

At last he spoke. "Christ came to save sinners," he said. "And only those who believe that they are great sinners will be saved. Paul persecuted the church; grace alone was sufficient to save him, the chief of sinners. You, good Jean-Louis, are a great sinner. Yet is Christ a far greater Savior. Flee to him alone."

"But will he have me?" I said in earnest now. "How can I be one of his elect?"

"All who flee in faith, my son," he said, seeming to gain new energy as he spoke, "are elect. Flee and live. Then tell the world of so great a doctrine of grace. Fall before the majesty of our great God, Jean-Louis, and acknowledge your sins, praying that he would make you increasingly conscious of them, so that you might hate your sin and embrace Christ's mercy."

Here he, with prodigious effort, raised his thin right hand and placed it upon my now-gray hairs, and continued.

"May his grace be poured upon you in ever-increasing measure. May his hand support and sustain you in your weakness, and may he bring you to his holy perfection in the kingdom of heaven, which he has bought for us—for you, my friend, Jean-Louis—by our Lord Jesus Christ. Now go in peace. And so shall I."

He passed from this life May 27, 1564. I recollect the clock tower striking eight in the evening some moments before his labored breathing ceased. We buried Calvin, as he had insisted, in an unmarked grave. Some believed it was his purpose that by so burying him, superstitious souls would not venerate his bones. But I knew better. Unpretentious Calvin simply did not believe he deserved a grand effigy over his remains.

"Tell the world of so great a doctrine of grace," so he had said. "Go," he had said, and so I determined to go. Nor was it a grappling decision where I was to go. Most of the students he had trained for ministry returned to their home towns, there to proclaim this doctrine of grace alone—and thence to martyrdom. I was resolved.

37

The End

So ends the confession of Jean-Louis Mourin. When I
arrived back in Picardy, in the village of Noyon-le-Sainte, I was
uncertain where to begin. With the blessing of Calvin's faithful
successor, Theodore Beza, and with his generosity I returned
with my own little copy of Olivetan's French Bible, with Calvin's
preface, and with sufficient means to find lodging. The house
known as Grain Place was vacant, and I secured it. It is from there
that I have written this all-unable account. But a vast change has
overcome me as I have penned these words.

Surely I will be discovered. I have just this day delivered a
sermon on the steps of our cathedral. I say sermon, but it was not
so good as Calvin would deliver, to be sure; yet it was true and it
was faithful, and that is enough for me.

At the last, they will discover me. I am as certain of the fact
as I now am that God's grace alone covers my sin. No one is as
intimate with their stratagems as I, Jean-Louis Mourin. I know
what lies before me, yet will I not shirk my calling. Even now,
they draw ever closer.

Pressed to the wall in a benighted alleyway, they are never far from me now. In the corner of my eye, indeed, I have seen them lurking. They consider me among the Huguenots, with whom they are remorseless in their rage. I am daily followed.

Sounds in the night awaken me. I am yet a man, and long to live. But I awaken to do as Calvin did: I pray, and commit my way to God. The noise may be merely a rat prowling in the street rubbish, a man staggering home, too long at the wine bottle, or a foolish woman trapped in her harlotries. Sounds in the night disturb my mind, but do not disquiet my soul, or shake me from my resolve. Sooner or later, in those night sounds, they will draw near. There is no doubt. Yet am I resolved.

I am a man and long to live. There are times when I am tormented by the dreaded anticipation of their poundings at my door. And the knowledge of what follows, at these times, wraps itself around my churning innards like the cold clutching fingers of the plague. Then I pray, and then am I resolved.

By nature, I am not strong. In body, yes, but in faith I am still an infant. Yet am I resolved. I long to be strong like some I have condemned in my time. When I think of what they will do to me, of their relentless cruelty, of the horrific effectiveness of their methods, of my certain and painful end at their hands, I fear. But when I think of my Redeemer, of grace alone for such as I—I am resolved.

At times I fear I may lose my nerve, and be a castaway. No, I must not dwell on such things.

I once believed that by penning this confession I could, by my penitential efforts, be cleansed in my tormented conscience. Thanks be to grace alone, I know better. Though expert at the bloody art of wrenching confessions from others, I am all unable as a chronicler of my own, yet do I vow that what I have penned is a true and faithful chronicle. Hence, I have written what I have written. Knowing that they draw near, I have carefully rehearsed how I shall conceal it. The niche is prepared; the stone is fitted; my method of concealment prepared, for certain it is, I will have little time when they come for me.

Knowing that the noose is drawn ever tighter about me, I am possessed with profound relief that my narrative, my confession, draws to an end. Still more am I possessed with confidence, not in feeble me, but in grace alone, by which I shall testify on the evil day, when they have come. I am resolved.

I write in haste. For I have heard them! Surely it is a commission sent by the bishop. Their boots thunder in the street before my house. "O comfort me in death's approaching hour, strong-hearted then to face it by thy power." They are pounding on the door with their fists!

"Ouvrez la porte!" they cry. "Au nom du roi, ouvrez la porte!"

In the king's name, they demand that I open to them. There are many of them. Now with pikes, or perhaps the butt of a harquebus, they thunder at my door. It splinters. Soon shall it be breached. God grant me stronger hope and sure! I must go. Conceal my confession from their view.

I am resolved.

The End

Timeline of the Reformation and John Calvin's Life

<table>
<tr><td>1384</td><td>Death of John Wycliffe, the Morning Star of the Reformation</td></tr>
<tr><td>1415</td><td>Martyrdom of John Huss</td></tr>
<tr><td>c. 1450</td><td>Birth of Jacques Lefevre d'Etaples</td></tr>
<tr><td>1483</td><td>Birth of Martin Luther</td></tr>
<tr><td>1492</td><td>Columbus discovers the New World</td></tr>
<tr><td>1509</td><td>Birth of John Calvin in Noyon, France, July 10</td></tr>
<tr><td>1513</td><td>Machiavelli writes The Prince</td></tr>
<tr><td>1514</td><td>Birth of John Knox of Scotland</td></tr>
<tr><td>1517</td><td>Martin Luther's 95 Theses</td></tr>
<tr><td>1519</td><td>Magellan circumnavigates the globe</td></tr>
<tr><td>1519</td><td>Leonardo da Vinci dies</td></tr>
<tr><td>1521</td><td>Luther at the Diet of Worms</td></tr>
<tr><td>1523</td><td>Fourteen-year-old Calvin goes to Paris to study</td></tr>
<tr><td>1525</td><td>Luther publishes Bondage of the Will</td></tr>
<tr><td>1526</td><td>William Tyndale's English New Testament published</td></tr>
<tr><td>1528-29</td><td>Calvin studies law in Orleans and Bourges</td></tr>
</table>

1529   Marburg Colloquy—Luther and Zwingli debate the Lord's Supper

1531   Calvin's father dies; Calvin returns to Paris

1532   Calvin publishes first book—a commentary on Seneca's *De Clementia*

1533   Persecution of Protestants increases in Roman Catholic France

1533   Nicholas Cop and Calvin flee Paris

1534   Henry VIII breaks with Rome, declares himself head of the Church of England; Cambridge Reformers laboring for gospel

1534   Calvin meets the aged Lefevre

1536   Calvin publishes first edition of *Institutes of the Christian Religion*, preaches in Geneva

1536   Lausanne debate; death of Lefevre; Tyndale martyred for English Bible translation

1538   Calvin and Farel are banished from Geneva; Calvin called to Strasbourg to pastor French-speaking congregation

1539   Calvin is asked to respond to Cardinal Sadoleto on behalf of Geneva

1540   Calvin publishes commentary on Romans, marries widow Idelette de Bure

1540   Loyola establishes the Jesuits; counterreformation and inquisition begin

1541   Calvin finally agrees to return to Geneva

1542   Birth and infant death of Calvin and Idelette's only child, Jacques

1543   Copernicus and the heliocentric theory

1546   Death of Martin Luther

1549   Death of Calvin's wife, Idelette

1552   Jérôme-Hermès Bolsec banished from Geneva

1553   Death of Protestant Edward VI of England; Bloody
        Mary begins burning of Protestants; English and Scottish
        refugees flee to Geneva

1553   Servetus burned in Geneva

1555   Latimer and Ridley burned by Bloody Mary in Oxford;
        300 Protestants martyred in England

1559   Calvin establishes University of Geneva and publishes
        final edition of *Institutes*

1560   The Scots Confession is approved by Scottish Parliament

1560   Jacobus Arminius is born

1564   Calvin's last sermon, February 6; his death, May 27

1572   St. Bartholomew's Day Massacre of Huguenots in Paris;
        20,000 French Calvinists slain

1572   Death of John Knox

1577   Calvin maligner Jérôme-Hermès Bolsec publishes
        fraudulent biography

Guide to Further Reading

(Selected sources for Calvin's voice in the novel)

Chapter 3
Fortune/chance: *Institutes of the Christian Religion*, Book I, chapter xvi, sections 8, 9.

Chapter 13
Persecution: Prefatory Address to Francis I, 2, 7, 8.

Chapter 17
Idolatry: *Institutes*, Book I, chapter x, sections 11,12; Book II, chapter viii, sections 16,17; Prefatory Address, section 6; *Tracts Relating to the Reformation*, by John Calvin, translated by Henry Beveridge, The Calvin Translation Society, 1844.

Chapter 18
Unity: *Institutes*, Book IV, chapter i, sections 6-13.
Conversion: *Commentary on the Psalms*, Author's Preface.
Imputed Righteousness: *Commentary on Romans* 3:22-25; 5:17.

Chapter 19
Natural Revelation: *Institutes*, Book I, chapter iv and chapter v; *Commentary on Hebrews* 12:1.

Chapter 20
Simony: *Institutes*, Book IV, chapter v, sections 9-11.

Chapter 21

Predestination/foreknowledge: *Commentary on Romans* 8:29; 9:13-26; *Institutes*, Book III, chapter xxii, sections 1-11; Book II, chapter iii, sections 12-14.

Chapter 22

Persecution/trials: *Institutes*, Book III, chapter viii, sections 1-11.

Chapter 24

Humility: Commentary on I Peter 5:5, 6.

Chapter 26

Lord's Supper: *Institutes*, Book IV, chapter xvii, sections 1-5.

Chapters 27 and 28

Purpose of *Institutes*: Prefatory Address to Francis I.

Chapter 29

Encouragement: Letter to Duchess of Farrara, February 2, 1555; *Letters*, p 165.

Chapter 30

Farel's influence: Theodore Beza, *The Life of John Calvin*, L. B. Seeley and Sons, Fleet-Street, London, 1834, p 8.

Chapter 31

The Bible: *Commentary on II Timothy* 3:16; *Institutes*, Book I, chapter vii and chapter viii.

Chapter 32

Lord's Supper: *Institutes*, Book IV, chapter xvii; *Commentary on I Corinthians* 11.

Chapter 33

Preaching: *Institutes*, Book I, chapter xiii, section 4; chapter vii, section 5; chapter viii, sections 1,2; *Commentary on a Harmony of the Evangelists, Matthew, Mark, and Luke*, Vol. 1, p 227.

Chapter 34

Predestination: *Institutes*, Book III, chapter xxii, sections 2-5; *Commentary on Romans* 8 and 9; *Commentary on Ephesians* 1:1-11.

Civil Government: *Institutes*, Book IV, chapter xx; *Commentary on Psalm* 2:22.

Chapter 35

Defense of Reformation: Letter to Sadoleto.

Submission to will of God: Letter to Pierre Viret, May 19, 1540; Letter to Farel, 1540, *Letters*, pp 62-66.

Brotherly love: *Commentary on John* 15:16, 17.

Church Discipline: *Institutes*, Book IV, chapters iv, v, and xii, sections 1-10.

Bolsec (scandal and criticism): *Institutes*, Book III, chapter xxi and chapter xxii.

Lord's Supper: *The Life of Calvin*, Theodore Beza, p 71.

Michael Servetus: Letter to John Frellon, February 13, 1546, *Letters*, p 79.

Chapter 36

Grief: Letter to Viret, April 7, 1549; Letter to Farel, April 11, 1549, *Letters*, pp 104-108.

Music: *Commentary on Genesis* 1:20; *Institutes*, Book III, chapter xx, section 32.

Last Words and Death: *The Life of John Calvin*, Theodore Beza, pp 99-103; Letters, pp 249-261.

"Doug Bond's latest novel introduces many to a largely invisible or prejuducially ignored character: John Calvin. This historical fiction brings Calvin back from an unwarranted oblivion. Thanks to Bond's vivid writing style and thorough acquaintance with the period, readers now have a looking glass into the life and history of a great man. I am pleased to commend this fine book to readers."

—DAVID W. HALL, executive director, Calvin500

"In this book Bond helps the reader grasp the humanness of Calvin, the manner of life in 17th-century Europe, and the real struggle for the gospel. This is a great entryway into the life of Calvin and the Reformation in general. It is entertaining and spiritually edifying, so I commend it heartily."

—RAY VAN NESTE, director, R. C. Ryan Center for Biblical Studies, Union University, Jackson

"Douglas Bond takes us on a journey to Calvin's times and places in a manner most colorful, convincing, and captivating. I felt like I was there."

—PAUL S. JONES, organist and music director, Tenth Presbyterian Church, Philadelphia

"The events and ideas of John Calvin are captured in a lively historical fiction, giving the famous theology a heart and voice. Douglas Bond's eye for cultural detail frames the debates of the day in a specific time and geography, resulting in a fresh vision for our own times. Well done."

—MIKE SUGIMOTO, visiting professor, Pepperdine University, Lausanne, Switzerland